THE A-Z OF CLASSIC CHILDREN'S TELEVISION

THE A-Z OF CLASSIC CHILDREN'S TELEVISION

Simon Sheridan

Reynolds & Hearn Ltd
London

This book is dedicated to
Mum and Dad, and my grandparents,
for the wonderful childhood
they gave me.

First published in 2004 by
Reynolds & Hearn Ltd
61a Priory Road
Kew Gardens
Richmond
Surrey TW9 3DH

A CIP catalogue record for this book is available from the British Library.

ISBN 1 903111 27 7

Designed by Peri Godbold.

Printed and bound in Great Britain by Biddles Ltd, King's Lynn, Norfolk.

CONTENTS

'Of course, when you hibernate you're much younger when you wake up...'

Tove Jansson,
Moominvalley in November (1970)

ACKNOWLEDGEMENTS

I owe enormous thanks to the terrific interviewees who made this book such a pleasure to write: Lo Cole, Brian Cosgrove, Maurice Dodd, Hilary Hayton, Dick Horn, David Jason, Peter Lang, Pamela Lonsdale, Peter Lord, David McKee, Graeme Miller, Gordon Murray, Donald Packham, Nigel Plaskitt, Isabel Ryan, John and Priscilla Ryan, Gay Soper, Bobbie Spargo, Jane Tucker and Anne Wood.

And all of the following gave me valuable help:
Oliver C Bradbury, John Cary, Alex Chidley, Alison Cole, Janie Conley and Alison Cook at Aardman Animation, Paul Cotgrove, Ben Elliss, Jane Gray-Wallis, Jane Gregory, Adam Hargreaves, Fiona Holland, Maya Kemp, Debbie Masling, Karen Morgan, AJ Read at Cosgrove Hall Films, Cassius Rayner, Robert Vickers, Mark Wood, Mark Wyman. Also: Animation UK, The British Film Institute, Birmingham City Library, Bristol Central Library, Bristol Zoological Gardens and Tracy Weston at the BBC Written Archives Centre.

I want to express my gratitude to all those friends who gave me encouragement in this project: Linda, Charlotte, Dan, Katie, Philip, Alex, Jonny, Heidi, Rachel, Hilary, Liz, Laura, Jenny, Gillie, Nick and Phil & Debbie. Special respect goes to the indefatigable Mark Powell.

Thanks also to Kenneth Sutherland, who reminded me what I was like aged seven.

FOREWORD

I was the voice of Danger Mouse. Well, that's to say, I still am Danger Mouse! I've always completely adored cartoons, so it's no surprise that I ended up voicing one of the best!

I came from a working class family. My father was a fishmonger and my mother a char lady. However, my mum would escape from the drudgery of real life by going to the cinema. When I was a little boy she'd always take me with her. I'd have been something like seven or eight years old and she'd drag me along to the local Gaumont or Odeon to watch some romantic Hollywood movie. I usually thought the film was a bit soppy, but I'd sit there patiently because I knew that when the intermission started I'd be in for a treat. Cartoons! That was it for me! I thought Bugs Bunny or Daffy Duck were just *so* amazingly wonderful. Looking back, I think I had a great affinity with cartoon characters even then. After all, they gave me great material to impersonate. Cartoon characters fascinated me and I'd spend hours mimicking their voices. Those early days really started my great romance with animation.

Doing voices for cartoon characters is no different from acting in something like *Only Fools and Horses,* where you are actually *seen.* You still have to use exactly the same skills. I always admired the actor Mel Blanc, the voice of so many of my Warner Bros cartoon heroes. His talent was for breathing genuine life into a character and making it utterly convincing. I tried to emulate him, because I never wanted people to watch the cartoon and hear the voice and immediately say 'Oh, that's David Jason!' I wanted the audience to hear the voice and say 'Oh, yes, that's Danger Mouse!' You really have to invest yourself 100 per cent into the character and make the audience *believe.*

I first became Danger Mouse in the late 1970s. At the time I was known a little bit from *Open All Hours,* but I certainly didn't think I was famous. At around the same time I'd worked on a partly-animated film called *The Water Babies,* for which I'd provided some of the cartoon voices. The main star was James Mason and I can distinctly

remember, as a green young actor, thinking 'I'm working with a bloody legend here!' It was amazing. Little did I know then that a white mouse with an eye patch would be just around the corner and that eventually university students would be writing theses on him! I auditioned for the job like any actor would, but when I saw the character drawn on paper for the first time I was struck by how classical he looked – better than Disney! As soon as I met Brian Cosgrove, *Danger Mouse*'s director, I knew straight away I wanted to play this amusing rodent-James Bond-type character. Brian and I clicked immediately, and I shared his belief that Danger Mouse had to have a life of his own. I wanted to make him *real* for the viewers and I felt very strongly about what he should be like. Danger Mouse was silly; he was ridiculous; he was daft, but I did take him very seriously.

As we progressed with the series over time, the better the Danger Mouse character became. The writers were getting better, we as actors were understanding our characters more and everybody started having a tremendous time. Terry Scott – who played Penfold – and I would have such fun ad-libbing. We'd be in the recording studio and we'd be flying! I always knew how well we were doing if Brian's glasses misted over – meaning he'd be crying with laughter. If we achieved that, then I knew we were all working well.

I can honestly say it was brilliant getting paid to have fun all day. We were creating something wonderful for an innocent young audience, but in order to do it we had to be a little bit childlike ourselves. We were always pushing ourselves: me, Terry, Brian, the writers and the animators, but we worked out of a genuine desire to entertain people. That was our driving force; and when I think about *Danger Mouse* today it still makes me happy. I'm immensely proud that it's now considered a children's television classic.

David Jason
Buckinghamshire
March 2004

INTRODUCTION

When I was a small boy I watched an inordinate amount of television. She'll not like me for saying this, but I think my mum actively encouraged me to watch as much TV as humanly possible. For that I will be eternally grateful. This book is about the children's television I was raised on, but it would actually be ten times the size if I included absolutely everything I was glued to. I really liked *Rainbow*, I adored *Chorlton and the Wheelies* of course, but my childhood is also liberally peppered with intense memories of 'grown-up' telly, when watching TV during daylight hours was still a cardinal sin. In the early 1970s ITV introduced a scrumptious menu of afternoon programmes which my mum and I eagerly devoured. After Hartley Hare's insane rantings on *Pipkins*, the TV stayed defiantly switched on for a diet of *Crown Court, The Cedar Tree, Emmerdale Farm* (when cows still made up the supporting cast), *General Hospital* and *Afternoon Plus* with Mavis Nicholson. The latter discussed 'women's problems' We loved all these shows, and would get extremely irritated if International Open Golf or Racing from York infiltrated our quality time. These are the programmes I recall before I started primary school, but my TV nostalgia extends to long summer holidays too and times when I was off sick, which must have been quite often considering how vividly I remember the muddy wellies standing next to Annie Sugden's Aga.

I lived in a large town, which, even to this day, cannot make up its mind exactly where it is supposed to be. Is it the south Midlands, or is it the top of the West Country? Here was the dilemma – which TV region would we get? Ten miles down the road you could pick up HTV West from Bristol, but we were stuck with ATV from Birmingham, which was fine by me as I knew no better and inadvertently enabled me to watch *Tiswas* some years earlier than the rest of the UK. The downside, particularly for my parents, was the fact that our regional news seemed to come from another world completely. I had little idea where Wolverhampton and Walsall were

on the map (although, Dudley was another matter since I'd visited the clinically depressed, head-swinging polar bears at the zoo there and never forgot it). But thanks to genial ATV news anchorman Bob Warman, I watched intently as the latest burglaries, stabbings and arson attacks from the so-called 'Heart of England' filtered into our house. My father attempted to mumble or cough over anything too upsetting that Warman might have said, but I shall never forget his face when I innocently asked him what 'flasher' meant.

By the time dad arrived home for his tea at 5.30 pm the TV set was still on after another marathon session of bewigged judges, blanket baths and cottage loaves, finishing with a bit of *Magpie* for good measure. We always watched the local news with our tea and it became a family ritual. My elder brother and sister and I would sit in the dining room while one of my parents would open the door into the lounge and wheel in the unwieldy Rediffusion telly, with the fake wood surround, to stand by the dining table. This could be a tricky manoeuvre since TV sets in those days were the size of small caravans and the aerial lead could easily get caught around the wheels and turn the screen to fuzz just at a crucial moment when Bob Warman was talking about the mugging of an old age pensioner in Birmingham. TV news seemed to go on for an age back then. As soon as the ATV news had finished its daily diet of murder and mayhem, one of us would have to go up and change the channel (remote controls were just a fanciful dream in the mid 1970s) to *Nationwide* on BBC1, where the tone was lighter, but not always. I clearly recall the announcement of Sid James' death solemnly delivered over a montage of clips from *Carry On* films and *Hancock's Half Hour* and a tearful interview with Barbara Windsor. Babs' blubbing completely put me off my liver sausage sandwich (white bread, of course) and Arctic Roll.

Invariably the only television programmes my father could stomach in those days were news or current affairs. My mother's love of TV encompassed just about everything, but my father had no patience for 'crude' shows like *Are You Being Served?* or anything else he deemed to be corrupting our morals or exposing us to 'common people'. He worked incredibly long hours in those days. He'd pop in for his tea and an hour of news then go straight back

out to work again in the evening so we could get away with watching Benny Hill without interruption. However, if he was around and happened to hear the opening bars of the *Coronation Street* theme tune, or even worse *Grange Hill*, he'd be in the lounge quicker than the Six Million Dollar Man to demand we turn it off. My sister and I got pretty wise to this after a while and would kneel by the TV set and turn the volume down immediately before the music started, check the coast was clear, and then turn up the sound again just before Ena Sharples came on. Soon we had this procedure timed like a military operation.

I must state here and now that I was a bigger fan of ITV than the BBC and this has made me somewhat, but not overly, biased about some of the programmes in this book. I repeatedly hear from my contemporaries that they were banned from watching ITV because it 'wasn't quality' This is patently ridiculous, but in the 1970s it was a firmly held belief nevertheless. One of my aunts once famously declared to my mother, over tea at her house, that she 'only watched the BBC because there's nothing worth watching on ITV.' We rapidly made our excuses and left. This ITV/BBC division meant that some kids were only allowed to watch *Blue Peter* and not *Magpie* or *Multi-Coloured Swap Shop* and not *Tiswas*. I was permitted to watch both and nothing was banned since my mum considered all TV to be 'good for you' Ahh happy days, why can't more mothers have that refreshing outlook on life? We had the *Radio Times* and the *TV Times* delivered each Tuesday when we were kids. In those days the *Radio Times* only carried BBC listings and the *TV Times* only programmes on commercial telly. I hated the *Radio Times* because, apart from the colour cover, its listings were printed in black-and-white on nasty, coarse newsprint. The *TV Times* (still my favourite magazine to this day) had lots of colour, felt nice to hold and was choc-a-block full of glamorous ads for Players No 6 and Martell Cognac (both contraband items in our household). I used to vent my spleen over the *Radio Times* by regularly defacing whoever was on the cover, whether it be Mike Yarwood or Fanny Craddock, variously giving them gappy teeth, bulging warts and stitch marks around their necks *à la* Frankenstein's monster. My parents pleaded with me not to do this, as they couldn't bear to look at the

magazine any more and had to tear off the cover and throw it in the bin.

In many ways my childhood was idyllic. Apart from watching as much TV as I could get my eyes on I was a pretty normal kid who liked drawing Spider-man pictures with felt tips, eating Neapolitan ice cream, setting fire to *Star Wars* figures, following the adventures of Scared Stiff Sam each week in *Whoopee!* and playing on the swings at Old Pat's, the local playground. My time spent at primary school was perhaps the most blissfully happy period of my life. I attended the local C of E primary – a vast redbrick Victorian building that had been much built on and expanded. It was a pretty eccentric place with a cast of teachers straight out of a St Trinian's movie. Nowadays primary school teachers are all bright young, go-getting 20-somethings with big ideas about how to develop young personalities and achieve goals. My teachers were a pretty decrepit bunch of elderly bogie-picking spinsters, lesbians in thick woolly tights and one-eyed carp fishermen who let us do whatever we wanted, just so long as they could get on with the *Telegraph* crossword quietly in the corner.

My formative school days are a blur of colour and vitality: of building puppet theatres, doing never-ending projects on witches (the occult was big at our school) and stepping into the literary worlds of Moomins, Mrs Pepperpot, Green Knowe and Bottersnikes and Gumbles. We were always drawing and painting and cutting things out of card and sticking silver milk bottle tops onto them. Even during PE, it seems. One year we memorably had to draw fanciful pictures of what we thought we'd all be doing on the eve of the millennium. My painting, which still exists, was of myself wearing a suit of armour and walking a robot dog (no doubt inspired by *Doctor Who*'s K9) on a giant conveyor belt up a mountain. Funny then that I really did spend New Year's Eve 1999 feeling sick in a Devonshire pub after having just downed another cocktail, called a Furry Fanny, in a pint glass and chatting to a girl, rather ingeniously dressed up as a giant packet of Marlboro Lights.

Outside of class the playground ruled supreme; a racing track of small boys wearing *Incredible Hulk* T-shirts and girls using their skipping ropes as *Wonder Woman* lassoes. Overseeing this potentially

catastrophic state of affairs was sometime dinner lady, toilet cleaner and vomit-cleaner-upper Mrs Mustoe. A lady of some advanced years with a dyed dirty blonde perm and permanently dressed in a gingham polyester tabard, Mrs Mustoe (or 'Mrs Mustard' as we hilariously nick-named her) ruled the tarmac with an iron fist, albeit one in a pink Marigold rubber glove. If it rained heavily we were frog-marched back inside and allowed to sit in the main hall and watch television. ('Sit up straight with your legs crossed!' boomed Mrs Mustoe.) The school's ancient old TV would be trundled in and 'something suitable' would be found for us to goggle at. And it was rarely a frontal lobotomy on *General Hospital* either. TV watching at primary school was usually only reserved for 'special occasions' like NASA rockets being launched or members of the royal family being assassinated, so any excuse to turn on the box was greeted with huge enthusiasm. However, BBC2's educational morning shows like *Words and Pictures* and *You and Me* left my compatriots and I pretty non-plussed, since their content was too overtly obsessed with learning. That's not what we went to school for. If we got *Camberwick Green* or *Bod* we could barely contain ourselves.

Compared to ITV, the BBC never offered much in terms of 'daytime' television in those dark days. There was no breakfast telly, no home makeover shows featuring effeminate men discussing wallpaper swatches and certainly no televised car boot sales. (Actually, perhaps that's a good thing.) But 30 years ago it was slim pickings all round and stay-at-home mums, the unemployed, striking bin men and the infirm and incontinent must have cursed the BBC every single morning. It was a toss-up between the now legendary *Pages from Ceefax* and 'Programmes for Schools and Colleges'. The latter included such treats as *Science Session, Maths Workshop* (later excitingly renamed *It's Maths!)* and *Developments in Social Work*. In fact *Developments in Social Work* was sometimes repeated on BBC1 on a Saturday morning too, in case you missed it first time round. Thank God somebody invented *Multi-Coloured Swap Shop* in 1974. Thousands of needless suicides were instantly prevented. BBC2 was even worse. You'd get 20 minutes of *Play School* at 11.00 am, only to be followed by six hours, yes *six hours*, of beardie-weirdies on *Open University*, or worse still that

chubby-faced girl playing noughts and crosses with a stuffed clown on the Test Card. Suddenly *Pages from Ceefax* seemed quite exciting.

Today's children with their suffocating diet of Cartoon Network, Fox Kids, Boomerang, Nickelodeon and CBeebies would find it difficult to comprehend that in the years following the Second World War the only form of televisual children's entertainment was a single channel broadcasting the *very* limited adventures of a mute, moth-eaten donkey. The BBC's *For the Children* strand had started in 1937, but didn't really take off until it was relaunched after the war with the introduction of *Muffin the Mule*. The show's presenter was Annette Mills, a middle-aged woman with a perfectly pitched BBC voice, who sang songs whilst playing the piano. She had been a mainstay of *For the Children* for some time before realising that her audience might prefer to watch a donkey instead. Mills approached famed British puppeteer Ann Hogarth and allegedly asked: 'Can I have one of your puppets as an accompaniment to my songs?' 'Certainly not,' replied Hogarth tersely, 'but you can provide the musical accompaniment to one of my puppets!'

Muffin made his theatrical debut in a five-minute slot on 4 August 1946. Miss Mills sat at her piano whilst Hogarth stood out of shot behind a curtain and manipulated the dappled mule in time to the songs. It was all jolly good fun, with Muffin refusing to take a bath or go to bed and generally misbehaving with his animal friends. As the series progressed Peregrine the penguin, Peter the pup, Oswald the ostrich, Louise the lamb and Prudence kitten all made appearances too, but it was the weekly chorus of 'We want Muffin, Muffin the Mule. We want Muffin, always playing the fool,' which really got everyone going. There were attempts to change the format and somebody called Crumpet the clown tried to muscle in on the act, but the kids thought he was creepy and he had his BBC contract terminated. It is *Muffin the Mule* who became the four-legged founding father of children's telly. He's also partly responsible for the next 60-years' worth of furry, felt, boggle-eyed, zip-mouthed, dancing, singing uppets. *For the Children* was retired in 1950, immediately replaced by the *Watch with Mother* umbrella. Kids' television was barely out of nappies at the time, but the era has still

managed to produce some of the most enduring characters in small screen history.

Watch with Mother was the brainchild of Freda Lingstrom, the then head of children's programming at the BBC. Lingstrom wanted to emphasise the bond between mother and child (only daddies went out to work in those days) and devised a series of new programmes that could be enjoyed by both generations. It's doubtful that watching a wobbly-limbed, pyjama-clad juvenile delinquent running after a teddy bear was as stimulating for a mum as it was for her three-year-old, but I could be wrong. I suppose it depends on whether the mother had been drinking gin all afternoon. *Watch with Mother*'s first big star was *Andy Pandy* (the pyjama boy I was just talking about) and such was his popularity that Lingstrom commissioned further series to fill the 3.45 pm slot. Mr Pandy was originally only broadcast on Tuesdays, but by 1953 he had been joined by *The Flowerpot Men* (on Wednesdays), and *Rag, Tag and Bobtail* (a puppet hedgehog, mouse and pregnant-looking rabbit). Two years later *Picture Book* (a forerunner for *Jackanory*) was busying itself on a Monday afternoon and then *The Woodentops* (the everyday tale of people made of... wood, and their big spotty dog) had arrived on Fridays. Of them all it was Bill and Ben, *The Flowerpot Men* who made the biggest impression. In fact impression is the operative word since end-of-the-pier comedians were still doing impersonations of their 'flobadob' language 25 years later in *New Faces*, usually alternating with a bit of Frank Spencer, for good measure. Bill and Ben's unusual parlance – actually called 'Oddle Poddle' to the uninitiated – became *Watch with Mother*'s unofficial trademark. What was not so documented was the fact that the phrase 'flobadob' originated from puppet creator Hilda Brabban's own brothers (also called Bill and Ben). As kids they used the expression whenever they farted in the bath.

Watch with Mother became a byword for quality kids' TV series, but throughout the 1950s and early 1960s the BBC failed to invest in any new episodes of their perennial favourites. *Andy Pandy* and *The Flowerpot Men*, in particular, over-stayed their welcome by enduring nearly 20 years of solid repeats. It wasn't until the advent of colour television that some new programmes finally escaped from

the toy box to the goggle box. By the early seventies monochrome string puppets finally gave way to the more sophisticated Technicolor pleasures of *Camberwick Green, Trumpton, Mr Benn, Teddy Edward* and *Fingerbobs*. The *Watch with Mother* banner was starting to anger the Women's Liberation movement and by the end of the decade it was quietly dropped altogether, only to be replaced some years later by the less controversial, but totally meaningless *See-Saw*.

Daytime programming was always a much bigger deal for ITV, who filled up their afternoon schedules with the likes of *The Galloping Gourmet* and *Paint Along with Nancy* Curiously, though, most of their daytime series were aimed squarely at an adult audience. Then, in 1972, after a successful lunchtime run of America's *Sesame Street*, ITV began to play catch-up with the Beeb, investing in more homegrown children's series. Suddenly, ground-breaking pre-school shows like *Rainbow, Pipkins, Animal Kwackers* and Keith Harris' *Cuddles and Co* – well perhaps not *Cuddles and Co* – all began to erode the BBC's once vice-like grip on kids' educational entertainment. Not surprisingly the BBC did not like the competition one bit. 'It wasn't rivalry as such,' remembers Pamela Lonsdale, the creator of *Rainbow*. 'It was more that the BBC put themselves above everybody else in producing children's television. I went to a European Broadcasting Union conference during this period and all the ITV producers were on one side of the room and all the BBC people were on the other. It was a case of never the twain shall meet. I thought it was rather silly, but I then got talking to Cynthia Felgate, the producer of *Play School*, and for the very first time both BBC and ITV children's departments mingled. The BBC actually stopped being frosty and smiled!'

Even though ITV was beginning to kidnap lunchtime viewers away from the BBC, by the mid-1970s the old *Watch with Mother* slot was becoming less and less important to the corporation. Teatime telly was the new ratings battleground. For much of the 1970s the BBC1 early-evening news bulletin was broadcast at 5.40 pm each weekday. Children's programmes like *Grange Hill* and *Blue Peter* finished at around 5.35 pm, leaving a five-minute slot conveniently filled by some of the best British animation of the era, including *Ivor the Engine, Roobarb* and *Captain Pugwash*. As parents

sat down in sitting rooms across the country to watch the news, their children were still glued to the box for the latest instalment of *The Magic Roundabout* Because these sacred five minutes attracted such a large cross-section of grown-ups and children the BBC viewing figures were often immense. Viewing figures of six and seven million were not uncommon for a single episode of *The Wombles*, although ratings peaked in 1980 with *The Amazing Adventures of Morph*, which scaled the incredible heights of 11 million viewers. Peter Lord, the co-creator of Morph, the little plasticine man, explained to me why those short programmes were so vital to children's television. 'God knows there wasn't much work around really in the 1970s,' he comments, 'but we were starving young animators back then and we really wanted to go somewhere with Morph. We were watching series like *Paddington* and *The Wombles* in the pre-news slot and that really was the Holy Grail to animators back then. It honestly was. We knew as consumers what an impact that time slot had. It had huge adult-child crossover appeal and it was just a great window for animators to use. To be brutally honest, most producers of children's series hoped to sell a lot of toys off the back of it too. I mean, Wombles toys were just everywhere back then.'

Arguably the most famous production company making five-minute cartoon classics throughout the 1970s and 1980s was British animation studio FilmFair. To them the 'Holy Grail' slot was their bread and butter. The jolly FilmFair symbol at the end of series like *Paddington* and *The Perishers* was something I always looked for when I was a child and by the age of six or seven I could spot one of their productions a mile off. Even then I knew FilmFair equalled quality, but by the early 1980s the five-minute slot had been squeezed out by efficient TV schedulers. The very last FilmFair show of this kind was *The Moomins*, the second series of which debuted in 1986. Exactly a decade later, Montreal-based animation studio Cinar gobbled up the company and its vast library of characters. Their more recent remakes of 1970s FilmFair series – like *Simon in the Land of Chalk Drawings* and *The Wombles* – have been made depressingly trans-Atlantic. Happily, many of the series in this book have refused to go away and have endured in their original versions, thanks to

more recent releases on video and DVD. The resurgence of interest in classic kids' telly can probably be pinpointed to the 1988 release of a BBC video called, no surprises here, *Watch with Mother* This 75-minute tape contained original fuzzy black-and-white footage of Bill and Ben and Spotty Dog and was the first British video to sell over a million copies. Surprised by its success, and realising that childhood nostalgia was suddenly big business, the BBC released a whole slew of follow-ups in 1989, including the VHS adventures of *Andy Pandy, The Magic Roundabout* and even edited highlights from *Play School.* Each generation has its own childhood TV favourites and by the 1990s series like *Fingerbobs* and *Jamie and the Magic Torch* were experiencing their second coming on lushly packaged video and DVD. Whilst other companies began jumping on the kids' TV nostalgia bandwagon, it was the BBC who were the first to hit on a very interesting phenomenon: children's television is an incredibly evocative shared experience between adults everywhere. It inexorably binds people of a certain age together – more so than sex, football or religion.

Regardless of class or social background, nearly everybody who grew up in the 1970s can instantly remember Zippy and George, Great Uncle Bulgaria and the Soup Dragon, or can hum the theme tune to *The Adventures of Rupert* when plied with Carlsberg. Not everybody has an opinion on the situation in the Middle East or whether the concept of a British Royal family is outdated. But ask a group of people down the pub if *Rainbow*'s pink hippo George is male or female and you've got a parliamentary debate on your hands. I have been incredibly fortunate to interview some of my childhood heroes for this book, including George the pink hippo's mother, so I actually know the answers to the questions that have tortured me for a quarter of a century. As a boy I'd never have imagined in my wildest dreams that some 25 years later I'd be socialising with Fenella the Kettle Witch in a country garden in Cheshire, eating spicy Lebanese dishes with Morph in Bristol, walking the dog with Mary from *Mary, Mungo and Midge* in a Sussex churchyard or reminiscing with Hartley Hare at the Brent Cross shopping centre. But it's all true. I've met them all and sometimes it was quite a surreal experience. For instance, witness the following encounter:

I am sitting in the grand lounge of the Savoy Hotel with chanteuse Gay Soper. A totally charmless waiter with too much gel in his hair serves us a pot of tea (costing an exorbitant £11; my grandfather was horrified when I told him later) and a selection of wafer-thin Scandinavian biscuits. The pianist strikes up Labi Siffri's 'It Must Be Love' on the old ivories and Gay launches into her Pootle voice. Gay is the voice of *The Flumps* you see. Pootle was the baby Flump. It's actually quite unnerving to see this incredibly glamorous blonde talking like a six-inch-high fur ball. She explains that his infamous husky voice was the result of adenoids. I nearly spill my Earl Grey. 'Your generation is incredibly nostalgic,' she says to me, but not in Flump mode now. 'When I was your age I just couldn't wait to grow up and escape my parents and do mad things. If I'd been sitting at home still watching *The Flowerpot Men* I'd have been terribly embarrassed.' Suddenly I *do* feel terribly embarrassed. I was sitting around watching *The Flumps* on DVD only the night before. I start shifting in my velvet-upholstered seat. 'Your generation is so different from mine,' she continues, 'but you know what, I think it's rather lovely. It's actually very sweet to be nostalgic for your childhood.' I breathe easy again.

Back in the 1970s, aside from Wombles pillowcases and cuddly Paddington Bear toys, TV series didn't enjoy the benefits of lots of tie-in merchandise. Actual Flumps were very thin on the ground. Naturally, there were those abundant *Blue Peter* annuals clogging up the shelves in WH Smith's, the odd *Muppet Show* hand puppet, *Take Hart* 'How to Paint' guides and some rather nasty 'action figures' from *The Perishers*, but that was about it. Today, with the huge boom in kids' nostalgia, you can't move for 'as seen on TV' clutter. The 1990s saw the origins of the sometimes sublime, often ridiculous, sentimental throwbacks to people's collective childhoods. Druggy dance remixes of the themes from *Roobarb*, *Sesame Street*, and even *The Adventures of Black Beauty* lured loved-up ravers to greenfield sites around Britain (trance outfit Urban Hype's number six hit 'A Trip to Trumpton' took children's telly to its logical conclusion). No student squat was complete without a poster of *Scooby-Doo* on the chimney breast and *Bod* T-shirts became *de rigueur* for any number of stag weekends in Newquay. From my own

student experiences there really wasn't anything quite as satisfying as watching videos of *Hector's House* at 4.00 am after a night out clubbing. The teeny TV torrent has continued unabated. HMV devotes whole swathes of its stores to classic kids DVDs. If you so desire you can lounge about watching *The Complete Mary, Mungo and Midge* on your widescreen plasma telly, wearing a *Bagpuss* g-string and *Hong Kong Phooey* socks, whilst eating toast spread thickly with Mr Small strawberry jam followed by a slice Tesco *Clangers* cake. Or maybe that's just how my life is.

Advertisers and marketing men see the value of childhood nostalgia too. The theme tune to *Jim'll Fix It* has been bastardised for the Co-op (with suitably inappropriate new lyrics about 'buy one get one free'); Zippy promotes the joys, and horrors, of Marmite and the capricious occupants of *Hector's House* have come out of retirement in France to advertise internet banking for Virgin, to name but a few. It seems that old puppets never die; they just get covered in mildew in a box in the attic. That is until they get stitched up for a TV comeback. In recent years various kids' favourites from the 1970s have become what the tabloids like to call 'cults' This is particularly true of the stars of *Rainbow*. Nowadays, it's not unusual to find Geoffrey trading awkward banter with a foul-mouthed American rapper on *Never Mind the Buzzcocks*, Bungle 'guest starring' on risqué BBC2 sitcom *Two Pints of Lager and a Packet of Crisps* or Zippy and George spinning records at a gay nightclub in the West Midlands. In the autumn of 2002 the puppets even released a disco version of the *Rainbow* theme tune featuring the mono-limbed Zippy shouting 'C'mon, put your hand in the air, George!' A pre-school puppet going all post-modern is not without its risks, however. Zippy and George were stolen out of the back of Geoffrey's car when he stopped off for a wee at a service station on the M4. After a newspaper appeal they were returned unscathed, but George was later punched in the face by a drunken reveller at a charity event in London. All charges of GBH were later dropped.

Whilst some of the stars of *Rainbow* have expressed an interest in doing a new late-night adults-only TV remake, several of their contemporaries have already enjoyed a television rebirth, albeit without any dirty jokes. *Andy Pandy, The Flowerpot Men, Postman*

Pat, *The Basil Brush Show*, *Noddy* and *Captain Pugwash* have all been sexed up for the new millennium. *The Magic Roundabout* is back on the big screen and, unbelievably, even *Muffin the Mule* has come trotting back, although his strings have been neatly snipped. In several instances where the original series' creators have died, their legacy has been handed down to their children. Bobbie Spargo, Lo Cole and Adam Hargreaves have now replaced their fathers' paintbrushes with computers for, respectively, the new *Willo the Wisp*, *Bod* and *Mister Men*.

Back in the 1970s actors of the calibre of John Le Mesurier, Arthur Lowe or Leonard Rossiter would do kiddies' voice-overs as a favour or because it could be squeezed in between 'proper' jobs. Nowadays, however, children's TV programme makers fight tooth and nail over the likes of Martin Clunes, Dawn French, Alan Bennett and Joanna Lumley, paying them thousands of pounds just to secure their services and give their series a little extra kudos. Series aren't made in half measures either. In the good old days series like *Bod*, *The Flumps and Chorlton and the Wheelies* were commissioned in 13 part chunks (13 being quarter of a calendar year) and episodes were recycled endlessly, perpetuating the myth that many of these shows had hundreds of episodes. (I continually hear: 'What! *Mr Benn* only had 13 episodes? No, that can't be true.') Now TV networks demand huge packages of 52 or 104 episodes at a time, and, where once just a handful of animators toiled over Madame Cholet, now vast teams of artists create the very same thing. The original 1970s series of *The Wombles* has only seven names listed on its credits. The 1990s version has over 100. And I know which one I think is better animated.

This book does not aim to catalogue every single kids' TV show ever created. Please don't look for a chapter on *Teenage Mutant Ninja Turtles* or *The Teletubbies* because you won't find one. I've nothing against Tinky Winky personally, but I just wanted to celebrate the golden age of kids' telly of my childhood when Brian Cant screamed 'I like peace, I like quiet,' at the top of his voice in *Play School*, when the presenter of *Fingerbobs* was allowed to be a heavy-metal rocker in his spare time, Hartley Hare could say 'Hello big boy' to a tortoise at lunchtime and Chris Tarrant made children

cry on live Saturday morning TV by stuffing custard pies in their faces. How often do you see that nowadays? Not enough, if you ask me. Perhaps I'm just watching classic kids' TV through rose-tinted Elton John specs, but I'm sure television used to be more dangerous and surreal when I was a child. Bod could throw an apple up in the air and it would stay up. *And nobody would question it.* Today's programme makers have to *explain* everything to children. Series are shown to 'focus groups' in church halls who decide whether green furry hand puppets are scary or not. The whole point is that kids want their TV shows to be dangerous and insane. Surely children still love seeing Beaker getting his nose ripped off when Dr Bunsen Honeydew's latest experiment goes disastrously wrong on *The Muppet Show*?

Perhaps in 30 years' time the Sunny Delight generation will write about their wonderful subversive childhoods watching *The Fimbles, The Animals of Farthing Wood* and *Fireman Sam* and I will be proved totally wrong. But alas, this tome has to end in the early 1980s, at a time when I traded in *The Clangers* in favour of *Hart to Hart* ('When they met, it was murderrr!'), Frankie Goes To Hollywood and masturbation, but not necessarily in that order. It's only now that I'm getting the odd grey hair that I realise what genius programmes I was watching as a kid. Has there honestly ever been anything better than *Jamie and the Magic Torch*? Was any year ever as good as 1977? Well, most probably yes. I mustn't get too carried away, but if I'm an *Animal Magic* anorak or a *Jamie* junkie I must hide it well. 'You're very level-headed,' master animator Brian Cosgrove tells me after I've spent five minutes enthusing about Officer Gotcha and Mr Boo. 'I've met some guys and you'd think they were talking to the Pope and not me. They're saying, "Oh my God, this is the man who created *Danger Mouse*." And I'm thinking, "You're grown men for God's sake!"'

I'm a grown man who's gone back in time and enjoyed a second helping of cartoons and puppets and I've loved every single minute of it. Watching these programmes has made me laugh like Chorlton the Happiness Dragon, weep till my eyes were redder than Noddy's tunic and left me yearning for my youth all over again. However, it's still a source of continued amazement to the people who created

my kids' TV heroes that books like this ever get published in the first place. 'It's great fun to revisit your childhood and to remember the pleasure things gave you back then,' Brian Cosgrove says. 'It's still a genuine surprise to me that our shows had such an impact on the adults of today. At the time I had no idea I was creating icons, or whatever you want to call them. You just don't know that at the time. You're just having a lot of fun. I'm lucky to have helped create characters which people still adore after all this time. That's a wonderful feeling.'

THE A–Z OF CLASSIC CHILDREN'S TELEVISION

THE ADVENTURES OF BLACK BEAUTY

ITV / Produced 1972-1974 / An LWI Production for London Weekend Television / Created by Anna Sewell / Produced by Sidney Cole / Directed by Charles Crichton, Ray Austin and Gerry Poulson / Edited by Ray Helm / Music by Denis King / Starring William Lucas (Dr James Gordon), Judi Bowker (Vicky Gordon), Stacy Dorning (Jenny Gordon), Roderick Shaw (Kevin Gordon), Charlotte Mitchell (Amy Winthrop), Stephen Garlick (Ned Lewis) and Tony Maiden (Albert) / 54 episodes / First broadcast 7 October 1972

Perspicacious horses and athletic children have always made for good wholesome family entertainment. A horse is a horse of course but whilst American TV could only muster a common old nag called Champion we had a real thoroughbred: a big black steed which galloped around the English countryside to the accompaniment of a beautiful, rousing theme. Ah yes, the music. Who could possibly forget it? Written by Denis King and entitled 'Galloping Home', the theme tune of *The Adventures of Black Beauty* has proved to be even more enduring than the excellent show it accompanied. This majestic 1970s series was based on a book written by Anna Sewell in 1877, for which she was reputedly paid just £20. But 20 quid doesn't get you very far, especially when you've only got months to live. Poor Ms Sewell died shortly after the book was published and never lived to reap the huge reward from her equine hero. Her one and only novel has sold some 30 million copies since her untimely death and has spawned numerous movies, TV series and some rather nasty American animation.

ITV already had a horse-sized hit with *Follyfoot,* a children's Saturday serial made in 1971 about a sanctuary for rescued fillies,

when the network commissioned a new stable mate. The real resurgence of interest in Sewell's four-legged creation had begun the same year when Britain's foremost child actor, Mark Lester, starred in a big screen adaptation of the story. The worldwide success of the cinematic tearjerker prompted London Weekend Television to cash in with a spin-off. *The Adventures of Black Beauty* bears scant relation to Sewell's original novel, which was written as a 'horse autobiography' documenting the cruelty Beauty had to endure as a cab horse in Victorian London. In this TV adaptation the ebony steed, with the white blaze on his forehead, is transported to rural Rickmansworth in Hertfordshire (masquerading as fictional village Five Oaks) to have adventures of a different kind with the well-to-do Gordon family. Widowed doctor James Gordon (played with debonair relish by actor William Lucas) and his firm but fair housekeeper Amy (Charlotte Mitchell) cast watchful eyes over a brood of mischievous children who just can't help getting into trouble with more villains than you'd find banged up in Wormwood Scrubs. Gordon's headstrong daughter Vicky (played by ex-ballerina Judy Bowker), his soppy son Kevin (Roderick Shaw) and their friend Albert (Tony Maiden) have a frustrating habit of attracting thieving gap-toothed gypsies, unscrupulous magistrates, horse-rustlers and any number of scowling baddies in top hats. Their faithful horse Beauty plays his part too, neighing a lot and rearing up on his back legs with his hooves flailing about in the air. Beauty soon becomes well versed in saving children from mortal danger, but you do get the distinct impression that having to include the four-legged beast into the ever more elaborate storylines was a source of frustration for the programme's team of resourceful writers. In real life there was more than one equine actor. The main Beauty was too temperamental to be ridden and was regularly substituted with a variety of other steeds (one good at rolling on his back, another better at pawing the ground etc) all with stuck-on white patches applied by the make-up ladies.

By the second series, in 1973, lead actress Bowker left for green pastures new. I always thought her porcelain features looked a little too delicate to be careering around the Hertfordshire countryside (minus riding helmet) on the back of a huge black stallion. Stacy Dorning arrived to take her place as Jenny Gordon, the doctor's previously unseen 'other' daughter. Her character nonchalantly explains that she's been 'away at school' and nobody bats an eyelid. Actually Dorning is far better than her predecessor and her piles of curly blonde hair and headstrong characterisation injected the series with a new energy. Also joining was the incomparable Stephen Garlick as Ned, the housekeeper's soap dodging, cheroot smoking *Cock-er-nee* nephew. With scruffy urchin Ned on board the childhood mischief continued unabated with attempted murder, arson, kidnapping and ghostly apparitions coming thick and fast. Naturally, the kids always play second fiddle to the clever horse. 'We *always* felt as though we were being upstaged,' recalls Stacy Dorning. 'You've only got to watch it – Beauty solved everything! It wasn't us. We were just the also-rans. It was always 'Well done, Beauty,' or 'Good horse, Beauty' I still hear it in my dreams – 'Well done, Beauty...*Beauty!*'"

The series' emotionally manipulative storylines, sensitive performances from the juvenile leads and high production values made *The Adventures of Black Beauty* a must-see 1970s Sunday teatime programme. A nifty pre-titles sequence promised the excitement to come and, at times, the three minute commercial break after the 'End of Part One' cliffhanger was almost too much to cope with. The series regularly boasted more action and excitement than *The Sweeney* and *The Professionals* put together, courtesy of stylish direction from ex-Ealing comedy stalwart Charles Crichton and Ray Austin (*The Avengers*). Thanks to a generous helping of 54 episodes, made over the space of just two years, and continually repeated, the programme extended its shelf life right until the mid-1980s. In the 1990s *The New Adventures of Black Beauty* arrived, reuniting Stacy Dorning and William Lucas, but transporting the action to New Zealand. However, it is the original series which has such an enduring feelgood factor about it, mining the same uplifting vein that *The Darling Buds of May* would later exploit. It always looks sunny, the scenery is lush and green and at the end of every episode you'll come away with a self-satisfied nostalgic glow. *Black Beauty* is the classiest looking series in this book, no contest. And that incredibly sentimental scene of the magnificent horse running in slow motion through a field of golden corn, accompanied by Denis King's romantic theme, is as spine-tingling now as it was 30 years ago.

THE ADVENTURES OF CHAMPION

BBC TV / Produced 1955-1956 / A 'Flying A' Production / Created by Gene Autry / Directed by Frank McDonald and George Archainbaud / Starring Barry Curtis (Ricky North), Jim Bannon (Uncle Sandy) and Ewing Mitchell (Sheriff Powers) with Champion as himself and Blaze as Rebel / 26 episodes / First broadcast (UK) 15 July 1956

The most wondrous thing about *Champion the Wonder Horse* (as the series was better known in the UK) was not that the equine hero could untie knots, open five-bar gates and kneel on the floor, but the fact that the BBC shamelessly inflicted this show on unsuspecting children for over 20 years. Originally broadcast in the summer of 1956, the corporation was still repeating it in the late 1970s. I vividly remember the grainy black-and-white episodes being shown endlessly every Saturday morning throughout the school holidays. If you were really unlucky it would be sandwiched between some Laurel and Hardy two-reelers or, worse still, Buster Crabbe in *The Adventures of Flash Gordon*. It was like colour telly had never been invented.

The original Champion was a steed owned by Gene Autry, the so-called 'Singing Cowboy'. Legend has it that Autry was discovered warbling in a telephone exchange by America's most beloved cow-poker Will Rogers. The star was so impressed with his yodelling that he helped him get a recording deal and by 1932 he had enjoyed his first hit with the melancholic 'That Silver Haired Daddy of Mine.' It rather brings a tear to the eye doesn't it? Not only could Autry sing, he could also act, well kind of. He went on to star in nearly 100 Westerns between the 1930s and 1950s, always playing the same role: that of 'Gene Autry'. However, perhaps to take the audience's minds off Mr Autry's dubious acting abilities, a horsy sidekick was introduced and Champion was born. The chestnut-coloured stallion was immediately successful with audiences and Autry was generous enough to reward the horse's loyalty by giving him his own TV show.

Only 26 episodes of *The Adventures of Champion* were made in the mid-1950s, but by then the original Champion was a bit long in the

hoof so a new 'TV Champion' was introduced. Thankfully you couldn't see the join and his fans were none the wiser. The series followed the escapades of Ricky North, an irksome freckle-faced scamp with a Brylcreemed flick. Oh Ricky North, how I hated everything about you – your nasty all-American face, your annoying squawky voice and your unswerving devotion to your cheerily patriotic 'Uncle' Sandy. Set in the turbulent 1880s, the stories were all exactly the same. Young Ricky would inadvertently get tangled up with surly horse rustlers, dirty cattle ranchers, masked bandits and ruthless oilmen. It was all in a day's work home on the range. Thankfully Ricky had befriended a wild stallion named Champion after saving a weak foal from a herd. The horse, grateful for Ricky's act of charity, immediately allowed himself to be domesticated and using a sixth sense could warn the boy of impending disasters. It was all that *Lassie* kind of stuff. You know the score – Champion would whinny shrilly, rear up and paw the air with his thrashing hoofs. This, naturally, translated as 'There are cattle rustlers down by Dead Man's Creek and we must go there and save the herd.' Quite brilliant. If I had a horse as clever as this I'd have sold it to the circus long ago, but Ricky North was a simple mid-western boy who doted on animals and also had a similarly talented German Shepherd called Rebel. Champion's acts of daring-do were accompanied by a song performed by Frankie Laine which was sung something like this: *'Champ-yun thu Wun-der Hoss'* and pointed out the similarities between the four legged star and lightning flashes, whizzing arrows and mighty cannonballs. None of these were true. Champion was certainly no *Black Beauty* and he had not one ounce of class.

The series was not the resounding success in America that had been hoped and it was cancelled after just one season. Strangely, it had a bigger fan base on this side of the pond thanks to those never-ending repeats and the continued publishing of Champion annuals and cartoon strips. Champion's 'dad' Gene Autry retired from TV producing, replaced this famous horse twice more (the fans still didn't cotton-on) before finally giving it all up and buying the California Angels baseball team. But what of the original TV Champion the Wonder Horse? Well, his hooves were immortalised in the cement pavement outside Hollywood's famous Chinese Theatre. Thereafter he was put out to grass and finally died in 1991, at the grand old age of 42.

THE ADVENTURES OF RUPERT BEAR

ITV / Produced 1970-1976 / An ATV Production / Created by Mary Tourtel / Produced and Directed by Mary Turner and John Read / Written by Marcia Webb and Jill Fenson / Narrated by Judy Bennett / Theme Song performed by Jackie Lee / 156 episodes / First broadcast 28 October 1970

In a dark corner of my parents' loft lives a Rupert Bear doll. He's about 12 inches tall, but he's getting steadily shorter every day. Made out of moulded foam by the legendary 1970s toy company Bendytoys, poor Rupert is now slowly crumbling to dust. His internal wire frame is poking out of his left paw and his ears are flaky and brittle. He stands next to an equally toxic-looking Pinky and Perky and a large plastic Donald Duck on wheels, so he's in good company. Don't feel sorry for him though. Feel sorry for me, as he's my only reminder of one of the greatest kids shows of the 1970s – *The Adventures of Rupert Bear*.

If you want to buy a DVD of this lunchtime classic, don't bother; there isn't one. And if you'd like to have a root around in ATV's extensive archives you won't be satisfied either because overzealous staff wiped most of the tapes back in the 1980s. I should imagine the same two things I remember best about *Rupert Bear* are the things that caught your imagination too, and neither was actually Rupert himself. First is the famous theme tune and second is a nasty little woodland sprite called Raggety with a twiggy nose and a bad attitude.

Let's start with chanteuse Jackie Lee and her syrupy sweet rendition of one of the most recognisable TV tunes of all time.'Rupert, Rupert the bear. Everyone sing his name…!' OK, OK, I know it doesn't look much on paper, but I'm telling you this was one fabulous song! Although *The Adventures of Rupert Bear* has been absent from the television since 1981 (when it was last repeated), when most fans think of the series they recall the bouncy tune which topped and tailed each of the 11 minute episodes. The song has been much revived on compilation albums over the years and is still beloved by

the Schooldisco.com generation, who can do all the accompanying actions on the dance floor. We mustn't forget that the single was even a hit, reaching number 14 in January 1971 and staying in the charts for nearly four months. Never doubt the consumer power of three year olds. Dublin-born Ms Lee toured and recorded under a number of pseudonyms, but didn't enjoy any degree of success until she sang the theme to a dubbed Yugoslavian children's series called *White Horses*, a top ten hit for her in 1968. Thereafter she rather cornered the kiddie market providing the vocals to both *Rupert Bear* and, in my humble opinion, her masterpiece, *Pipkins*.

Once you've got that Jackie Lee song lodged in your head you instantly get transported back to the lush greenery of Nutwood and the quaint wood-built home of Mr and Mrs Bear and their son Rupert. Mr Bear is a pipe-smoking traditionalist, never seen out of his three-piece suit and pedal-pushers. Mrs Bear is the homely type. Always dressed in her apron she tends to her families needs, baking cakes, cleaning and polishing and using a bit of lick on her handkerchief to wipe a dirty smudge off her son's cheek. Rupert is an eccentric little boy, easily recognisable around the forest since his parents insist on dressing him in a pillar-box red sweater and sunshine yellow check trousers and matching scarf. He personifies all that is spiritual, innocent and exciting about childhood and his adventures take him to far away kingdoms where princesses and sea serpents dwell, where Chinese conjurers make magic, evil elves live in dingy caves and where flying chariots swoop over mountains and down into unexplored valleys. Rupert takes it all in his stride and somehow always manages to return home just in time for tea.

Rupert Bear is a real star. He's older and wiser than Mickey Mouse, Winnie the Pooh, Larry the Lamb *and* Andy Pandy, and as a consequence is more likeable than all of them. His sparkling eyes, happy smile and squidgy white face make him a British legend and he never looked better than in *The Adventures of Rupert Bear*. The string puppet series was commissioned by ITV for their early afternoon children's slot, but was later moved, permanently, to lunchtime. Only 13 episodes were made at first, but the series was such a runaway success for the channel that it eventually ran for six years and clocked up a colossal 156 individual adventures.

The show's success can be partly attributed to the household name appeal of its main character. Rupert first appeared in the pages of the *Daily Express* on 8 November 1920 created by Mary Tourtel, the wife of one of the paper's news editors. The newspaper's circulation went up and Rupert was soon a mainstay of Fleet Street, just as he still is today. Tourtel had to give up the strip, due to failing eyesight, and she reluctantly handed over Britain's favourite bear to ex-advertising artist Alfred Bestall in 1935. It was Bestall who expanded Rupert's Nutwood adventures over the next 30 years, by introducing new characters and refining the look of Tourtel's original creations. Considered to be the definitive Rupert artist, it is Bestall's drawings that provided the blueprint for the TV series.

The people charged with making Rupert move in 3D were John Read, a former director of photography, and Mary Turner, a puppeteer. Both had worked extensively with Gerry Anderson on his groundbreaking series *Fireball XL5* (1962), *Thunderbirds* (1964) and *Captain Scarlet and the Mysterons* (1967). What they didn't know about making puppet series wasn't worth knowing. Pre-production on *The Adventures of Rupert Bear* started in 1969 with the intricate carving of the individual puppet heads. Apart from Rupert and his parents there were the bear's odd bunch of zoological schoolmates – best friend Bill Badger, Ferdie and Freddie the fox twins, Podgy Pig (a bit of a porker, him), Edward Trunk the elephant boy, and my own particular favourite Pong Ping the Pekinese. Pong had a great face – like a cross between Sid James and a cabbage, and in the opening titles he grinned like some sort of creepy oriental dragon. I found him both revolting and loveable at the same time, probably because I pitied his unconventional looks. More frightening viewing was to come with the introduction of one of my all time childhood horrors – Raggety the twig boy.

In the Rupert cartoon strip the little bear was often taunted by a vile, intimidating little forest troll named Raggety. I hated the pictures of him in my Rupert annuals, as he would always seem to be suspended mid-air, face contorted and twiggy limbs flailing all over the place. Raggety was a horrible spindle-shanked freak and the 3D puppet series only made him more of one. To look at, he is a cross between The Great Gonzo from *The Muppet Show*, a giant sultana, a

bluebottle and a bonsai tree. It's not a nice image I know, yet it's one that has haunted millions ever since. Possessing a level of scariness only matched by the Child Catcher in *Chitty Chitty Bang Bang*, Raggety's scraggy, wooden body, saucer plate eyes and screechy voice was perhaps the most repulsive thing in 1970s kids' TV. But then again, there was Larry the Lamb. The super staying power of *The Adventures of Rupert Bear* series surprised everyone at ITV who had never expected such a positive reaction from terrified pre-schoolers. Parents also knew that Raggety was an excellent device for making naughty children behave themselves: 'Stop that noise and eat you tea,' Mums and Dads shouted across the land, 'or Raggety will come and get you!' It worked every time.

The end of the 1970s saw a feature film spin-off being mooted for the series, bankrolled by none other than ex-Beatle Paul McCartney, a lifelong Rupert fan. The superstar musician had started writing a musical score for the film (although how he hoped to better Jackie Lee is a mystery), but sadly the project fell by the wayside. McCartney moved onto other things, and then in the early 1980s revived his idea, but this time for an animated short. The finished film *Rupert and the Frog Song* (1984) was about as far removed from the ITV puppet show as you could get. Part pop video, part cartoon adventure, the film won a BAFTA and frog-spawned an annoyingly catchy top ten hit with 'We All Stand Together' the following Christmas.

The film prompted renewed interest in the character but a 1988 BBC series, *Rupert*, narrated by Ray Brooks, only used a camera panning slowly over Bestall's static illustrations. The 65 episode, Canadian-produced, *The All New Adventures of Rupert* (1991-1997) was an improvement, but still paled in comparison with the definitive 1970s puppet version. Rupert now has an American accent and when Raggety appears, which isn't very often, he's about as scary as an elderly wood pigeon.

ALBERTO FROG AND HIS AMAZING ANIMAL BAND

BBC TV / Produced 1975 / A Bodfilms-BBC Production / Created and Written by Michael and Joanne Cole / Directed by David Yates / Drawings by Joanne Cole / Narrated by Maggie Henderson / 13 episodes / First broadcast 23 December 1975

Mmm, milkshakes are great comfort food. Banana, vanilla, chocolate and strawberry. All absolutely delicious, but what about lime milkshake? Lime-flavoured? LIME!!!? Who's ever fancied a lime milkshake? How utterly disgusting. Sharp citrus fruits and milk surely do not mix! Perhaps it's just an amphibian thing, because frogs adore lime-flavoured milkshakes. It might not be to human tastes, but to a frog a green lime milkshake is pure nirvana. And there is no frog more famous for his love of milkshakes than Mr Alberto Frog, the conductor with the internationally renowned Amazing Animal Band.

Alberto plays second fiddle (though not literally, as the marmosets are in charge of the violins) to the star of *Bod*. This 15 minute *Watch with Mother* classic started with a little bald lad and finished with a loose-limbed frog waving his baton about. For some teeny viewers Alberto was just an irritation tacked onto the end of a cartoon with deep philosophical meaning, but, for millions more, choosing the milkshake flavour was their reason for getting up each morning. Whilst the *Bod* segment of the show was vibrantly animated, Alberto's limited budget only stretched to still paintings with a camera slowly panning over them. He was simple and he didn't actually move, but that milkshake was so damn addictive you just didn't care. 'Alberto was originally just conceived as a filler for the rest of the *Watch with Mother* slot,' explains Lo Cole, the son of *Bod*'s late creator Michael Cole. 'The *Bod* cartoon only lasted five minutes so the rest of the timeslot had to be filled on a very tight budget. I didn't realise how popular the frog was at the time because it was just very cheap telly.'

Michael Cole's wife Joanne painted the creature characters in vivid goulash primary colours and actress Maggie Henderson provided the

voices. And there were plenty of varied voices too because Alberto's Amazing Animal Band has a massive amount of musicians. In one particular episode Alberto boasts that he has 105 members. You'd be hard pressed to count half that many on-screen, so we'll just take his word for it. The orchestra consists of chimpanzees on cellos, marmosets on fiddles, cats on clarinets, squirrels on flutes, hippos on the French horns, a kangaroo on cymbals, ostriches on double bass, ducks on the trumpets, tigers on trombones, an elephant on the tuba, a gnu on the xylophone, mice scurrying along the piano keys and a zebra banging away on the drums. It's not an easy ensemble for a little frog to manage, least of all because the musicians are liable to eat each other. Alberto's beastly band is world famous (he even does a Royal Command Performance for the King and Queen of Elsewhere), but he's just as happy playing at the local bandstand to grateful OAPs. Alberto is also quite content searching for lost canaries, cheering up depressed dogs and playing soothing music to battery hens who have downed tools. ('I 'aven't 'ad a cluck out of 'em for weeks!' moans the farmer to his froggy friend.) In many ways Alberto is an amphibian Pied Piper. His musicians blithely follow him wherever he goes, as he mediates in people's problems and soothes their anxieties with his strangely medicinal music. He's cheap, too, because Alberto never charges for his services. He has only one weakness in life.

At the end of (nearly) every episode the grateful recipient of Alberto's symphony asks the clammy-skinned conductor what payment he requires. No money ever changes hands, but Alberto will spend a moment or two pondering his reward. 'Well... Ummm... Errr...,' he stutters. And here's where one of television's greatest moments comes into play. The hippos knew what he's going to ask for. So do the ostriches. The frog-tired members of the animal orchestra know their bandleader's peccadilloes all too well. Alberto is a milkshake junkie. And he's not ashamed. 'I wouldn't say no to a milkshake,' pipes up Alberto after a predictably long pause. Viewers know exactly what he wants, but the agony doesn't end there. After all, what flavour is he going to choose?

Throughout Britain under-fives clung to the edge of their sofas, gripped with suspense. 'I bet it's lime,' say the cats. 'It's going to be

chocolate,' thinks hippo. 'No. It'll be strawberry,' say the chimpanzees. PLEASE, don't let it be the lime. Let it be chocolate! We're now screaming at the TV. Maggie Henderson squeezes every last drop of tension from the scene and then...'I think I'll choose choc-o-late!' says Alberto calmly, totally unaware of the mental torture he's causing in sitting rooms across Britain. Chocolate! 'Hippo was right!' says Henderson, smugly. 'Were you?' Thousands of children breathe a collected sigh of relief. 'That milkshake segment really seems to hit a note for kids. Everybody remembers it,' laughs Lo Cole. 'It must be the repetition that is so appealing because children know exactly where Alberto was coming from. He just *has* to get his milkshake and that is that!' The motto of this story is that if you ever have a frog round for tea, make sure you've got some Nesquik in the cupboard.

THE AMAZING ADVENTURES OF MORPH

BBC TV / Produced 1979-1980 / A Morph Ltd Production / Directed, Animated and Written by Peter Lord and David Sproxton / Produced by Patrick Dowling / Edited by Alan Trott / Narrated by Tony Hart / Voices by Peter Harwood / 26 episodes / First broadcast 13 October 1980

Everybody's favourite five-inch tall plasticine man was born in Bristol in 1976 as a companion for artist-extraordinaire Tony Hart, in his long-running TV series *Take Hart.* Created by Peter Lord and David Sproxton, the founders of the internationally renowned Aardman Animations, Morph's *Take Hart* adventures rapidly became the *raison d'etre* of the show and in 1979 work started on a spin-off series – *The Amazing Adventures of Morph.* What is most amazing is that Mr Hart agreed to take a back seat and let his little squashy mate take all the glory, but agree he did. In fact, did Morph actually become more popular than his silver haired co-host? And was there even some professional jealousy? 'Erm, not really,' admits Peter Lord modestly, 'but people would flatteringly say that Morph was their favourite part of *Take Hart.* I mean he was funny and disobedient and

totally different from the reassuringly gentle pace of the rest of the show. Tony didn't do gags, but that's why Morph was there. He did the jokes!'

The veteran artist still played his part in the new series, as the calm narrator and also briefly appearing on screen in his bohemian art studio, but this time, the real focus is what is going on *under* the table. The naughty little brown man with a button nose and mitten hands still lives in a wooden pencil box on Hart's desk, but a whole new metamorphic world lies beneath. Also transferring from a supporting role in *Take Hart* is Morph's pugilistic mate Chas, the sort of plasticine bloke you'd find down the pub telling tall stories and getting drunk very quickly. He can't get pissed on kids' TV though, so instead he gorges himself on lemonade, loses his temper and ends up having 40 winks with his head in a comic instead. When Morph and Chas aren't scrapping they're morphing through the table to mess about in a subterranean society where people relax in yoghurt pots, eat their dinner on an England's Glory matchbox and do peculiar things with doorknobs. This *is* the amazing world of Morph after all, or perhaps more like a modelling clay version of Mary Norton's novel, *The Borrowers*.

The new series introduced a host of new Morphs, which proved, without a shadow of a doubt, that these plasticine creatures could actually reproduce somehow, despite not having any visible sexual organs. 'The BBC strongly advised us that we needed more characters for the spin-off series,' explains Lord. 'Now I know how scientific it is when you make a kids' TV show. I didn't in the 1970s. You just did it. It would have been difficult to tell a story with just Morph and Chas so we had to invent some more very quickly.' Head of the new household is a cantankerous old man named Grandmorph, equally proud of his Santa Claus beard as he is of his mastery of the skateboard. There's also Gillespie, a big clumsy blue giant – very much the Bernard Bresslaw of the plasticine world – whose gentle meditation is in stark contract to his terrifyingly heavy eyebrows. A hysterical, sulky, ginger-haired tomboy called Delilah represents the sympathetic female character. She's doing a home study course in plumbing and is jealous of her pretty girlie friend Folly, who always catches Morph's wandering eye because she's made of sparkly aluminium foil. ('We used some deplorable stereotypes really,' chuckles Lord when he thinks about his old characters, 'but you fall into stereotypes when you are making something new.') An exceedingly ugly kleptomaniac alien called Gobbledegook, some 'very small creatures', which look like Smarties, and a nailbrush, which thinks it's a dog, also make regular appearances. 'Beyond the Morph segments in *Take Hart* we didn't really have any experience of making self-contained episodes in a series, so it was a learning experience for us. Patrick Dowling, *Take Hart*'s producer, came on board just in case it didn't work. But it did succeed and pretty spectacularly at that!'

Within a few episodes of *The Amazing Adventures of Morph*'s debut in October 1980, the series was racking up viewing figures of well over ten million, something that still amazes Peter Lord to this day. 'We got *a lot* of million,' he laughs. 'The series was huge, but what pleased me most about the show's success was we had naughty characters which children loved. It was very important that Morph misbehaved and that Chas was ostentatiously bad. Chas is loud and raucous and probably likes dirty jokes. Morph is a bit more pompous and self-important and thinks Chas is his intellectual inferior, but Morph also has preposterous optimism too. Our characters had an edge to them unlike...' Lord chooses his words carefully, '...well *other* teatime series had blameless characters doing blameless things and they were bland. Morph and Chas trick and tease each other and they could act. It is very important to remember that, because they were made of plasticine, we could change their faces. We could make them look devious or sneaky or sulky or whatever. Whole storylines in *The Amazing Adventures of Morph* were motivated by reprehensible actions, which I always thought was a good thing. Children love all that!'

The Morph character has been in continual production for over 25 years now, appearing in all of Tony Hart's TV series and getting a second flush of stardom with his own series *The Morph Files* in 1995. Whilst Aardman's technically stunning *Wallace and Gromit, Chicken Run* and *Creature Comforts* productions have somewhat overshadowed his achievements, Morph is still the plasticine daddy of them all. Aardman's Bristol offices now bulge with Oscars and BAFTAs but it is Morph who has been awarded the ultimate accolade: a *Blue Peter* badge, and not even Gromit got one of those. 'I have such great affection and enthusiasm for Morph,' explains Peter Lord. 'I no longer animate him, sadly, but he continues his life and he'll always be with me because he's part of my heritage. I remember the old days with great fondness. Under the hot studio lights he'd go quite hard and fall over.' Lord looks misty-eyed for a second. 'You know, sometimes even his arms would drop off.'

ANDY PANDY

BBC TV / Produced 1969 (colour version) / A Westerham Arts Film Production / Created and Written by Freda Lingstrom and Mary Adams / Narrated by Vera McKechnie / Singing by Valerie Cardnell / Music by Maria Bird / 13 episodes / First broadcast (colour version) 5 January 1970

Along with a dapple-coloured mule and a couple of knuckle-heads made out of terracotta pots, *Andy Pandy* is one of the big boys of British kids' TV. This rather unlovely puppet was co-created by the then head of BBC children's programming Freda Lingstrom, who had consulted child psychologists at the Ministry of Education before feeling safe enough to unleash him on the viewing public. He made his first wobbly appearance as part of the *Watch with Mother* strand in July 1950. Only 26 black-and-white episodes were made but, in an era when children's TV was still in its infancy, the BBC kept on showing them. Unbelievably these early episodes were repeated some 34 times in less than 20 years. I have little recollection of Mr Pandy, but my mother swears I was a big fan in the early 1970s, but only when Andy went Technicolor.

After two decades of black-and-white adventures – always ending with Andy and his two chums, Teddy and Looby Loo, safely tucked up in a picnic hamper at the conclusion of each show – the BBC commissioned 13 new colour episodes. The trio returned unchanged, as did the *Thunderbird*-esque strings, which kept them nimble on their toes. The quaint Victorian piano music still tinkles in the background, accompanied by the high-pitched shrill of singer Valerie

Cardnell. Andy himself probably looks a lot worse in colour. He's a sickly, pasty-faced individual in a blue striped pyjama suit and a three-cornered hat. His waxy complexion and curled upper lip give him the look of a teenage Irish race-goer at the Cheltenham Gold Cup who's downed way too much Guinness. In fact his trembling hands and nodding head indicate that he may well have been a recovering alcoholic. Rarely has there been a more unattractive pre-school hero, but since virtually all the action is (puzzlingly) filmed in long shot we don't get to see his pallid features too closely.

By today's standards *Andy Pandy* is a pretty primitive show. In fact by 1970's standards it's a primitive show. The mute marionettes wobble all over the place ('Teddy needs a rest after falling flat so often,' we are told) and austere narrator Vera McKechnie dominates the proceedings by barking out orders willy-nilly. 'Don't touch that!' 'Hurry up!' 'Go over there now!' she shrieks. She saves her worst tongue-lashings for poor Looby Loo, the drippy rag-doll with the woolly lips. The script stipulates that girls do not like the same things as boys; therefore Looby is denied the pleasures of the trampoline, the sandpit and the hobbyhorse. Even buns and milk are off limits. If she dares to even get close to Andy and Teddy she is ordered off screen forthwith. 'Andy and Teddy are playing together. You mustn't go there,' McKechnie warns Looby sternly. 'Run away Looby!' Just what is she so scared of Looby seeing? Oh, actually here we go. Andy is pushing Teddy round the garden like a wheelbarrow. 'Do you like being a wheelbarrow Teddy?' she asks politely.

Yes, the show is traditional, and remembered with great fondness by its fans, but what is so apparent now is how startlingly sexist and embarrassingly dated it is. In its first black-and-white incarnation Andy was rubbing shoulders with *The Woodentops*, so he knew no better, and, hey, it was the early 1950s. But by the time this remake of *Andy Pandy* was shown, we'd already had the more realistic view of family life in Alison Prince's *Joe*, the feminist adventures of *Mary, Mungo and Midge* and even Valerie Singleton wrestling lions on *Blue Peter*. The colour *Andy Pandy* really was the final remnant of 'old school'-style kids' telly, trading on gender stereotypes and pre-war notions of 'proper behaviour'. However, the BBC had paid for the new colour episodes and got their money's worth repeating them a further 15 times until 1976, when Andy was finally put back in his tatty picnic basket.

Amazingly, against all the odds, the pyjama-clad lad did return in 2002, but this time superiorly animated by Cosgrove Hall Films. He looks somewhat different now; the strings are gone and a more friendly *Noddy*-esque face has replaced Andy's once-sozzled features. Most revolutionary of all, his put-upon, felt-faced ragdoll sidekick is now described as 'a real modern twenty-first century girl.' This can mean only one thing: after half a century Looby is finally allowed to play 'wheelbarrows'.

ANIMAL MAGIC

BBC TV / Produced 1962-1983 / A BBC Bristol Production / Originally produced by Winwood Reade / Originally directed by George Inger / Presented by Johnny Morris with Tony Soper, Gerald Durrell, Keith Shackleton and Terry Nutkins / Theme tune: 'Las Vegas' by Laurie Johnson / 454 episodes / First broadcast 13 April 1962

When you were little did you honestly think camels spoke with clipped Home Counties' accents? Well, if you did you must have been either pretty stupid or more likely a fan of British TV's best-ever natural history entertainment show, *Animal Magic*. The first wild animal series to be specifically aimed at young children was BBC's *Zoo Time* in 1956, presented by naturalist and body language expert Desmond Morris. Now Desmond certainly knew his leopard's spots from his tiger's stripes but he had one failing. *He couldn't do funny voices.*

This was soon hastily rectified in 1962 with the birth of the long-running *Animal Magic*. That show's presenter was a little Welsh man with a kindly face and wavy silver hair. And he was excellent at funny voices. Johnny Morris had originally worked on a farm in Wiltshire, but found his true vocation using his wonderfully expressive tones on radio in 1946. At first, he was only known to listeners in the West Country, but his big break came seven years later when he was asked to front *The Hot Chestnut Man* (1953-1961) on TV. A forerunner to

Jackanory, the series enabled Morris to exploit his greatest strength – communicating to children without patronising them. One episode of *The Hot Chestnut Man* was filmed at Bristol Zoo with Morris starring alongside permanent resident Rosie the elephant. That episode was so successful that the BBC approached him to present a new zoological series. The pilot episode of *Animal Magic* showed Morris taking a nap under a tree on Bristol's famous green space, the Clifton Downs. As Morris sleeps he dreams he's applying to become a keeper at the nearby zoo. He gets the job and within minutes is kitted out in the uniform and peaked cap. This image of Johnny as zookeeper extraordinaire stuck fast and for the next 454 episodes he played the role with surprising believability and a smattering of comic timing that Norman Wisdom would have been envious of.

'He was a natural with the animals and a natural in front of the cameras,' recalls his good friend and real-life head keeper at Bristol Zoo, Donald Packham. 'People honestly thought he really was a real zoo employee. They'd arrive at the zoo expecting to see him mucking out the elephants, but when he wasn't there we had to tell his fans he was on his day off!' In fact Morris had his own uniform especially made and whenever zoo staff had replacements an extra one was tailored for the TV star.

After a day's filming at the zoo Morris would return to his house and watch the day's rushes. He'd then write a script and add his distinctive voice-over later. It appeared that his animal friends really were talking to him and Morris was able to give them their own individual personalities and curious peccadilloes. Oscar the orang-utan became a mischievous gravel-voiced cockney; Flo the giant anteater was a delicate namby-pamby and Gustav the hippo was a greedy German glutton. One of his most famous co-stars was Dottie, the sensitive ring-tailed lemur who chattered nervously and was fed jelly tots by the children's presenter. Morris's talent for anthropomorphism became his trademark and it was impossible to look a camel in the eye without imagining it speaking in a haughty, superior voice. 'Camels are the easiest to give voices to,' commented Morris, 'because they are always chewing and moving their mouths.'

Despite being middle-aged when fame finally found him Morris insisted on doing all his own stunts. He clambered, unassisted, onto

an elephant's back, brushed a crocodile's teeth without gloves and was flung to the ground by a doleful dromedary. Dottie the lemur bit him on the ear and drew blood during one day's recording. 'In the early days all the shows went out live,' recalls Donald Packham. 'It meant that anything could happen. Johnny and I had to wrestle a temperamental tapir to the floor totally live on the show once. We did the interview lying on the floor desperately holding onto this creature.'

One of Bristol Zoo's tetchiest inmates was Audrey the blue and yellow African macaw. 'She had a very colourful vocabulary and always seemed to sense when a party of schoolchildren or a vicar were near her cage,' chuckles Packham. 'She really did know an extensive range of swear words.' Against the zoo's advice the BBC producers invited Audrey in their BBC Bristol studios to feature her in a live programme. She behaved impeccably until right at the end of the show. 'As Johnny was saying goodbye, the parrot squawked "bollocks!" at the top of her voice and we just all fell about laughing,' recalls Packham.

As *Animal Magic* progressed over its mighty 22 year reign on TV its content had to modernise too. The programme became less about chimpanzee's tea parties and giving elephants showers with hosepipes and more about conservation. Morris was ably assisted by a series of co-presenters including Gerald Durrell, Keith Shackleton and Tony Soper and filmed items at other zoos as far away as Japan, Germany and Africa. By the time the show had reached its 1970s heyday Morris had a new assistant, Terry 'Nutkins' Nutkins, a balding hippy who had hand-reared a sea lion from just a few weeks old. Gemini, as was her name, became a huge star of the show and Johnny even released a seven-inch single in tribute to her. Needless to say 'Geminee Geminii' did not exactly set the charts alight.

The dream-team pairing of the comical, but kind-hearted, Morris and his youthful sidekick Nutkins gave the show it biggest viewing figures, but there were rumblings at the BBC that talking animals were becoming old hat. 'There was a feeling at the BBC that it wasn't right that Johnny was still providing voices for the creatures,' explains Donald Packham. 'They wanted the show taken off air because the felt it was corrupting children. It was plainly rubbish. Johnny never did any harm. He knew children weren't stupid.'

After the 42nd series had finished in 1983 Morris was called to the higher echelons of the BBC and told that his services were no longer required. The show's axing was a body blow from which Morris never really recovered. 'He was absolutely devastated,' recalls Packham. 'That show was his life and he loved it. He was never quite the same afterwards but he still enjoyed coming to Bristol Zoo and he did talks for children there. The public still absolutely adored him.' However, Morris was not one to mope about. His knack for storytelling never left him and he wrote his autobiography *Around the World in 25 Years*, as well as continuing to work extensively on radio. He still kept abreast of conservation issues and was campaigning against the controversial Newbury by-pass in his late 70s. In the spring of 1999, after years away from children's television, Morris was invited to provide animal voices once again, but this time for the inmates of Marwell Zoo in Winchester for a new ITV series called *Wild Thing*. Now a sprightly 82 years old, his TV comeback was announced triumphantly in national press. 'It will be nice,' he said philosophically. 'My sort of stuff is dead and buried, but they have found that a lot of children still like me.' Sadly, just three days later Morris collapsed at his home in Hungerford and was rushed to hospital. He never fully recovered and on 5 May 1999 he died at a nursing home. His friend and co-star Terry Nutkins paid affectionate tribute to him: 'He was just, for want of a better word, a magic person.'

BAGPUSS

BBC TV / Produced 1974 / A Smallfilms Production / Written and Produced by Oliver Postgate / Illustrations and Puppets by Peter Firmin, Babette Cole with Linda Birch, Jean Firmin and Charlotte Firmin / Music by John Faulkner and Sandra Kerr / Narrated by Oliver Postgate, John Faulkner and Sandra Kerr / 13 episodes / First broadcast 12 February 1974

In 1999 *Bagpuss* was voted Britain's favourite children's TV character in a nationwide poll conducted by the BBC. Naturally, when a cuddly fat moggy is awarded such a flattering accolade, opportunistic merchandisers' eyes light up with £ signs. As a result, never has a 1970s puppet been marketed so ruthlessly into the millennium as *Bagpuss* has. The transition from *Watch with Mother* to a sparkly concession in Harrods has made the saggy cloth cat into a marketing success story. Take your pick from *Bagpuss* mousemats, *Bagpuss* Nokia phones, yawning *Bagpuss* alarm clocks, *Bagpuss* toothbrushes, inflatable *Bagpuss* chairs, and last, but not least, those interminable *Bagpuss* toys with suction pads which appear in car windows in every street in Britain.

Bagpuss is used to being a commodity. After all, he started life in a shop window anyway, but an unusual shop window where nothing was ever for sale. The shop was called Bagpuss & Co, owned by a little Victorian girl named Emily. Unlike most little girls who liked to stay at home playing with their dolls' houses, Emily busied herself going through bins and hedgerows looking for discarded junk. Each week she placed a broken object in the shop window among the old toys, wooden nick-nacks and silly trinkets. The opening sequence of the show was identical for each episode – Emily in her tidy pinafore dress creeping about with a wicker basket with a secret 'thing' in it. I used to find it all a bit eerie actually, especially when Emily whispered a magic incantation and the sepia-tinged photos slowly flickered into colour: 'Bagpuss, dear Bagpuss, Old fat furry cat-puss, Wake up and look at the thing that I bring....'

Sabrina the teenage witch has nothing on Emily, that's for sure. Emily's beloved stuffed cat Bagpuss awakes first and when he begins yawning so his friends come to life too. Emily promptly leaves her 'thing', usually a broken statue, a dirty shoe, a rusty tin bucket, a broken necklace or a tatty raffia toy and does a runner, leaving her magical friends to, literally, pick up the pieces, and uncover a tale and a tune.

The masterly Oliver Postgate wrote the stories and the puppets were created by his partner Peter Firmin, the father of Basil Brush. Lovely, cuddly old Bagpuss is a corpulent bundle of pink and yellow stripes and boasts the most expressive puppet face ever. The plump feline looks continually incredulous, like a startled old granddad shaken from his comfortable slumber. Bewildered and befuddled, Bagpuss is slowly pressed into action by a wooden bookend carved in the shape of a studious woodpecker. Professor Yaffle (Augustus Barclay Yaffle to his close friends) is a cynical, old-fashioned kind of bird, disapproving of frivolity and prone to opinionated outbursts. He'll have a poke about with his beak at the junk left by Emily and immediately write it off. 'Nyek, nyek, nyek. Ridiculous! Ridiculous!' he exclaims. 'It is all nonsense!' The nyek bit either seems to be a bit of a speech impediment or just Yaffle's way of verbalising his thoughts. Gabriel the banjo-strumming frog also strains to have a look at Emily's 'thing' while clearing his throat with an unpleasant 'hyuk, hyuk' sound, which still disgusts me to this today.

Gabriel's musical partner is Madeleine, a pancake-faced rag doll with terrifyingly piercing almond-shaped eyes. Apart from singing she doesn't do much, preferring to stare unblinking from her wicker chair and chide the over-enthusiastic mice, which swarm all over Emily's 'thing'. The mice are really the stars of *Bagpuss*. They get practical things done while the university-educated bookend barks orders and Madeleine shouts, 'Stop! Stop at once!' She's a bit of a spoilsport because the mice just want to restore Emily's lost object. They want to display it, clean and gleaming again, in the shop window, in the vain hope that its owner will come and collect it. 'We will rub it. We will scrub it,' sing the enterprising mice, as adept with brushes as they are with a needle and cotton or a duster. Poor Yaffle positively loathes rubbish. 'Well *that* is a pink elephant,' he says disgustedly, looking at Emily's latest arrival. 'It's made of straw, it's very tatty and hasn't any ears. I'm not surprised it looks sad!'

As well as playing deservedly dirty tricks on Yaffle with chocolate biscuits – definitely *not* made from butterbeans and breadcrumbs – the mice also form a musical collective. The tiny tenants of the Marvellous Mechanical Mouse Organ happily heave (or more accurately 'Heave! Heave! Heave!') organ rolls into their machine to create sweet folk music and a moving picture projected onto a little screen. *Bagpuss* fans could enjoy two wonderful stories an episode, either emanating from the Mouse organ itself or from Bagpuss's delightfully woolly thought bubbles. Peter Firman's meticulous drawings and three dimensional puppet characters illustrate the delectable stories. They range from the funny (an ancient king who weaves his silvery beard into a rug), the heartbreaking (the love between a Scotsman and a tartan 'Hamish' – a cross between a haggis and a set of bagpipes) and the jubilant (silly Uncle Feedle and his patchwork world). Feedle is the highpoint of the series for me, a foolish, whirling rag doll who builds himself a flippy-floppy fabric house which won't stay up until he stuffs it full of cotton wool. But only then the silly fool can't get through the door!

Sandra Kerr and John Faulkner's jolly olde English tunes provide the uptempo backing to all the stories. The *Bagpuss* revival has encouraged the original musicians to go back on the road to play the series' songs to hyperventilating audiences at folk festivals across the UK, excitedly waving their hands in the air and screaming 'Heave!' at the top of their voices. I know this to be true because I've met people who have done it.

There were only 13 episodes of *Bagpuss* made, repeated by the BBC a whopping 27 times until 1987. But he lives on, through car air fresheners, underpants and slippers. More importantly, the series is still vivid in people's memories. (Is there anything more traumatic than watching Charlie mouse being forcibly stuffed head-first into a brandy bottle?) As Oliver Postgate used to say at the end of each episode, Bagpuss is 'just an old saggy cloth cat, baggy and a bit loose at the seams. But Emily loved him.' And millions still do.

BARBAPAPA

BBC TV / Produced 1974 / A Polyscope Production / Created by Annette Tison and Talus Taylor / Music by The Paul Reade Ensemble / Narrated by Michael Flanders / 45 episodes / First broadcast (UK) 17 January 1975

Depending how posh you are, you can pronounce the name of this series as 'Babba-pappa' or 'Barba-par-par'. I always go for the latter, but this curious confection is not to be confused with the similar-sounding European character Babar. One is grey and has a trunk (therefore identifying him as an elephant); the other is an obese, legless, ectoplasmic blob who slides across the floor (and is a total freak of nature). Before we go any further it should be noted that Mr Barbapapa is French and his name derives from the slang word for candyfloss. Like candyfloss, Barbapapa is indeed shocking pink, incredibly sugary and makes you violently sick if you have too much. Knowing British children have sensitive stomachs the BBC made the sensible decision to broadcast only 30 of the 45 episodes made. Over on the continent, however, every last morsel of Barbapapa was gobbled up, along with his syrupy children.

Barbapapa was born in 1970 in a picture book written by Annette Tison and her husband Talus Taylor. Tison had been working as an architect in Paris when she met, and fell in love with, Taylor, an American mathematics teacher. Together they started writing for pre-school children and a big pink blob was the result. A number one bestseller, the book, and its many sequels, were turned into a cartoon series four years later and sold to an incredible 40 countries world-wide. The *Barbapapa* saga explains how a simple French boy, named François, is happily watering his flowerbeds when a 20 feet tall lump bursts through the soil and introduces himself. Despite his beautiful garden being completely destroyed, the lad takes it very well: 'François was surprised to see Barbapapa, but they quickly became friends....'

Big pink blobs, although difficult to explain to the neighbours, are very useful nevertheless, especially when they can change shape.

Barbapapa's greatest talent is being able to squeeze through railings; turning himself into a swing for the local children or morphing into an escape chute when people are burning to death in a block of flats opposite. In fact, so flexible is Barbapapa that he sometimes moulds his body into things that are disturbing, as well as helpful. I don't know quite why, but seeing him change into the shape of a boat or a school bus full of screaming children made me feel sick. Of course, the old shape-shifter doesn't have all the fun himself. Suddenly, Barbamama miraculously appears – also able to mutate, but black as the ace of spades and with daisies around her head. They had seven multicoloured kids too, all talented in their own way, despite having no legs. They were: Barbabravo (red and with muscles), Barbabright (blue and clever), Barbabelle (purple and vain), Barbabeau (black and, rather oddly, *very* hairy. He was an artist), Barbalib (tangerine and studious), Barbalala (green and musical) and Barbazoo (yellow and fond of animals). So we had nine transmogrifying terrors, just enough to spell out the letters of the series' name. 'They've got a lot of wild disguises. They can change their shapes and sizes,' went the theme tune.

In the UK version of the series the narration was provided by Michael Flanders, best remembered as one half of the comedy-musical duo Flanders and Swann. Flanders was an erudite man, the writer of several West End reviews and a star of the Broadway stage. Quite why he agreed to do *Barbapapa* is a mystery. It might have contributed to finishing him off too. Just weeks after the series started on BBC1 Flanders dropped dead, aged 53. In 1997 *Barbapapa* was repeated on French television for the first time in 20 years. The response from nostalgic viewers to episodes like 'Sheep Shearing', 'Milking Time' and, the rather controversial, 'Wine Party' was so positive that a brand new series was commissioned. This saw the amorphous family travel the globe. Fifty episodes of *Barbapapa Around the World* were made and again sold to every last corner of civilisation, except dear old Blighty, where the BBC rejected a second helping of cotton candy. The programmes were greeted with most riotous applause in Japan where Barbapapa is considered a god, and is on a par with cult figures such as Moomintroll, Hello Kitty and David Beckham.

BARNABY

BBC TV / Produced 1970-1972 / An Albert Braille Production / Created by Olga Pouchine / English version produced by Michael Grafton-Robinson for Q3 / Featuring the voices of Colin Jeavons, Charles Collingwood, Percy Edwards and Gwenllian Owen / Music by Mireille / 13 episodes (UK) / First broadcast (UK) 4 April 1973

Barnaby is his name so on no account whatsoever call him Jack or James. Never, ever. Don't make Barnaby angry. You wouldn't like him when he's angry. The thing is, his frustration is probably due to an identity crisis. After all, if you were a bear of indiscriminate breed you'd be temperamental too. Barnaby is short and red so he's not a grizzly, and despite having a white face and chest he's not a polar either. His blue eyes are a puzzle too, but he's hardly a panda. Who knows? Except that he looks like he's been knitted from an old sock. Oh, and he's got a bloody terrible singing voice. To confuse things further for the poor little chap, his real name isn't Barnaby at all. He was born with the name Colargol, which when said very quickly, sounds like the green liquid you squirt under the rim of the lavatory. Canadian readers may recognise him as Jeremy, which has nothing to do with cleaning products.

Colargol was born in the midst of France's sexual revolution in the 1960s and proved exceedingly popular with doting fathers who read the bear's storybook tales to their sleepy children at bedtime, before climbing down the drainpipe to meet their mistresses. Created by the matronly Olga Pouchine, the Colargol books were so popular across the continent that it wasn't long before an animation company, eager to set the bear's fluffy ears and bow tie in motion, approached her with an offer she couldn't refuse. French producer Albert Barille teamed up with Polish animator Tadeuzs Wilkoz and by 1970 the first 14-minute episode (of 52) had debuted on French television. Despite reservations from bed-hopping TV critics worried that the show would curtail their extra-marital affairs; the series was a massive hit. On the other side of the English Channel the BBC were also busy

eyeing up the diminutive Gallic bear. The corporation had already enjoyed successes with two other French-made series, *The Magic Roundabout* and *Hector's House*, and were always looking for other series to fill the *Watch with Mother* slot. The London-based animation company Q3 promptly bought up the rights to the first 13 episodes and translated them into English. It was decided that Colargol wasn't the sort of name to easily slip off a four year old's tongue, so he was hastily re-christened Barnaby. Actor Colin Jeavons, who had previously voiced Q3's *Joe* in 1966, was drafted into provide Barnaby's dulcet tones.

The British *Barnaby* explains how the pocket-sized hero longs to trill along with the birds in the enchanted wood. Sadly his voice is as palatable as Ozzy Osbourne's first thing in the morning, so he enlists the help of the 'King of the Birds.' He suffers the indignity of being dressed up in a big lace ruff and having a paper beak stuck on his gob, but it seems to work. Within minutes his caterwauling has become a beautiful carol. With a talent like this Barnaby sets about getting himself exploited, and quick. He signs up with Monsieur Pimoulou's circus and soon becomes the star attraction, but performance after performance asserts his right to explain his name is Barnaby. *Not* Jack or James. 'Barnaby the bear's my name. Never call me Jack or James. I will sing my way to fame....'

Ringmaster Pimoulou, a sneaky old rascal with more than a passing resemblance to Dick Dastardly, runs the sort of 1970s circus ring where animals get whipped and are made to jump through fiery hoops. (He also takes a close interest in his bikini-wearing Siamese cat acrobats, but we won't go there.) Thankfully Barnaby finally realises that there is more to showbusiness than being locked up in a cage every night and escapes to the North Pole (as you do). He also goes to jail and lands on the moon. He really needs a better agent. I live in hope that everybody's favourite egotistical French bear eventually found his way to the New York Academy of Performing Arts. After all, its catchphrase was: 'Fame! Remember my name!'

THE BASIL BRUSH SHOW

BBC TV / Produced 1968-1980 / A BBC Production / Created by Peter Firmin and Ivan Owen / Originally produced by Johnny Downes / Originally written by George Martin / Co-presented by Rodney Bewes (1968), Derek Fowlds (1969-1973), Roy North (1973-1977), Howard Williams (1977-1978) and Billy Boyle (1979-1980) / Basil voiced by Ivan Owen / 15 series / First Broadcast 14 June 1968

'Boom! Boom!' – one of the most memorable comedy catchphrases of the 1970s, brought to us courtesy of an 18 inch high fox called Basil. This was a truly incredible glove puppet; one that could attract 14 million viewers on a Saturday night, become the mascot of the Royal Navy's HMS Fox warship, regularly play the Royal Variety Performance, be invited to meet PM Jim Callaghan at 10 Downing Street, drive a Rolls-Royce and earn himself a cool £1,000,000 from lucrative advertising and sponsorship deals. This was no ordinary common or garden fox. In fact he wasn't the slightest bit common. He was dead posh.

Basil Brush had humble beginnings though. He was first launched on telly in 1963 in a little-known puppet show called *The Three Scampies* (no relation to Scampi from *Fingerbobs* incidentally) in which he played the sidekick to a Scottish hedgehog named Spike McPike and a human called Howard Williams. It was pretty basic slapstick stuff, but Basil's truculent tones and classy demeanour made him the real star of the show. And Basil certainly oozed class. Peter Firmin, later to co-create *Bagpuss*, allegedly made Britain's longest-living fox out of scraps of felt and tartan for less than £20. His friend Ivan Owen provided the haughty voice and a star was born. Dressed in waistcoat, tartan cape and sporting a cravat, Basil was a superior creation to those puppets that had gone before like *Muffin the Mule* or *Pinky and Perky.* Basil was a cad and a bounder and revelled in his ancestry; in fact he was partly based on comedy actor Terry-Thomas, right down to the gap-toothed look. 'I thought it would be nice to have a county fox,' recalled Owen, years later. 'Basil is a frightfully good counties name, don't you think?'

The positive audience reaction to *The Three Scampies* was heavily loaded towards its foxy star and before Spike McPike had even been put back into his dusty suitcase the BBC was approaching the bushy-tailed one for his own series. Basil got his big break in 1967 when he was signed up for a regular guest spot on *The Nixon Line* presented by David Nixon. Bald magician Nixon had been a household favourite since his early appearances on *What's My Line* and in the 1960s had been hosting his own variety shows. A genial presenter, with an endearingly hesitant manner, he was the perfect foil for the wisecracking fox. Basil was an instant hit with prime-time viewers, although his corny jokes have not dated well. 'Basil, how do you work?' asks Nixon, trying to work out where Ivan Owen's hand goes. 'Oh as little as possible, Mr Nixon!' replies Basil.

In 1968 the BBC gave Basil his own TV show. *The Basil Brush Show* ran for 12 years and became a staple of the corporation's Saturday night line-up, usually sandwiched between *Grandstand* and *Doctor Who*. The new half-hour programme comprised a bit of banter between Basil and his human 'straight man' (more of that later), a big production piece (usually in costume), a guest spot for the latest pop sensation and then a tale from the storybook, interrupted by Basil munching jelly babies, his favourite confection. The show was a magnet for guest stars and anybody who was *anybody* wanted to rub the fox up the right way. Pop groups like The Kinks, Herman's Hermits and Dave Dee, Dozy, Beaky, Mick and Titch all clamoured to appear on stage with the distinguished glove puppet. Basil had a definite eye for the ladies and was not adverse to staring, tail erect, at the heaving bosoms of Cilla Black and Lulu. *The Basil Brush Show* was a big deal for the BBC. Not only did it pull in millions of viewers, it also boasted some of the best production values of the 1970s. One week Basil would be starring in a skit about the French Foreign Legion, the next in a POW camp. He also enjoyed the company of his own orchestra and selection of leggy dancers. In many ways it was a 30-minute condensation of all the best bits from *The Stanley Baxter Show* or *The Black and White Minstrels*.

The best remembered part of the show was Basil's strained relationships with his human co-hosts. Ex-*Likely Lad* Rodney Bewes was the fox's first victim, but he only lasted 12 episodes. It's not surprising.

Ivan Owen had a habit of ad-libbing whenever possible and injecting slightly blue jokes and double entendres into the sketches. Not everybody appreciated them, but some presenters lasted longer than others. Bewes was replaced by Derek Fowlds (1969-1973), and then Roy North (1973-1977). Fowlds, who later went onto a starring role in *Yes, Minister* started the trend for being called 'Mister'. He was forever 'Mr Derek', but it was 'Mr Roy' who took the expression into the annals of history. Mr Roy – Basil's longest-suffering straight man – ruthlessly promoted the value of a floppy brown fringe and knitted tank top. For years I was convinced that he and Dave Bartram, the lead singer in Showaddywaddy, were one and the same person. Poor Mr Roy had to grin sweetly through Basil's really, really rotten gags. Example: 'A prune is just a worried plum. It's covered in wrinkles!' The scripts left an awful lot to be desired, but the kids, including myself, loved it. Basil's petrifying puns were always followed by his hysterical upper-class laugh and the 'Boom! Boom!' pay-off. On occasion he'd laugh so much he'd actually keel over on the desk.

When Mr Roy had taken about as many dreadful jokes as he could stomach, he was replaced by Howard Williamson (Basil's old sidekick from *The Three Scampies*) and then Billy Boyle (later the actor who played Ronald McDonald in the British TV adverts). Neither made a memorable impact and by 1980 the show was looking tired. Ivan Owen approached the BBC with an idea to make Basil a late night chat show host appealing to a more adult audience, but the corporation were not interested. Instead they axed *The Basil Brush Show* outright. The following two decades could be classed as Basil's 'lost years'. Although he made the odd guest appearance on *The Val Doonican Show* and was seen with Stu Francis on *Crackerjack*, the once famous fox was no longer a top-billed attraction. He briefly starred in an educational series for ITV in January 1983 called *Let's Read with Basil Brush*, but it did not showcase his humour to best effect. For a period in 1986 he was reduced to acting as a 'continuity fox' presenting the links between ITV children's programmes. For some odd reason he occasionally did this in drag and was unable to announce *The Moomins* without stuttering. The fox had lost every scrap of dignity he once had.

Fortunately, because of his associations with the Royal Variety Performances, Basil still had fans at Buckingham Palace. In 1987 he was

duly summoned to be the star turn at Prince William's fifth birthday party. He returned to production, although under much reduced circumstances, in 1990's independently made *Basil Brush's Cartoon Storybook*. The show, never shown on terrestrial television, presented Basil as a shadow of his former self, living in a hollowed-out oak tree (the shame of it!) and without a straight man to bounce off. All Basil did was provide the links between some unpleasant 1970s animation from Japan, voiced by a simpering American woman. It was the utmost humiliation.

However, by the end of the 1990s Basil was being fêted again. He made highly publicised, but bizarre, appearances on Frank Skinner's risqué *Fantasy Football League*, wrote a lively autobiography and was awarded a 'Lifetime Achievement Award' by the lads' mag *Loaded* in May 2000. By the end of that summer the BBC approached him to make a new show. There was no certainty that Basil's famous laugh would be revived by Ivan Owen himself, as he had sold the rights to his puppet in 1997, but to many fans there was only man who could fit the furry glove snugly. Sadly, disaster struck: Owen, the man who had provided Basil's incredible voice for over 30 years, suddenly died of cancer at the age of 73. The actor had always refused publicity throughout his life and was never photographed for fear that it would ruin the 'magic' of Basil. He died just as invisibly as he had lived, but there was life in the old fox yet.

The Basil Brush Show returned to the BBC in 2002, but this time as a domestic sitcom with intrusive canned laughter. Basil now resides with an eccentric suburban family and looks somewhat plumper and younger than he used to (a new puppet was modelled from Peter Fermin's original drawings). He's got a new voice too, but it's pretty convincing, especially at press conferences. 'When the producers approached me I had to ensure they appreciated my true standing as an international megastar,' Basil said in the national press. 'They offered me jelly babies and it was an offer I just couldn't refuse!' He's still a master of self-publicity too. In the summer of 2003 he made the tabloids again when he had his tail insured during a countrywide promotional tour. The policy promised to pay £1 million if Basil's nether regions suffered 'permanent damage'. Considering he's had a hand stuck up his backside for 40 years I'd have thought he'd have the constitution of an ox. Or should that be fox?

BATTLE OF THE PLANETS

BBC TV / Produced 1978-1979 / A Tatsunoko Production / Directed by David E Hanson / Produced by Sandy Frank / Music by Hoyt S Curtin / Featuring the voices of Casey Kasem (Mark), Keye Luke (Zoltar), Alan Young (Keyop and 7-Zark-7), Janet Waldo (Princess and Susan), Ronnie Schell (Jason) and Alan Dinehart (Tiny Harper) / 85 episodes / First broadcast (UK) 3 September 1979

Battle of the Planets was *incredibly* popular with eight-year-old boys. It had sleek spaceships, horrific monsters *and* effeminate robots. In the post-*Star Wars* universe it was the perfect teatime accompaniment to fish fingers and crinkle-cut chips. Scenes from the series could be endlessly re-enacted in the playground the following day, but, best of all, the show featured a character with a speech defect which was easy to mimic and perfect for annoying teachers. His name was Keyop and he spoke like this: 'Brrrrr-root-proot-toot-toot teeny-weeny'. Ah, happy days!

The programme that we watched spellbound (but mostly in dumb disbelief) in Britain in the late 1970s was actually adapted and translated from an original animated series made in Japan in 1972. Catchily entitled *Science Ninja Team Gatchaman*, the show ran for an incredible 105 episodes in its home country and was so successful that it spawned a further 100 episodes in two sequels called *Science Ninja Team Gatchaman II* (1979) and *Science Ninja Team Gatchaman Fighter* (1979). For a while, it seemed, the Japanese just couldn't get enough Gatchaman.

Naturally, all this Gatchaman stuff went straight over the heads of stuffy American TV executives whose only concern was how to make the incredibly violent series more palatable to children more used to *Yogi Bear.* At a cost of over $5 million, a team of Hanna-Barbera graduates, headed by producer Sandy Frank, tore the show to pieces, re-titled it, edited out all the gratuitous razor blade decapitations, re-wrote all the storylines and added new linking sequences with a friendly robot to jigger things along a bit. The best bit, however, was a glorious new opening theme tune. Sounding like the music for the

opening ceremony of a gay Olympic Games, the tune swirls and swoops in a *Charlie's Angels* versus *Star Wars* kind of way. Why some bright spark didn't add vocals from Amii Stewart or Tina Charles and release it as a single is anyone's guess.

The basic premise of *Battle of the Planets* is that Earth is constantly under attack by the dying planet of Spectra, which has used up all its natural resources and is actively seeking to plunder our world of all its lovely things. The ruler of Spectra is called the 'Great Spirit', a disembodied floating bird head who hisses out orders to his henchmen from a TV screen. You can forget about bird heads for a minute because the real villain of the piece was a seven-foot-tall theatrical drag artiste called Zoltar. Easily the freakiest baddie on 1970s telly, Zoltar got to camp it up with his red lipstick, unfeasibly large pointed bat-eared headdress, and laugh maniacally at given points during each episode. He really was a nasty sort. Each week the ever-persistent Zoltar would launch another fearsome plague on the world in the shape of a giant 'space terrapin', a 'space serpent' or a 'space squid'. You see some sort of pattern emerging here? In fact, by the end of the series it was all getting quite ridiculous, with Earth regularly being attacked by antagonistic armadillos, cuttlefish and furry seals.

The Intergalactic Federation was obviously disturbed by these terrifying events and sought to protect the Earth from attack. And whom did they choose to defend our liberty? Why, five orphaned teenagers dressed as poultry! G-Force are a motley collection of parentless youths with cerebonically-enhanced powers (a-hem!) who liked nothing better than donning skin-tight bird suits and saving the world. Mark was the leader – a butch, tousle-haired no-nonsense pretty boy who rather let the side down by being voiced by Casey Kasem, better known for bringing dopey drop-out Shaggy from *Scooby-Doo* to life. His side-kick was Jason, the arrogant impulsive one, and they were joined by a stroppy women's libber called Princess, continually flashing her white panties and 'Tiny' Harper, who wasn't, but was instead rather overweight and dull, and wore his lycra suit far too tight. Rounding off the team was Keyop, the one with the speech impediment and the character who embodied the show's bizarre appeal. Apparently Keyop was born from a single

embryonic cell in a Californian laboratory, but obviously something went very badly wrong. Standing only a few feet tall and dressed like a duck Keyop squealed like an imbecile and sported a pronounced overbite (just like one boy in the bottom class for English at my primary school). Together the teenagers make an unlikely band of feathery freedom fighters, but they are united by their well-worn catchphrase: 'Dedicated, Inseparable, INVINCIBLE!'

G-Force are called to arms whenever they get the call from Center Neptune, a top secret world defence base 900 fathoms under the sea off the west coast of the USA. Sending the five orphaned teenagers into perilous danger each week is a kindly, but desperately fey robot especially designed by the American animators to top and tail the action-packed storylines and provide what they call in the business some 'light relief'. The robot in question, 7-Zark-7, is in a wholly different class of animation from the rest of the stylish Japanese original and his R2-D2-inspired design is, frankly, rubbish. This 7-Zark-7 is a twittering, hypochondriac who endlessly worries about the children in his charge ('It's a good thing I don't need sleep,' he opines). Far camper even than Zoltar, 7-Zark-7 nevertheless asserts his heterosexuality by flirting with a disembodied female voice called Susan (played by voice-over artiste Janet Waldo, who a decade earlier had created Penelope Pitstop) who spouts disgusting double-entendres via an intercom on Pluto.

The show was a forerunner for the superior American cartoon series *Thundercats* (1985-1987), where the heroes weren't birds they were, um, cats, and the execrable live-action Japanese hit *Mighty Morphin' Power Rangers* (1993-1996). As for *Battle of the Planets*, the formula remained largely unchanged over the 85 American episodes. The brew was an intoxicating one: lots of American cod-philosophy about family values and world peace, and some painfully slow action all mixed up with the hallmarks of Japanese *anime*; namely close-up shots of gritted teeth, anguished expressions and beads of sweat rolling off furrowed brows, not to mention some regular underage knicker-flashing.

Confusingly, the series was re-issued for American television in 1987 under the title *G-Force* with the silly stories re-written for a second time. It was hastily re-edited and all the voices completely

re-recorded by different actors. As a consequence, the principal characters had to endure the indignity of being given even more ridiculous names. Tubby 'Tiny' Harper was saddled with the rather cumbersome moniker 'Hoot Owl' and Zoltar got a much-needed injection of testosterone when he was re-named 'Galactor'. However, best of all, the annoying Keyop was appropriately re-christened 'Pee Wee', which just about served him right.

BLUE PETER

BBC TV / Produced 1958- / A BBC Production / Originally produced by John Hunter Blair / Series Editors include: Biddy Baxter (1962-1988) and Lewis Bronze (1988-1996) / Presenters include: Christopher Trace, Valerie Singleton, John Noakes, Peter Purves, Lesley Judd, Simon Groom, Sarah Greene, Peter Duncan, Janet Ellis, Michael Sundin and Mark Curry / Over 3800 episodes so far / First broadcast 16 October 1958

Perhaps I should come clean before we go on. I have a very tentative connection with this series because I am one of those fortunate individuals who own a *Blue Peter* badge. Yes, a real *Blue Peter* badge. And not one I picked up at a car boot sale either. I won it fair and square. The memories are slightly hazy now, but some time during the 1970s *Blue Peter* got a bit obsessed with Himalayan expeditions and tales of big hairy beasts who lived in ice caves. They had a competition to find the best drawing of the so-called 'Abominable Snowman'. Being an artistic lad I excitedly rushed off my felt-tipped masterpiece to the BBC and waited patiently. Boy, did I wait patiently, but I didn't win. The first prize was a weekend in a cave with a Yeti, so maybe just as well. I was a runner-up though (in the 'five to seven category') and had my name read out on telly. They pronounced it wrong. Several days later I got my badge sent through the post with a letter signed by John Noakes, Peter Purves and the lissom Lesley Judd. It was photocopied.

I'm looking at my badge as I write this, but it's suddenly dawned on me that not once did I ever use it to get me free entrance to

'hundreds of British attractions'. In fact it's been sitting in a drawer for 25 years. Hold on a minute, while I make a telephone call… I've just spoken to a fiercely professional young lady in the *Blue Peter* office at the BBC. She tells me that I still *could* use my badge at 'hundreds of British attractions'. But at my age I'm going to be a bit shamefaced flashing my credentials over the counter at Wookey Hole. 'Do I have to wear the badge for the duration of my visit?' I ask her. 'That's up to you,' she says, desperately trying to get me off the phone. She's got a Bring and Buy sale to organise, I expect.

Dear old reliable, lovely, wholesome *Blue Peter*. It's the BBC's flagship children's television series, having made its debut at 5.00 pm on 16 October 1958. In those black-and-white days it was just 15 minutes long and went out once a week. The very first episode was presented by Charlton Heston's body double Christopher Trace and featured an item on mind reading. That was actually a bit spooky for *Blue Peter*. Playing with train sets was more their cup of tea. Trace and a succession of pretty co-presenters – Leila Williams, Anita West and the fabled Valerie Singleton – spent four years doing historical items on Henry VIII, inviting Shetland ponies into the studio and making things out of washing up bottles (the brand name was always obscured with black tape). It was all jolly good fun and then the show's creator, John Hunter Blair, departed and was replaced by the celebrated Biddy Baxter. By all accounts she wasn't the easiest person to work with, as plenty of ex-presenters have testified, but under her 26-year tenure the show scaled new heights of worthiness. It was Biddy who introduced the yearly charity appeals, started the cult of the *Blue Peter* pet and steered the programme into its new twice-weekly slot.

It was Biddy who also insisted that *Blue Peter* have an annual expedition abroad; so British children could laugh at all the Johnny Foreigners and be thoroughly glad that they lived in Britain. For married presenter Christopher Trace the first *Blue Peter* expedition to Norway was also his last. Whilst out there he shagged a pretty Scandinavian girl and when schoolmistress Biddy found out she hit the roof. Trace's contract was not renewed and he ended up driving a mini-cab around Norwich. With Trace's departure the programme entered its golden age, thanks to the introduction of two new male

presenters who were thrilled to bookend Ms Singleton. Former actors John Noakes and Peter Purves stayed in the job for longer than they should have, but they became synonymous with all that was fun and unpredictable about the series.

Yorkshireman Noakes rapidly became TV's action man doing feats of endurance far and above the call of duty. In 1967 he climbed, unassisted, 127 feet up the rigging of HMS Ganges and made headlines across the country. The following series he assailed Nelson's Column, without a safety harness, just so he could show viewers how to scrape pigeon shit off the plinth. Five years later he skydived five miles with the RAF Flying Falcons, but it was in 1975 that he nearly made an unexpected exit from the show. Hurtling on a sledge down the world famous Cresta Run in Switzerland, Noakes collided with a hole in the ice wall and completed the rest of his journey skidding on his arse at 80mph. Dragged off the slopes delirious and disorientated, Noakes was lucky to survive. Biddy and her 'firm but fair' producer Edward Barnes pushed their presenters to the very limit in the pursuit of ratings, but provided their daredevils with only minimal insurance cover. Noakes, in particular, has bemoaned that he nearly died just for £25 per show and several of his other embittered colleagues claim their stunts contravened health and safety regulations. In 1968 Valerie Singleton nearly had her spinal cord ripped out after a speed-boat stunt on the River Thames went disastrously wrong. ('I floated out from under Blackfriar's Bridge like a pooh stick!' she claimed.) A year later Peter Purves drove a stunt car through the side of a furniture van and the look of sheer terror on his face was palpable.

Even though Biddy had the canny knack of finding people who were prepared to die on camera, she also specialised in hiring the most awkward, desperately uncool presenters yet seen on TV. Noakes was a nice bloke, but his street cred was zilch. Watching him attempt to dance to 'River Deep, Mountain High' with new presenter Lesley Judd in 1972 is *just hopelessly awful*. The *Blue Peter* crew always made you cringe and that is what set them apart from the trendier, more relevant presenters on ITV's *Magpie*. In 1978 there was a mass exodus from the show. Noakes, Purves and Judd walked out and there was a very public dispute about a sheepdog. Noakes' constant companion during his time on the programme had been a hound called Shep.

The faithful collie wasn't the only pet to grace the series over the years. There was Fred the transgendered tortoise, who in fact turned out to be Freda, Patch who ate rat poison and expired, and two dogs called Petra. (The first puppy died and was swiftly replaced with a doggy doppelganger. After all, there was only so much grief a child could cope with.) The second Petra was vicious and the presenters hated her, but she was still rewarded with a bronze bust in the *Blue Peter* garden when she died, toothless and smelly, in 1977. Shep, however, was everybody's favourite canine. Immortalised in a song – 'Get Down Shep' by 'comedy pioneers' (a-hem!) The Barron Knights – the dog became as famous as his human co-stars. When Noakes quit he was told he could take Shep with him, but the producers later feared the pooch would be used to advertise dog food on ITV, a cardinal sin for an ex-BBC employee. 'God they were nasty,' recalled Noakes in a TV interview in 2003. Noakes never got to keep Shep, but advertised dog food anyway with a look-alike mutt called Skip.

Noakes, Purves and Judd's replacements were much less fun. In fact, it wouldn't be an exaggeration to say that the 1978-1980 era took the show to new depths of naffness. The perpetually squinting Christopher Wenner, grimacing Tina Heath (she looked like she drank vinegar cocktails) and lanky Simon Groom were subsequently dubbed 'the worst *Blue Peter* team of all time'. Wenner, an ambassador's son, and Heath, a born-again Christian, hardly lasted two years, but Groom became a fixture of the series for the next decade. A country boy from Derbyshire, Groom used to sit on his father's tractor and have lofty aspirations of becoming a film star. Roles for thespians were thin on the ground in the agricultural industry, so instead the Groomster became a part-time DJ down at the local church hall, wearing embarrassing John Travolta suits and adopting the name 'Neil St John'. 'I'd vaguely heard of *Blue Peter*,' Groom cheerfully admitted years later. 'I knew there was someone called John Noakes, but apart from that I knew nothing about it at all.' Groom always looked awkward and stiff in front of the camera and only seemed at home presenting those intolerable reports on silage-making from his father's bleak hill farm in Dethick.

It was former actor Peter Duncan who saved *Blue Peter* from the deep morass it had found itself in. Originally approached by the BBC in 1978, to take over from Noakes, Duncan had initially refused, but was coaxed back two years later by Biddy. However, Duncan didn't come without some less-than-pristine baggage and by the early 1980s *Blue Peter* seemed to create new tabloid scandals each month. As a young actor Duncan had appeared in a couple of X-rated films including *On the Game* (1973) and *The Lifetaker* (1975). The latter movie featured a naked Duncan romping on top of an actress and sucking on her breasts. When the newspapers found out they had a field day. *The Sun*'s predictable headline was 'Very Blue, Peter!' and Biddy was furious. It was the sort of scandal the tabloids adored. The brouhaha eventually settled down and Duncan happily accepted his dual role as *Blue Peter*'s new action hero and first male pin-up. If he wasn't hanging off Big Ben's clock face, he was donning revealing lycra leggings on the circus trapeze. In 1983 Duncan did something Noakes never could have dreamed of doing – recording a drippy ballad called 'Cold as Ice'. It reached the heady heights of 113 in the charts, but Elton John was kind enough to come on the show and give Duncan some much-needed pop tips. Naïve Groom was unaware that the pop superstar was gay and in the BBC bar afterwards commented on the leggy dancers from *Top of the Pops*. 'Hey, Elton look at all this crumpet!' he said excitedly. Elton made his excuses and headed for the loo where he bumped into Duncan. 'Has the tall, stupid one gone yet?' he asked the *Blue Peter* pretty boy. 'And d'you want to go for a curry?'

Duncan was strictly heterosexual, unlike the 13th *Blue Peter* inductee. Ex-gymnast Michael Sundin was hired to take over from Duncan in 1984, but how Biddy managed to miss his overt sexuality is anybody's guess. Short and *very* theatrical, Sundin was painfully out of his depth filming reports with the Royal Marines on Dartmoor and dipping sheep in disinfectant to stop them catching 'scab disease' on Groom's farm. A former dancer in Andrew Lloyd Webber's musical *Cats* and the choreographer for a dance group called 'Midnight Fantasy', Sundin was always going to be *Blue Peter*'s loose cannon. In 1985 the *News of the World* printed pictures of him cavorting in his underpants with a male stripper at Heaven, London's premier gay

nightspot. His contract with the BBC was terminated after barely nine months and Duncan was swiftly drafted back into action. As for poor Sundin, he tragically died of an AIDS-related illness in 1989, aged just 28. Another presenter to fall foul of Biddy's Thatcher-like grip on the series was Janet Ellis. A bubbly former actress, who famously had appeared wearing nothing but a vintage German army helmet, romping with John Thaw in a 1978 episode of *The Sweeney*, Ellis joined the programme in 1983. Ellis's marriage to TV producer Robin Bextor fell apart during her time on the show and she 'carelessly' got pregnant by another man. An exasperated Biddy allegedly told her to 'Marry at once, or quit.' Ellis stood her ground and her contract was not renewed.

By now the well-scrubbed façade of *Blue Peter* had begun to show some major cracks. The series' most infamous moment came when the Italian Sunken Garden was vandalised (good grief!). 'It was like someone hitting you in the stomach – hard,' claimed Simon Groom. 'The garden looked like a battlefield.' Well, not quite the Battle of Ypres, Simon, but quite messy nonetheless. Percy Thrower's daffodil bulbs had been uprooted; the antique urn smashed to pieces and the fishpond had been poisoned with oil. Worse was to come. 'The gnomon, the metal pointer from the centre of the sun dial, was *completely missing*,' recalled Groom. *Blue Peter* milked the story for weeks as teams of restorers came to put the garden back together. It wouldn't be a lie to say that plenty of viewers thought the whole incident was extremely funny. The crestfallen look on Groom's face was just priceless.

I've always maintained that this act of wanton vandalism was probably caused by aggrieved *Magpie* presenters, but more recently footballer Les Ferdinand has admitted that he took part in the smash and grab when he was a tearaway teenager. The *Blue Peter* scandals have continued unabated ever since because none of the presenters have ever really been allowed to grow up and step outside of the Wendy house. Allegations of cocaine use, sexual assault and rumours of substandard pantomime performances have haunted *Blue Peter* in more recent years, but there is still one ex-*Blue Peter* presenter you can always rely on to be sensible: Simon Groom now produces videos about steam trains from his offices in Chesterfield.

BOD

BBC TV / Produced 1975 / A Bodfilms-BBC Production / Created by Michael and Joanne Cole / Written, Designed and Produced by Michael Cole / Directed by David Yates / Animation by Alan Rogers and Denise Shackell / Drawings by Joanne Cole / Music by Derek Griffiths / Narration by John Le Mesurier and Maggie Henderson / 13 episodes / First broadcast 23 December 1975

Here comes Bod. Enigmatic, mysterious, asexual, serene, dreamy, droll: just some of the words used to describe one of Britain's most adored cartoon characters. What is Bod exactly? It's perhaps easier to start with what he *looks* like. Short and bald with a pointed nose and apple pips for eyes, Bod wears a triangular yellow dress and walks in an anatomically impossible way. Is he actually a little boy? Or is he a curious man-child hybrid? Is he even a *'he'* anyway?

'He is an entity and there's just no point trying to explain him,' says Lo Cole, probably tired of being asked what Bod *really* is. 'He's just a Bod and lives in Bodland and that is that.' Lo is the son of Bod's late creators Michael and Joanne Cole and the guardian of their considerable legacy. 'Bod is supposed to be racially ambiguous and asexual,' he continues. 'It was a very conscious decision by my father not to make him a black boy or a white boy or even a he or a she. Bod is neither a youngster nor an adult either and that reminds me of my Dad very much. He had a sideways approach to life, but he was also very wise, funny and full of life.'

In the 40 years since his first appearance, Bod still continues to confuse and amuse in equal measure. As a child I absolutely loved Bod, but I just thought he was a Chinese boy in a dress, and I took it for granted. 'I suppose he is Chinesey-looking,' admits Lo, 'but he was also influenced by the work Picasso did after the war, particularly his impressions of fauns and Pan. My parents lived in the south of France for about six months and they were heavily influenced by art during that period. They later moved to the English Lake District and I now understand that this was part of an exercise to create and develop

ideas for a character. Bod is very much a free spirit and a very sweet, funny character.'

He certainly is. Just witness this scene: Bod is invited round to his beloved Aunt Flo's for tea. As she's busy baking she politely asks him if he'd ring around all of their friends to invite them too. Bod agrees, but he's rather busy. He telephones Farmer Barleymow, who's struggling to get his cows into the cattle shed.

'Would you mind phoning the others, and asking them too?' says Bod; reluctant to make any more calls. 'I'm right in the middle of a jigsaw.'

Bodland is a peaceful place populated by just a handful of comical figures. Being an entity means Bod doesn't have any parents, in the traditional sense, anyway. His only relative is Aunt Flo, and he doesn't live with her. Flo is a nature-lover, prone to the odd pirouette around her rose bushes. Considering she looks like a top-heavy Russian doll this can't be an easy manoeuvre, even at the best of times. Flo has no romantic entanglements, but she's got a soft spot for PC Copper, the local Bobby with a heart of gold. He saves her from drowning at the beach one day by getting her to grab onto his helmet. Copper won't eat strawberries on duty, but he likes to take 40 winks in Flo's garden if the mood takes him.

PC Copper's best friend is Farmer Barleymow, a big benign agriculturist who rarely takes his hands out of his woolly coat. It must be cold on the farm, chasing after pigs and chickens all day. He likes to unwind by bouncing about on his bed, but only on his own. Dressed smartly in blue and walking up the muddy path to the farmhouse is Frank the Postman. Like PC Copper, he's never off duty, preferring to carry his hefty mailbag 24 hours a day. But who's he delivering to anyway? There's nobody else in the village (except for the enigmatic boatman at the park) and Flo's sister Alice from Down Under seldom writes. It's just as well that Bod's happy-go-lucky attitude touches them all. 'All the adults are like big kids really,' explains Lo. 'He keeps them young and it's a very sweet kind of enduring friendship they all enjoy.'

Bod first appeared in book form in 1962. Michael Cole originally wrote the stories for his own children and eventually four books were published by Methuen. Bod looked quite different then to how we

recognise him today. He was basically a stick figure living in a conceptual world. 'When my father wrote those early stories he felt that there were too few pre-school books that really meant anything,' explains Lo. 'He wanted to read something meaningful to his children and both he and my mother worked on many unpublished books. The early Bod stories are far more abstract and very different to what later appeared on TV.'

The little philosopher actually made his television debut on *Play School*, a full 18 months before he got his own series. One of Cole's original stories 'Bod and the Cherry Tree' was read aloud in May 1974 and proved popular enough with viewers for other Bod stories to appear. Cheered on by the positive feedback, Cole approached London-based animation studio David Yates Limited, with a view to turning the character into a cartoon. A new company, called Bodfilms, naturally, was set up and over the space of a year Bod was fattened up, his stick limbs replaced and his minimalist world was broadened to provide the framework for the forthcoming series. The BBC were happy to get behind the project too, partly because Cole was, at the time, a producer and scriptwriter for *Play School* and also the man behind previous *Watch with Mother* hits, *Fingerbobs* (1971) and *Ragtime* (1973), the latter featuring Maggie Henderson's talking wooden spoons and Fred Harris's unforgettable 'I am a Dachshund' song. 'I've always thought it was very progressive of the BBC to take on *Bod*,' believes Lo. 'My Dad had some very surreal ideas and *Bod* is full of quite oblique ideas, but he was very well liked at the BBC and they basically gave him free reign to make whatever he liked.'

Bod, the animated series, made its debut at 1.48 pm, precisely, on the day before Christmas Eve in 1975. The first episode set the level of absurdity by which the following 12 instalments would follow. In 'Bod and the Present' our hero, wearing a balaclava, trudges through the snow to deliver a Christmas gift to his beloved Aunt Flo. Soon his three friends are trudging behind him too, Frank the Postman, Farmer Barleymow and PC Copper, each carrying a gift of their own. Ultimately they get buried in a snowdrift and have to be saved by Father Christmas, who violently yanks them out of the ice. When freezing friends finally arrive at Aunt Flo's house they discover that they've all bought her identical gifts – new hats. No problem, Flo decides to wear all four bonnets at the same time. 'Oh what a hatty Christmas I'm having!' she beams.

The tale is typical of Michael Cole's magical writing style. Nothing much happens, but what does happen has a pastoral stillness about it. The stories aren't stories so much as floaty wisps of narrative driven by Bod's desire to do things his way. And his way is usually the way of his friends. Bod takes the lead, although he doesn't want to be a leader, and others follow. He spies a grasshopper and thinks he might hop after him. 'It's amazing what you discover when you follow a grasshopper,' he says as a wider world of nature suddenly becomes apparent to him. Before long Barleymow, PC Copper, Frank and Flo are all hopping behind him too, to the sound of a Jew's harp twanging. Bod has an innate calmness and an almost hypnotic ability to reassure and soothe. In the cartoon version of 'Bod and the Cherry Tree' Aunt Flo is miserable because the leaves on her cherry tree are falling off. Bod quietly explains that the leaves have to fall if blossom is to grow in the spring. This heartens his Aunt, but when the blossom comes it falls off too. Bod tells her that there's no point getting sad about it because when the blossom falls the cherries will come. He and Flo take time to admire the ripening berries. Soon everybody is staring at the red fruit...

'Aren't they coming along nicely?' says Frank to Barleymow.

'Very nicely,' says Barleymow, 'very nicely indeed. They're ripe for picking!'

'Yes,' says PC Copper. 'They're beauties!'

...and so on. The series is epitomised by its 'otherness'. It is startlingly different from any of the other animation of the era, probably because this 'otherness' has its roots firmly in Eastern philosophy. 'Bod is amazed by the simple things in life,' says Lo Cole. 'He can look at a grasshopper and be enthralled by it. Dad was very much like that in his life. He read a lot of books on Chinese philosophy and Bod was based on very profound Taoist ideas. He genuinely believed in presenting the truth to children – things like the cycle of life of a cherry tree. His ideas were very much from the heart.'

Michael Cole's Zen-like stories tend to draw heavily on the wonders of the natural world, through the simple appreciation of birds and blooms, fruits, the seaside, even raindrops. Bod subconsciously encour-

ages his grown-up friends to connect with their inner-child and enjoy building sandcastles, pretending to be clucking chickens, flying kites and having impromptu picnics. In fact, there's nothing more exciting for PC Copper than eating one of Aunt Flo's Victoria sponges, even more so than piloting the police helicopter. Some Bod episodes luxuriate in Cole's deliciously cryptic sense of humour. One day Bod throws an apple high up in the air, just because he can. But it doesn't come down again. He waits and waits in silence until his jolly auntie appears:

'I'm waiting for an apple I threw up in the air,' he says nonchalantly. 'It hasn't come down.'

'Oh it will,' says Aunt Flo, unimpressed. 'They always do.'

In the most fondly recalled instalment of the series Bod dreams about strawberries and cream whilst asleep in his bed. When he awakes he can't think of anything else and walks around in a dizzy trance. Everybody blithely follows him until they all fall down a dark manhole. At the bottom of the hole is a gigantic bowl of strawberries, smothered in double cream. That's it. Nothing else happens. 'But isn't that marvellous?' enthuses Lo Cole. 'It has such a surreal humour to it. A massive bowl of strawberries down a manhole! How fantastic would that be?'

Well, who can argue with that?

Actor John Le Mesurier fuzzily narrates each TV story. Best known for his role as Sergeant Wilson in *Dad's Army* (1968-1977), Le Mesurier brings a sleepy, often bewildered, charm, which perfectly mirrors the placid visuals. 'He was an absolutely inspired choice,' enthuses Lo Cole. 'He was just perfect for the pace of the show. My father was a huge fan of *Dad's Army* and had previously worked with Arthur Lowe and Clive Dunn during the 1960s, so working with Le Mesurier was a natural progression.' Another secret of *Bod*'s aural success was the charismatic music. Ostensibly provided by *Play School* presenter Derek Griffiths, each character was given their own theme tune, mirrored by their bizarre way of walking, which was quite a sophisticated idea at the time. PC Copper bends his knees to the sound of a 'pom, pom pom', Bod lurches to a penny whistle tune and Frank's legs move in a crazy circular movement to a clarinet.

Because each *Bod* cartoon barely lasted five minutes, the rest of the *Watch with Mother* slot was filled with a suspenseful episode of *Alberto*

Frog and his Amazing Animal Band plus a selection of guessing games, riddles, songs (usually endless aberrations of 'Ten Green Bottles' to the sound of a tambourine) and an infamous game of Bod Snap, overseen by Maggie Henderson. It was terribly exciting.

'Bod and Frank? No, that's not a snap!'

'Bod and Aunt Flo? No, that's not right either!'

'Two Flo's! Yes SNAP!'

As with many BBC series *Bod* only lasted 13 short episodes. When first screened the programme received an unprecedented amount of positive feedback from children. The series initially finished in March 1976, but by July it was being repeated all over again. Michael and Joanne Cole went on to work on other children's series including *Pigeon Street* (1981) and *Fingermouse* (1985), but *Bod*, remained their all-time favourite. *Bod* really is a masterpiece of British animation; probably the only children's TV character who embodies true spiritual feeling with an ethereal timelessness. Moreover, it's arguably the most tranquil cartoon you could ever watch.

Sadly Joanne died of cancer in 1985 and Michael in 2001, just as he was working on a comeback for his follicularly-challenged creation. 'He really loved the fan mail he got regarding Bod,' recalls Lo. 'He saw Bod as his legacy and wanted me to be involved in it. Before he died we were working on a new book, but he only managed to do rough notes for it because he was ill.' Lo, and his sister Alison, finally completed the resulting tome – *Bod's Way* – published in 2002, to great critical acclaim. A further book called *Bod's New Leaf* came the following year. 'He always wanted Bod to continue and if he was alive now he'd be thrilled and amused about people seeing Bod as a cult figure,' says Lo. 'Bod has never dated has he? He's a very modern character who still has plenty to say about life. He has a totally unique, dateless aura about him if you like, and I'm glad that my Dad's legacy is still intact.'

CAMBERWICK GREEN, TRUMPTON AND CHIGLEY

BBC TV / Produced 1966, 1967, 1969 / A Gordon Murray Puppets Production / Devised and Produced by Gordon Murray / Written by Gordon Murray and Alison Prince / Animation by Bob Bura and John Hardwick / Sets by Margaret and Andrew Brownfoot / Puppets by Gordon Murray / Music by Freddie Phillips / Narration by Brian Cant / 39 episodes / First broadcast 3 January 1966, 3 January 1967 and 6 October 1969

'Whee, whee di-dum, boing', 'Whee, whee di-dum, boing.' There's no better sound in the whole wide world than the rhythmical 'whee, whee di-dum, boing' of Windy Miller's creaking windmill sails. Windy is a cheery old yokel, keen to uphold traditional values and a man whose sole purpose in life is to listen to the 'whee, whee di-dum, boing' all day. The horrid monster mechanical mills in the town have taken much of his trade, but he still has his pride. Colley's Mill is in his blood. 'If the mill was good enough for my father and good enough for my grandfather it is therefore good enough for me,' he explains passionately to Farmer Bell, his only remaining customer. 'Besides, the modern machinery doesn't make such a nice noise!'

Camberwick Green is all about tradition, rural customs and plenty of reassuring old-fashioned noises. The tiny town has all you would expect from a post-war English community – a baker, fishmongers, a post office, a doctor's surgery, a chimney sweep on his bike, and a garage servicing vintage cars. There's a scattering of brightly coloured houses around a quaint village green, people wave cheerily at each other, stop to chat to PC McGarry on his beat and stress… well, stress doesn't exist at all. It's a quintessentially British way of life, a bygone age, before rural communities had to endure mobile telephone masts causing schoolchildren to vomit, illegal immigrants burning down their holding centres and northern relief roads running roughshod through the cowslip-covered flower meadow. Ah, those were the

days, before the ills of the twenty-first century. Puppeteer Gordon Murray created this idyllic fantasyland of Trumptonshire, a quiet British county where people lead enriching, happy lives and where the fire brigade are far too busy saving cats out of sycamore trees to put out fires.

'I'm absolutely delighted that people still love *Camberwick Green*,' says an excitable Murray, now in his 80s. 'It made quite a splash when it was first screened in 1966 and the BBC showed it for 20 years solidly. Then Channel 4 broadcast it for another seven years and it ended up that the children of the children who first watched it were now watching it. And now of course there are the DVDs, and the model figurines made by Robert Harrop Designs. It's all just marvellous!'

Murray certainly has a passion for his work, and who can blame him, since his *Camberwick Green, Trumpton* and *Chigley* series are some of the best-loved and most exquisitely produced pre-school series of all time. Murray had been a professional puppeteer before he joined the BBC in 1955. Over a period of nine years he produced numerous puppet shows for the network, including the magical kingdom of *Rubovia* (1955), *The Toytown Story Adventures* (1956) starring Larry the Lamb, and the original black-and-white episodes of *Captain Pugwash* (1957), as well as individual musicals and puppet operas. 'I had a wonderful time back then,' he recalls enthusiastically, 'but the BBC was changing and I wanted to do something else. When I left in 1964 I think they were rather cross with me actually and for the next 12 months they left me out in the cold.' The following year the corporation finally approached him to do a new puppet series to complement the likes of *Andy Pandy*. 'I wasn't keen to do something for the *Watch with Mother* slot,' he says, 'as I would have found it impossible to create a 15 minute episode featuring something like a little boy and his bear. I wanted to reach a slightly older age group and have more elaborate stories.'

Murray came up with *'Candlewick Green'*, a series about a small town and its loveable inhabitants. 'When I read the contract somebody had misspelled it as *Camberwick Green*,' he chuckles. 'I didn't actually mind because it was a good title anyway and I was hard-up and needed the money. I just signed the contract!' It took the puppet master and his team of animators, headed by Bob Bura and John

Hardwick, exactly a year to make the 13 episodes, each focusing on one of the town's loveable eccentrics. There's Peter Hazel the postman, who slams the post-box door with unnecessary ferocity, and enjoys a stolen waltz with Mrs Dingle the postmistress; Mickey Murphy the master baker, whose cream puffs are famous throughout Trumptonshire; Thomas Tripp the happy-go-lucky milkman and, best of all, Mrs Honeyman, the chemist's wife and championship-winning local gossip. Mrs Honeyman, always cradling her baby, is happy to offload her infant to any passing tradesman, just so she has her hands free to gesticulate. She'll hurriedly pass on the latest tasty titbits she's earwigged in the post office queue. 'Have you heard the latest?' she chatters. 'There's a robin's nest in Paddy Murphy's bicycle basket!' Well, who'd have thought it?

The denizens of *Camberwick Green* are introduced at the start of each episode from within a decorative musical box, sitting on Gordon Murray's desk. It gaily spins round and the top slides off into six triangular shapes before a chimney sweep, a fishmonger or a corn miller pops up. It is an image recalled with surprising accuracy by millions of adults who were brought up on the series.

'Here is a box. A musical box. Wound up and ready to play.
But this box can hide a secret inside. Can you guess what is in it today?'

Affable *Play School* presenter, Brian Cant, handles narration duties, extracting information from the nodding Camberwick Green-ians, like a dentist pulls teeth. 'Hello Doctor Mopp, are you very busy?' he asks sternly. 'A lot of illness about? No! I'm very glad to hear it. Are you off on your rounds? May we come with you?' And off we go on another gentle rollercoaster ride of lumps, bumps and rheumatic pains. The best-loved characters actually live on the outskirts of the town. The red-suited soldiers of Pippin Fort, a military academy, guard the town (from what, we don't know) and are overseen by the efficient Captain Snort. Mrs Honeyman's always having a crisis and the troop are called out in their 'humpity, bumpity army truck' at a moment's notice.

On the other side of town resides Windy Miller, a dextrous man by all accounts, since his windmill's sails never hit him even though they swoop violently over his front door. How does he do it? 'He's just

used to it,' explains Gordon Murray, cheekily. 'He never gets caught out because he times it so well. The truth of the matter is that it was all a happy coincidence. We built that windmill to fit a TV screen and didn't want the sails too high up in case the film camera cut them off. I built them so they would rush past his front door and fit in shot. Funnily enough it's what everybody asks me about!' I'm absolutely amazed that the sails *don't* thwack Windy. He likes a tipple on the job, you see. Whelks washed down with a couple of flagons of homemade cider are the perfect accompaniment to milling corn. But what did the BBC think of one of their kiddies' series featuring a man, drunk on the job? 'They didn't mind,' laughs Murray. 'I wanted to put some adult humour into the programmes because I didn't want to put off parents from watching too. My motto was that grown-ups should not be embarrassed by my puppets!' The first broadcast of *Camberwick Green* in 1966 was a tremendous daytime hit for the BBC and within months they had approached Murray to ask for further instalments. 'I was delighted of course,' says Murray, 'but I said to them "Let's move up the road a bit, to a posher market town," and that's how I came up with *Trumpton.*'

'Here is the clock. The Trumpton clock.
Telling the time steadily, sensibly. Never too quickly. Never too slowly.
Telling the time for Trumpton!'

So recites Brian Cant over the opening sequence to 13 episodes of *Camberwick Green*'s slightly more upmarket neighbour. *Trumpton* is a bustling market town with a grand town hall inhabited by a vain, egocentric mayor. The town proudly boasts its very own fire brigade, but the mayor prefers to fritter away taxpayers' money on using the firefighters to get his three-cornered hat out of a tree. It's been blustery in the town recently. Miss Lovelace, owner of the fancy milliners, is having trouble with her yapping Pekinese – Mitzi, Daphne and Lulu. 'They get so excited when it's windy,' she wails. 'I think it blows their fur up the wrong way!' The matronly Miss Lovelace glides around the square like a Dalek, although naturally, with more grace. As with many of the Trumptonshire lady residents her skirts reach right to the ground. ('It saved on having to animate any more legs,'

quips Murray.) Limiting the number of fires in the town also saved money. Flames are very difficult and time-consuming special effects. The trusty firefighters – here they come, and I know you've been waiting patiently for this – Pugh, Pugh, Barney McGrew, Cuthbert, Dibble, Grubb – are, as Murray explains: 'just happy to be part of the community. Fires are almost incidental.' To clear this up once and for all, Pugh and Pugh are twin brothers and Barney McGrew is the only one with a Christian name and a surname. 'It's purely that it sounds better for the rhyme,' says their creator.

By 1969 the Trumptonshire chronicles had become a trilogy. *Chigley,* helpfully subtitled *'near Camberwick Green, Trumptonshire'* made its debut in October of that year and introduced one of Murray's best ever characters, Lord Belborough of Winkstead Hall. Belborough is a splendid fellow, a down-at-heel aristocrat who's been forced to open his stately home and gardens to the plebs so that he can afford to have the roof replaced. 'Some people objected to Lord Belborough,' says a perplexed Murray. 'Apparently he promoted the upper classes and I was told that it was not suitable for children. How ridiculous is that? I mean, he pays for the six o'clock dances each day doesn't he?'

Indeed he does. At 6.00 pm sharp the whistle blows at *Chigley*'s main employer, the CCB factory (that's Cresswell's Chigley Biscuits to me and you). Out pour the proles, whose only source of enjoyment is when the refulgent Lord Belborough gets his organ out for a tune in the park. The *grand seigneur* of Trumptonshire gives rides on his vintage steam engine too, with the help of Bracket, his faithful, plodding manservant. Bracket's there in a flash, whenever the phone rings, but when Cant says he 'hurries to find Lord Belborough' nothing could be further from the truth. In the time it takes the butler to trudge down the marble corridors you could make a cup of Ty-Phoo and have drunk it.

Belborough's theme tune when he takes to his railway line is one of late composer Freddie Phillips' finest:

'As time flies by when I'm the driver of the train.
And I ride on the footplate, there and back again.'

Sadly, not all the characters have steamed off into the sunset. What

of the rumours that the residents of Trumptonshire all ended up on a bonfire in Sussex? Where was the Trumpton fire brigade when you *really* needed them?

'They'd all, unfortunately, had their day,' Gordon Murray admits, without the slightest wisp of melancholy. 'To be truthful the figures had gone very peculiar and were falling apart. I thought they were quite unhygienic. Rubber bodies and ping-pong-ball heads are not made to last, you know.' Murray's daughter gave one of the soldiers of Pippin Fort to a friend of hers in the mid-1980s, who kept it in a shoebox ('He only came out for dinner parties'), but the fate of the other 80 or so characters was not so glamorous. 'Yes, it's true,' says Murray excitedly. 'I threw them all on a bonfire in my back garden. Windy Miller, Doctor Mopp, Chippy Minton, the lot! As I said, they'd had their time and I felt no guilt at all. They were a good team while they lasted, but they had to go. Anyway, I must say I've enjoyed my puppet life very much!'

CAPTAIN PUGWASH

BBC TV / Produced 1973-1974 (colour version) / A John Ryan Studios Production / Created by John Ryan / Produced, Written and Drawn by John and Priscilla Ryan / Filmed by Bob Bura and John Hardwick / Narrated by Peter Hawkins / Music by Johnny Pearson / 30 episodes / First broadcast (colour version) 16 September 1974

When it rained during playtime at my school one of three things happened. 1) We'd sit in the library reading in silence (not a good option if you were hyperactive and wanted to re-enact the latest episode of *Doctor Who* from the previous weekend). 2) Watch the school television set wheeled in from the headmaster's office (preferable to choice 1, but the *Pages from Ceefax* weren't really designed to be enjoyed by seven year olds). 3) Play a game of 'Pirates' in the school gym-cum-assembly hall. The latter choice was easily the best and the one we invariably demanded. One of our aged teachers would instruct us to build a historically inaccurate pirate galleon out

of benches and climbing frames and we'd all clamber aboard and proceed to rape and pillage. On second thoughts there was no rape. Just pillaging. But we all wanted to out-do each other in the naughtiness stakes for one simple reason. The very baddest pirates were forced to *walk the plank*. The plank was actually just another bench, but with a poke from the teacher's cardboard cutlass we'd eagerly tiptoe down it, to meet our deaths in shark-infested parquet flooring.

Pirates were big news when I was a nipper. At school fancy dress parties they'd always be a surfeit of seafaring marauders compared to, say, Luke Skywalkers. Britain's most famous filibusters – Captain Pugwash and the crew of the bad ship Black Pig – no doubt inspired most of this pirate craze. Pugwash was a regular part of BBC teatimes during the 1970s. In the pre-news slot his catchphrases: 'Stuttering starfish!' 'Scuttling cuttlefish' and 'Jumping jellyfish' became household expressions to children and adults alike. He must have had a thing about fish.

Those colour *Captain Pugwash* episodes are what most of my generation remember, but the jolly smuggler actually first set sail two decades before in the pages of boys' comic *The Eagle*. Artist and writer John Ryan created Pugwash in 1950. Ryan, the son of a British diplomat, had spent his early childhood in Rabat, Morocco. 'Rabat is on the river Bou Regreg,' he recalls, 'and it was very close to where the infamous Barbary pirates had their headquarters in the seventeenth century. I think that's perhaps where my great interest in pirates came from.' Ryan left school aged 18 and immediately signed up to fight the Japanese in Burma during World War II. When Ryan returned to the UK, aged 23, he considered himself to be 'rather old to be an art student.' Undeterred he enrolled at the now-defunct Regent Street Polytechnic in London. 'I learnt absolutely nothing about art there,' he chuckles, 'but I did meet my future wife Priscilla there, and I couldn't have made Pugwash so successful without her.'

When John and Priscilla married, a close friend gave them a rather unusual gift. 'He said that he couldn't afford a wedding present,' says Ryan, 'but he could give me a good introduction. That introduction was to Marcus Morris, the editor of *The Eagle* comic.' *The Eagle* was the most popular boys' read of the era, although it strove to be too principled for its own good. 'I was told by Marcus that he only

wanted strip cartoons with a high moral tone,' says Ryan, with a giggle. 'So I did a strip about Bad King John. He gave it a perfunctory glance, twitched – he never laughed, just twitched his shoulder, you see – and told me to go away and draw something really funny instead.' One of the characters the young artist came up with was Captain Horatio Pugwash, a portly pirate who sailed the seven seas looking for treasure chests bursting with bounty, but usually failing in his attempts. The original Pugwash eventually sank without trace when *The Eagle* decided he was too juvenile for their readership. Ryan replaced him with the more contemporary 'Harris Tweed – Extra Special Agent.' Pugwash, however, refused to drown and Ryan continued his marauding in a series of beautifully drawn picture books published by The Bodley Head (the 13th publisher he had approached with the idea).

The Captain is not the most philanthropic children's character, yet young readers have adored his bounteous adventures in books for over half a century. 'Pugwash represents cowardice and greed, which I believe are strong in all of us,' says John Ryan. 'He wants to pinch the money off the table, but is terrified by the arm of the law gripping his shoulder. He wants to kiss the girl, but is fearful of the slap in his face. Children relate to that, I think.'

In the wake of the books' huge success, a friend of Ryan, who was working for the BBC at the time, suggested that pillaging pirates were just what the broadcasting giant was looking for. By 1957 the first of 50 black-and-white episodes of *Captain Pugwash* had aired. Television animation presented a problem for Pugwash's creator. 'Animation was, and still is, an incredibly complex business,' he says. 'Thousands of drawings have to be produced and I knew I could never hope to do that.' Instead Ryan created a uniquely eccentric alternative. Using flat cardboard cut-out puppets, animated by levers and tiny brass paper-clips, Ryan created the famous fluid movements for the Pugwash cartoons. Amazingly, just 40 or 50 individual pictures and backgrounds were used for each instalment. 'I suppose it was a crude way of animation,' says Ryan, 'but it saved us so much time.' The early episodes were filmed live, with John and Priscilla operating the puppet levers just out of shot. Even more surprising is that for a while the series was broadcast live too, so any fluffs were hard to disguise. For

nearly 20 years Pugwash's hysterical, nasal, voice was provided by actor Peter Hawkins, the man behind *The Flowerpot Men*. 'He was an incredibly skilful chap,' says Ryan, affectionately. 'He did the voices for all the characters and had this most amazing range. He was always spot on. But he was a very funny man too and we had to sit him behind a curtain because he'd distract us with his funny faces!'

Pugwash and his motley bunch of incompetent smugglers – Master Mate (who sleeps with his teddy bear), Pirate Willy, Barnabus and chief sausage fryer Tom the Cabin Boy – set sail in their vain search for buried loot, but invariably get gobbled up by giant fish rather than digging up golden doubloons. Hot on their tail is a lusty Cornishman called Cut Throat Jake, Pugwash's archenemy and a man with the hairiest knuckles this side of Land's End. Pugwash and his crew put on a bit of weight for television in comparison to their book adventures. The most noticeable change was their fat necks. 'Yes, I suppose they have got quite wide heads,' concedes John Ryan. 'But because their facial movements were operated by levers, these had to be hidden behind very wide necks. My wife, Priscilla, was incredibly good at doing the lip-sync and rolling the characters' eyes!'

John Ryan's pirate is not a particularly successful freebooter. He's been known to travel hundreds of miles across the oceans to locate the treasure on a tropical isle. But only Pugwash would forget to pack a spade. Undeterred, he still imagines himself to be the finest racketeer in the business. In one of Pugwash's 30 colour adventures, made in the early 1970s, he is awarded the prestigious 'Pirate of the Year' gong, despite being the only seafarer in the competition. 'It's hardly surprising really,' he boasts, holding his trophy aloft. 'After all it's obvious that I'm the bravest, most successful, and of course most handsome, buccaneer afloat!' Aside from false modesty, Pugwash's stuttering, bumbling ineptitude in running a watertight vessel is alarming. In one episode his crew threaten to mutiny:

'Ship's biscuits is unfit for 'uman consumption, Captain. They're full o' weevils!'

'Rubbish man! What's wrong with a few weevils?'

'The men cannot eat 'em, Captain. Reckon it's cruelty to weevils!'

Sadly for Pugwash it was Master Mate (or, at least, somebody who *sounded* like him) who sailed The Black Pig into its most treacherous

seas. In 1991 jocose journalist Victor Lewis-Smith made unsubstantiated claims about the series in the now defunct *Sunday Correspondent*. Lewis-Smith alleged that several of the Pugwash characters had smutty names. Other national newspapers repeated the slur and before long an urban myth was sweeping the nation. Apart from sullying John Ryan's peerless reputation, the untruths jeopardised the author's frequent visits to schools where he told Pugwash stories and drew illustrations for children. Ryan successfully sued and, in characteristic generosity, immediately gave the money to charity. By the time the new animated *Adventures of Captain Pugwash* left port for ITV in 1998 the rumours had been exposed as falsehoods. Pugwash still isn't the best buccaneer ever to sail the seven seas, but no one could criticise his perseverance in trying to find that elusive fortune. 'I'm pleased to have had Pugwash with me all this time,' says John Ryan, wistfully. 'He made quite a bit of money for me in his day, even if he didn't find any treasure!'

CHORLTON AND THE WHEELIES

ITV / Produced 1976–1978 / A Cosgrove Hall Production for Thames Television / Devised and Produced by Brian Cosgrove and Mark Hall / Directed by Chris Taylor / Written by Brian Trueman / Edited by Dave Street and John McManus / Narrated by Joe Lynch / Music by Joe Griffiths / 39 episodes plus Christmas Special / First broadcast 27 September 1976

Can there honestly be a greater love than the one between a big fat, daft dragon from Halifax and a foul-tempered, hyperventilating witch from Wales? I seriously doubt it. Having said that, this is a one-sided love affair. The dragon sees goodness and love in everyone. The witch hates everything, even Christmas. Nobody knows exactly where Chorlton the Happiness Dragon came from. He arrived one day inside an egg, which materialised on the gloomy, cold surface of Wheelieworld. The lady responsible for all this misery is Fenella the Kettle Witch – a grimacing, fist-clenching stressed-out sorceress. From her viewpoint at Spout Hall (a black kettle on stilts) she keeps a

steely eye on her kingdom of discontent, but the arrival of a huge colourful egg ('Very big, very cheerful and very daft') causes her no end of trouble.

The egg cracks open to reveal Chorlton, a big green lummox in a Rastafarian hat, who breaks the wicked spell. Happiness and laughter are immediately restored to Wheelieworld and the inhabitants are free to trundle around again on their three little wheels. Fenella is understandably furious. 'I can't stand it,' she shrieks. 'All that goodness!' Her magic is useless on Happiness Dragons and for 39 episodes gormless goodness and eviscerating evil battle it out. 'There is absolutely no badness in Chorlton's character,' says Brian Cosgrove, the series' co-creator, and one half of Cosgrove Hall Productions. 'He loves everyone. He even thinks horrid Fenella is adorable and that is a nice clear message for a young audience.'

The Wheelieworld inhabitants are an odd looking bunch. Ruled over by Queen Doris and King Otto, the Wheelies are basically just big heads on wheels, who whizz about their town at high speed. Legend has it that Brian Cosgrove invented them after a particularly vivid dream. Had he been eating too much cheese the night before, I ask? 'Yes, I had a dream about heads on wheels,' he admits. 'I tell you, there are times when I feel so embarrassed about this, but I guess when your head is steeped in children's TV oddities it had to happen. It's funny because although the series originated from the Wheelies, they actually became secondary to the relationship between Chorlton and Fenella. They are the key elements to the show.'

Chorlton's undiminished love for the old hag in the Tommy Copper fez brings together some of the most hilarious moments in kids' telly. It doesn't matter how many times Fenella stamps her foot and swears ('Ffestiniog!'), the innocent dragon still wants to give her a kiss and a cuddle. He refers to her as his 'little ole' lady' and lavishes endless compliments on her. 'Hey missus, you're a right tonic you are', 'Isn't she nice?' and 'Give us a giggle love!' are just some of his classic declarations of love. Fenella is not impressed. She's just infuriated. And she'd be better off at her kettle home drinking sour milk and eating boot polish butties. Spout Hall is also home to the harridan's disrespectful henchmen – her 'Oirish' telescope, Reilly (nicked from Dun Laoghaire Pier), the German spellbook Claptrap

Von Spilldabeans ('Achtung!'), the sneaky, sniggering Spikers, and lastly, Fenella's fungus-faced Chinese toadstools, the Toadies. The witch has a son too – a teenage giant called Clifford, so big that you only ever see his right leg. 'I have no idea who the father is,' admits Cosgrove, 'but he was a brave chap to have tangled with Fenella!'

Brian Trueman, an ex-Granada TV newsreader and current affairs presenter, wrote the series' wonderfully waggish scripts. His slightly surreal style of prose was not dissimilar to that of Eric Thompson, the man who re-invented *The Magic Roundabout* for British television. 'It's probably a bit more anarchic than *The Magic Roundabout*,' believes Cosgrove. 'There was a gentleness in *Magic Roundabout* scripts, but *Chorlton* is more crazy, I think. The scripts had lots of different levels. They were bright and colourful for kids, but some of the dialogue went right over children's heads. In that way *Chorlton and the Wheelies* had a wide appeal to younger kids and their older siblings. We never made shows that were gentle and twee, you know – Victorian parlour stuff. We had to produce series that gave us pleasure and matched our sense of humour. There is a child in all of us and we never lost that.'

The series is stuffed with cute references and barmy ideas. In the very first episode the Happiness Dragon is at a loss to know where he's come from. He is christened only after reading a label on the inside of his egg. It reads 'Chorlton-cum-Hardy', the area of Manchester where all Cosgrove Hall's productions were made. In another instalment a travelling salesman from Glasgow, named Angus McBargain, flogs the Wheelies a job lot of skateboards so they can enjoy the latest 1970s craze. Just to reiterate, the Wheelies *already have wheels*. It's absurd, but it's inspired. Only once did the series' off-the-wall humour cause upset. Fenella's spellbook was decorated with a Star of David-like symbol; yet spoke with an exaggerated Germanic accent. Some sensitive Jewish viewers took offence. 'That was a very innocent mistake to make,' says Cosgrove. 'It threw us totally.'

Chorlton, made in tandem with the even more delicious *Jamie and the Magic Torch*, helped establish Cosgrove Hall Productions as the most innovative animation studio in the country. Their fabulous cartoon and puppet shows set the Herculean standards which others tried to follow. 'When we started out making those series nobody was

watching us you see,' admits Brian Cosgrove. 'We didn't have anybody vetting us or censoring us. Nobody looked at the script too closely. We went into the recording studio and had fun ad-libbing. You couldn't get away with that now. As soon as you get a big success people from the top floor come downstairs and want to watch and keep an eye on things. The anarchy goes out of it. Anarchy is the lifeblood of *Chorlton and the Wheelies*. And it's nice to be crazy!'

THE CLANGERS

BBC TV / Produced 1969-1970, 1974 / A Smallfilms Production / Produced and Written by Oliver Postgate / Designed by Peter Firmin / Narrated by Oliver Postgate / Music by Vernon Elliott / 26 episodes plus one special / First broadcast 16 November 1969

Deep, deep in the outer reaches of the universe is a calm, serene orb sailing majestically among a myriad of stars. It's a bleak, cold, blue-coloured world covered in craters and doesn't look in the least bit hospitable; yet here live a family of cuddly whistling aliens. They're pink, knitted and eat disgusting food, but they are beloved of the British public. *The Clangers* debuted on British television just months after NASA sent its first man to the moon. It was a timely broadcast, perfectly capturing British schoolchildren's fascination with outer space. Earthlings fascinate the Clangers too, although Mother Clanger prefers to use the American flag, left behind by a passing astronaut, as a tablecloth. You see, on the planet of the Clangers everything stops for tea. But not tea as we know it.

Arguably, *The Clangers* is the greatest ever creation of Oliver Postgate and Peter Firmin, the men who made animated magic in an eighteenth-century cowshed, near Whitstable in Kent. It was in this barn where Ivor the Engine first smoked, where Professor Yaffle first pontificated and where blue string pudding was originally served at teatime. The Clangers are creatures of habit and they get quite temperamental if they don't get their meals at the specified time. Mother Clanger is a whiz with the pudding, but for a main course her

woolly brood demand green soup, and that has to be collected from their scaly neighbour, the benevolent, burbling old Soup Dragon. As Postgate's sanguine narration explains, she's a tireless worker 'day in, day out, slaving over a hot volcano' and all for what? I'll tell you what: the Clangers angrily waving their empty mugs in the air and kicking up a stink. 'Soup, yes, delicious soup, lovely soup,' mutters one Clanger, desperate for his next fix.

There are just five main Clangers – Major, Mother, Grandmother, Small and Tiny – plus a handful of aunties and uncles, but their desire for soup gratification goes on, unabated. Resembling fat, squishy mice with elongated noses and expressive ears, the Clangers have more than a passing resemblance to Postgate's earlier knitted creations, *The Pingwings* (1960), although, of course, they were penguins. But they look like they were probably cut from the same cloth, or at least, knitted from the same wool. The inhabitants of Planet Clanger are a peace-loving bunch motivated by their desire for green consommé, but also by an inherent curiosity about the objects that collide with the surface of their barren world. The Clangers have discovered, to their cost, that it's a dangerous place to live. Robust, yet surprisingly skimpy, suits of armour (all colour-coded) are their favoured daywear and each crater has a dustbin lid on it, which can be clanged tightly shut when iron chickens inexplicably fall from the heavens.

Actually, the Iron Chicken's misfortune is entirely the Clangers' doing. There she is, sitting pretty in her metallic nest, hatching out silver eggs when the pink aliens fire a rocket in the air and, inadvertently, bring her down with an almighty crash. Mrs Chicken, who, incidentally, sounds like Norman Collier doing his infamous poultry impression in a cave rather than at the Royal Variety Performance, gets her own back by trashing the place. Despite Postgate's assertion that she is 'a very polite Iron Chicken' she munches the leaves off the copper trees and steals soup out of the soup wells. The Soup Dragon, unsurprisingly, goes berserk and gives her a good bashing over the head with a big stick. She's a martyr to her nerves, that Soup Dragon. When she's broody she's even worse. My tip is if you see her with an egg, get the hell out of there. Just as eccentric, but no less loveable are the Froglets – orange amphibians who live in a deep underground pond and whose preferred mode of travel is a top hat. They also have

the most beautiful eyelashes this side of *Vogue* magazine. In addition to the 26 ten-minute episodes, those wide eyes briefly returned in a political spoof called *Vote for Froglet.* Screened on election night, 10 October 1974, Small Clanger and a Froglet try to canvass some votes for their campaign, presumably by promising to slash VAT on blue string.

Aside from the poetic residents of the planet, proper respect must be paid to Peter Firmin's astonishing sets. *The Clangers'* subterranean world has more than a touch of the *Barbarellas* about it. The cosy caves are a maze of macaroni branches, elegant yellow flowers, copper tin lids and music trees bedecked with glimmering musical notes. It looks like a comforting place to live and the philosophy of the series seems to be that the Clangers' way of life is infinitely preferable to our own. Their altruistic world is carefully built on neighbourliness, courtesy, mutual respect and ladles of green soup. In Postgate's illuminating autobiography *Seeing Things*, he reveals that the Clangers even had friends in high places. 'An engineer from NASA is reputed to have described *The Clangers* as "a valiant attempt to bring a note of realism to the fantasy of the space programme"', he writes. It poses the question: do the Americans know something we don't?

CLOPPA CASTLE

ITV / Produced 1978-1979 / An ATV Production / Created by Mary Turner and John Read / Directed by Mary Turner / Photography by John Read / Written by Anna Standon and John Kane / Voices by Charles Collingwood and Judy Bennett / Theme song performed by Rainbow Cottage / 52 episodes / First broadcast 11 January 1978

It was medieval hi-jinks aplenty when children of the 1970s went behind the walls of *Cloppa Castle* I must confess this puppet series was a favourite of mine as a kid, but latterly I'd forgotten all about it until I started writing this tome. Quite how Queen Ethelbruda departed to the dark recesses of my mind for the past 20 years is

tragic since she had such an impact on my formative years. Looking like Bernard Manning in drag, Queen Ethelbruda was a formidable lady with the same ability to reduce healthy young men to jelly as Margaret Rutherford or Dame Edith Evans once had. Not only did Her Ladyship have her stately residence in which to shelter from rampaging marauders, she also had a responsibility towards her sappy family. Cloppa Castle is the stone-built (or at least, polystyrene) stronghold of the Bygones, a feudal clan of eccentric Anglo-Saxons. Tough-as-old-boots Ethelbruda, a matriarch of alarming girth, is forced to take charge since her timorous husband, King Woebegone, and languid offspring Prince Idlebone and Princess Tizzibel, couldn't manage a piss-up in a brewery, let alone run a fourteenth-century domiciliary.

First transmitted the same year that super soap *Dallas* premiered, *Cloppa Castle* also owes its ongoing storylines to the fractious fight for oil. Ethelbruda owns extensive reserves of the black stuff, but her enemies are desperate to get their mucky hands on it. Step forward grizzled, hairy Beosweyne and his Hasbeene clan. (Hasbeenes versus Bygones, geddit?). Cretinous Yorkshireman Beosweyne wants the oil, but even more so he wants a bit of royal respect from his minions. 'I'll capture the oil wells,' is his frequent moronic cry, 'and I'll be king o' the castle!' Old Ethelbruda is having no funny business near her battlements, however, and has to rely upon her ramshackle army of old retainers to defend her honour. Over two marvellous series *Cloppa Castle* presented impressionable British children with a lunchtime diet of slingshots, sharpened battering rams, grappling hooks, bows and arrows and huge airborne boulders. Alas, I don't recall any vats of hot burning oil being poured over the ramparts, though.

The man in charge of the matronly monarch's security is a hefty oaf named Elbow. Fiercely loyal, but intrinsically weak ('Hold those doors men! Our queen don't want no visitors today!') Elbow sadly spends most of his waking hours bullying a little shrimp in a tin helmet called Osmosis. (You could never accuse the *Cloppa Castle* writers of character name fatigue.) Osmosis (catchphrase 'Excruciating!') is a dim-witted fool of epic childhood proportions. Having become recently reacquainted with his gibbering Frank Spencer-like voice and trembling over-sized bottom lip, I wonder how

I ever slept at night for worry. Taunted by his fellow soldiers about his physical shortcomings ('Big Boy' is the usual insult) the pigeon-toed lad also can't string a proper sentence together. *Cloppa*'s opening sequence has the illiterate Osmosis stranded up a ladder spelling out the name of his home on a wall: 'Coppel Saclet' and 'Cloppe Sactle'. He was probably educated at Grange Hill School.

Puppet masters Mary Turner and John Read are the people responsible for bringing these comical castle calamities to ITV, but just like their other two 1970s successes – *The Adventures of Rupert Bear* (1970-1976) and *Here Comes Mumfie* (1975-1978) – *Cloppa Castle* has sadly disappeared into obscurity. The series' theme tune has managed to attain some level of notoriety though. This pulsating glam rock extravaganza, reminiscent of the best work by The Glitter Band or The Sweet, is 1970s kitsch at it very worst. Recorded by the fabulously named Rainbow Cottage, from glamorous Wigan, the rebel-rousing theme explodes with histrionic vocals and wonderfully naff lyrics: 'A jolly bunch of chaps they are, the friendly enemy. And everyday at three o'clock they all sit down to tea. Living in harmony at Cloppa Castle!' which is blatantly untrue.

CRACKERJACK

BBC TV / Produced 1955-1984 / A BBC Production / Originally produced by Johnny Downes / Starring Eamon Andrews (1955-1964), Leslie Crowther (1960-1968), Michael Aspel (1968-1974), Ed Stewart (1973-1979), Don MacClean (1974-1977) and Stu Francis (1980-1984). Featuring Ronnie Corbett, Peter Glaze, Jan Hunt, Little and Large, Bernie Clifton and The Krankies / Over 400 episodes / First broadcast 14 September 1955

'It's Friday. It's five past five and it's CRACKERJACK!' You read right. Five *past* five. In fact it could just as easily been five o'clock, too, because, contrary to legend, *Crackerjack* wasn't always scheduled at its famed 'five to five' home. The very first episode was broadcast at 5.15 *on a Wednesday*! Thereafter it zig-zagged around the schedules, only settling into its catchphrase slot in the 1970s. By this stage the series

had entered its 'golden age' or was in terminal decline, depending on your opinion of the velour tracksuit-wearing host Stu Francis. We'll come back to him later, because *Crackerjack* is a lot more than just grape crushing.

I hereby declare that I was not a fan of the show, in any of its incarnations. It typifies all that was wrong with the BBC's kiddie 'light entertainment' shows of the era – under-rehearsed, unfunny, terminally embarrassing and all-too desperate to please, populated with woefully un-hip 'variety acts'. Nevertheless, the series ran for 29 years and regularly pulled in massive audiences of boy scouts so I must give credit where it's due. Readers perhaps want me to dish the dirt on The Krankies in the 1980s, unaware that *Crackerjack* actually started way back in 1955, under the helm of *This Is Your Life* host Eamon Andrews. Variously referred to during his career as 'Mr Bland' and 'Seamus Android', the rather shy, awkward Andrews would not have been my first choice to control a bunch of unruly schoolchildren and make tired music hall acts look interesting. It is one of the mysteries of British showbiz that Andrews was so enduringly popular. Children and adults alike loved him and *Crackerjack* was just one of a string of hits for the quiet Irishman.

Thankfully for Andrews, he was the straighter-than-straight man to a succession of talented comedians including Jack Douglas, Ronnie Corbett and Leslie Crowther. In between some astoundingly silly comedy sketches and wretched songs, viewers were treated to a game show section entitled 'Double or Drop'. Devised (and later copyrighted) by Andrews himself, this silly vignette involved miserable-faced youngsters being hauled out of the audience to stand on a pedestal to answer questions. For every question correctly answered they would be handed a prize, which in those days was probably a chemistry set or a *Dandy* annual. However, and here comes the stinger, if the poor child got a question wrong they would be handed, wait for it, a rubber cabbage! As the boy or girl struggled to balance cabbages and prizes things would invariably clatter to the floor. In the case of the chemistry set there was most likely sulphurous emissions too. The winner – usually the child with the longest arms – would run off with the booty whilst the loser got a consolation prize: the infamous *Crackerjack* pencil.

Easily the shoddiest BBC prize ever (even worse than the *Blankety Blank* cheque book and pen), the *Crackerjack* pencil was, nonetheless, much sought after by 1950s schoolchildren with clipped vowels. During the first 15 years of the show some 2,000 of these pencils were given away to salivating *Crackerjack* viewers. During the 1970s the BBC gave the show a bigger budget and ink pens superseded the pencils. These were innocent days of course. Give a child a pen on a kiddies' game show nowadays and they'll most likely stick it up your arse.

Perhaps fearing the worst, Eamon Andrews deserted the show in 1964 (for a while taking his cabbage-themed quiz with him) and his comedy co-host Crowther was promoted to anchor-man. It was during Crowther's gushing reign that Her Majesty The Queen visited the show's studios at London's Shepherds Bush Empire. Her visit, in November 1961, was notable for a royal revelation that would shake the Empire. The Queen whispered in Crowther's ear that she, too, was a big fan of the show and regularly watched with the teenage Anne and Charles. *Crackerjack* was soon enjoying audiences of 7.5 million, buoyed up this royal seal of approval, but sadly the show's content did not improve. A little man with Brycreemed hair and thick specs called Peter Glaze soon joined Crowther. The comic, an understudy for The Crazy Gang and a dead ringer for Norman Wisdom's cinema stooge Edward Chapman, stayed with the show for over two decades. I'm sure he was a lovely man, but his cringe-worthy routines, particularly when paired with the show's resident crumpet, Jan Hunt, probably still haunt the theatre today.

Crackerjack always yearned to be achingly funny and topical, but it NEVER was. Because it was filmed live in front of an audience of teachers' pets, boy scouts, brownies and girl guides the comedy never rose above the level of excruciating. Children's laughter rang out perfectly on cue, but it was always flat and lifeless, trailing away into oblivion. Crowther's gang inflicted weekly gut wrenching 'parodies' of current pop hits, but seeing middle-aged men pulling faces and dressing-up as the Beatles was just mortifying. His favourite skit involved a piss-take of 'Michelle' by the Fab Four. Whenever Crowther sang 'Michelle, my belle' he would ding-ding his bicycle bell. Did children *really* enjoy this level of sophistication? Crowther

departed in 1968, by which time real pop acts like Lulu, Cat Stevens and The Hollies were happily guest starring. Genial Michael Aspel took over until 1974, during which time *Crackerjack* resorted to custard pies being flung about and Gary Glitter was conducted sing-a-longs with cub scouts. The crappy jokes continued throughout the 1970s: 'When is an artist like a horse?' asked Glaze. 'When he draws a cart!' replied Aspel. All this met with howls of artificial merriment. Throughout the rest of the decade cheesy new hosts Ed 'Stewpot' Stewart (with the big nose) and Brummie Don MacClean (with the massive teeth) went through the motions with Little and Large, Bernie Clifton (and his comedy ostrich) and the ever-reliable Peter Glaze. There was absolutely no let-up from this sickening parade of cheap patronising junk.

Both Stewpot and MacClean were troupers and probably enjoyed the money the BBC was paying them, but by the dawn of the 1980s a new host was looming large on the kids' telly horizon: his name was Stu Francis. It could be argued that *Crackerjack* only hit the pinnacle of dreadfulness when Francis arrived with his pseudo-Bucks Fizz fashions, relentlessly cheerful demeanour and 'joke' book crammed full of forgettable catchphrases. For the last four years of *Crackerjack*'s life the series endured some of the most low-budget end-of-the-pier shenanigans in its chequered history. Francis, an ex-holiday camp performer hailing from Lancashire, made the series his own. The show descended into self-indulgent pantomime, with Francis conducting the newly resurrected 'Double or Drop' and the high speed 'Take a Letter' and 'It's In The Box' games whilst avoiding the numerous pratfalls of resident comedians The Krankies. Thanks to *Crackerjack* The Krankies brought their own particular brand of transvestite schoolboy humour to the widest possible audience. They persuaded millions of impressionable minds that a middle-aged Scots woman could happily dress up as an eight-year-old boy and sit on her husband's knee without any feelings of shame. The Krankies' fearsome war cry of 'Fan-dabbi-dozi' entered the nation's vocabulary, but they had serious competition in the catchphrase stakes. Stu Francis' screen persona was one of a slightly camp Blackpool bingo caller. He played upon the fact that he wasn't terribly tall or muscular and launched into a catalogue of self-deprecating one-liners. 'Ooh, I

could crush a grape!' was his most memorable, but let us not forget the others. 'Ooh I could test drive a Tonka!' 'Ooh, I could rip a tissue!' and 'Ooh, I could jump off a doll's house!' are other examples of his wit and wisdom. His threat of 'Ooh, I could wrestle an Action Man!' is too horrible to contemplate. I don't wish to denigrate Francis' effeminate, and highly emotive, comedy routines, because babies and grandmothers throughout Britain absolutely adored him. However, many did not, including those in the higher echelons of the BBC.

By the mid-1980s The Krankies had been replaced by a chubby 'comedy magician' called The Great Soprendo (later becoming Mr Victoria Wood), and guest 'stars' included ventriloquist Keith Harris and his green duck Orville, a homeless Basil Brush and top disco icons Hazell Dean and Limahl. It was a step too far for the BBC's schedulers and Stu Francis' plans for kitsch world domination were nipped in the bud. In the autumn of 1984 word finally filtered down from the Director General's office that *Crackerjack* was to be yanked from the schedules, just short of its 30th birthday. Francis' immediate reaction was to tour the provinces with his own stage show 'Stu Francis and the Stars of Crackerjack', co-starring The Chuckle Brothers. I never witnessed it, so I will let you draw your own conclusions.

CRYSTAL TIPPS AND ALISTAIR

BBC TV / Produced 1972-1974 / A Q3 London-BBC Production / Created by Hilary Hayton / Designed and Written by Hilary Hayton and Graham McCallum / Directed by Richard Taylor / Produced by Michael Grafton-Robinson / Music by Paul Reade / 50 episodes plus Christmas special / First broadcast 28 February 1972

She was a little girl with big hair. Really big purple hair, which looked like candyfloss. And she was probably a hippy, (but she didn't take LSD). He was a big hulking dog who could ride a bike. They were completely inseparable. This colourfully innovative BBC teatime series has been jokingly dubbed 'Crystal trips with Alistair' over the years because so much of its amazingly psychedelic imagery is crudely lumped in with the hedonistic flower power movement of

the late 1960s. 'Yes, I admit she probably was a bit of a hippy,' concedes *Crystal Tipps'* creator Hilary Hayton, 'but there was nothing else to it. We made the series for fun and people loved it. If they wanted to read anything else into it they can, but I assure you we certainly weren't out of our skulls on drugs making it!'

A graduate of Leeds Art College, Hayton moved to London in the early 1960s. 'Although I never actually studied at the London's Royal College of Art, I hung out in that social scene with people like David Hockney and it was all very exciting,' recalls Hilary. 'I was working in advertising at that time when, quite by chance, I got an invitation to visit the graphic design department at the BBC. I tell you, I was blown away. I thought to myself "Wow this is magic!"' Luckily for Hilary, somebody in the department was off ill and she was asked to fill in, on a five-week contract. Those five weeks ended up being 16 years. Hilary's beautiful design work was so sought after that she was commissioned to produce the memorable opening titles to *Play School* and *Jackanory*, but it was a chance meeting with an ice-cube maker that was to change her life. I'll let Hilary tell the story:

'I've never really publicly spoken about this before,' she laughs, 'but I doubt it matters now. The pool of animators for children's television programmes all worked on the sixth floor of the BBC building's east tower. Well, there was a tea bar on the ninth floor we all used and one day I happened to notice an ice-making machine in the corner of the room. I was drinking my tea and staring at the name on the machine. There was a plaque that read "Crystal Tips". I thought "What a terrific name" and it stuck in my mind. I then started noticing the company's delivery vans driving around West London with Crystal Tips written on the side and I knew I had to create a character to fit the name. All I did was add an extra 'p' in her surname. I didn't want to get into trouble, after all!'

By the late 1960s Hilary began making drawings of a pretty rosy-cheeked girl in a stripy pinafore dress and a pile of triangular-shaped curly hair on her head. Her constant companion became Alistair, a big awkward dog with humungous paws and a loveable languorous face. Pleased with her designs, Hilary was asked to produce a short film of her new characters for a competition held by the European Broadcasting Unit. In all, 13 countries competed and *Crystal Tipps and*

Alistair was such a success that Monica Simms, the head of BBC children's programmes, commissioned a series of 25 episodes, quickly followed by a further 25. 'I was still working on *Play School* when they asked me to make a series of my own,' explains Hilary, 'so we used an outside company called Q3 to co-produce the series.' Q3 was the mastermind of ex-BBC producer Michael Grafton-Robinson and Hilary enlisted the help of fellow animator Graham McCallum to create the intricate cut-out figures, which typified the final look of the series. 'I think Graham and I adopted the characters of Crystal and Alistair slightly,' chuckles Hilary. 'We'd do a spot of role-playing in the BBC offices with me acting out Crystal's role and Graham doing the dog. It was really very funny.' *Crystal Tipps and Alistair* has no narration, so it was up to the late Paul Reade's wonderfully expressive harpsichord to convey emotion and pace. 'He was a wonderful musician from *Play School* and knew just the right sort of tempo for the scenes that we mimed out in front of him.'

The series bears all the trippy hallmarks of other Pop Art style productions of the era, including The Beatles' cartoon *Yellow Submarine* (1968) and Terry Gilliam's animated inserts for *Monty Python's Flying Circus* (1969-1974). 'That's interesting actually,' says Hilary, 'because that was just the style of that time. Pop Art was big then and we loved those bold psychedelic images that leapt off the page. I don't think it was a conscious decision to make it look trendy. It was just a style we were happy working with.' The animation's intriguing backgrounds are also exemplary. Hilary uses different textures, collages and snippets from Victorian scrap albums and photocopies of French Old Masters. Crystal's ornamental brick-built cottage is an eclectic mix of patchwork fabrics, wallpaper swatches, magazine cut-outs, chintzy patterns and smooth luminous shapes. It is this refreshing style which has made the series so enduringly special.

The *Crystal Tipps* stories themselves are simple, yet disarmingly persuasive. Each episode takes a wry look at everyday activities like decorating, spring-cleaning or keep fit. Eating cakes at the dinner table was a popular pastime too. Other episode titles speak for themselves, embracing nature and freedom: Bird, Butterfly, Fishing, Seeds, Seaside, Flowers and Pussy. The supple leading lady can throw herself about with vigour (thanks to her well-articulated cut-out limbs) and

has the strength of will to pick up her big hefty lump of a dog. Alistair is a bit of a clumsy old hound and innocent little Crystal isn't averse to teasing him. Custard pies in the face, tickling sticks and soakings from a hosepipe are just three of poor Alistair's torments. 'But I don't think he's as stupid as he looks, though,' counters Hilary. 'Crystal can be a bit bossy and naughty, but that dog of hers can still ride a bike!' Crystal's age has long been a matter of debate. She acts like a young girl, but she is free from any sort of adult supervision and is presumably old enough to hold a pilot's licence since she buzzes around her garden in an aeroplane. The comedic interplay between girl and pet, and the absence of voices, made *Crystal Tipps and Alistair* a popular overseas export for the BBC. Throughout the world people seemingly identify with the purple-permed girl and her often indignant looking pup with the uncontrollable legs. 'I still get people saying to me "I have a friend who is the real Crystal Tipps. She looks just like her" or "there's a Crystal Tipps in my daughter's class at school."' says Hilary. 'So I know she's out there somewhere!'

DANGER MOUSE

ITV / Produced 1981-1992 / A Cosgrove Hall Production for Thames Television / Devised by Brian Cosgrove, Mark Hall and Mike Harding / Produced by Brian Cosgrove and Mark Hall / Executive Producer John Hambley / Directed by Brian Cosgrove / Written by Brian Trueman / Starring David Jason (Isambard the Narrator/Danger Mouse/Nero), Terry Scott (Penfold), Edward Lelsey (Baron Greenback/Colonel K) and Brian Trueman (Stiletto) / Music by Mike Harding / 87 stories / First broadcast 28 September 1981

What is it about cartoon mice? Mickey Mouse, Jerry Mouse, Mighty Mouse, Midge Mouse, Speedy Gonzales, even Pixie and Dixie. Why are mice so irresistible to animators? 'What I'd like to say is why has there never been an incredibly successful cartoon panda!' asks *Danger Mouse*'s co-creator Brian Cosgrove. I'm thrown for a moment. Pandas? 'Well, I mean pandas are predestined to be good cartoon material. No human could design a bear to look like that,' says Cosgrove. 'Pandas look incredible don't they?' I have to agree, but it poses the question: why didn't he create *Danger Panda* instead? 'Mmm,' he ponders for a second. 'I don't know. It just seemed right and proper that he should be a mouse!'

Danger Mouse had been a suave secret agent waiting to happen on Cosgrove's desk since the early 1970s, at a time when the legendary animator was still working in his attic. 'The original idea was inspired by a 1960s series called *Danger Man* starring an actor called Patrick McGoohan,' he recalls. 'He played a sophisticated English spy, but as the James Bond films began to come out regularly, more and more influences from Bond crept in too. Basically *Danger Mouse* was a rodent parody of spy films!' The mouse remained on the back burner as Cosgrove, and his partner Mark Hall, concentrated on the seminal *Chorlton and the Wheelies* and *Jamie and the Magic Torch* series. That is until 1979, when Cosgrove Hall Productions started work on a pilot episode. 'The character of Danger Mouse started off very James Bond

looking,' recalls Cosgrove. 'We had him in a tuxedo and a bow tie, but we didn't really like it. Then we put him in a white catsuit and all the people in the merchandising and copyright division at Thames Television said: "You can't do that. He's got to have colour!" We said no. We liked him in white and we stuck to it.'

Apart from the strange anomaly of a mouse wearing a *cat*suit, *Danger Mouse*'s most striking item of clothing is his black eye patch. The young Cosgrove had paid close attention to a famous advertising campaign for Hathaway shirts when he was an art student in Manchester. The long running poster campaign, devised by David Ogilvy, portrayed a grey-haired, moustachioed model with an eye patch. 'When we were designing *Danger Mouse* this male model came back into my mind,' says Cosgrove. 'So I put the mouse in an eye patch. Simple as that! Nobody knows if he's got an eye under that patch or not. You don't know, do you? There could be a mysterious device hidden behind!' As well as a missing eye, the world's greatest secret agent is also tail-less. 'The reason for that is it was too difficult to animate,' chuckles the animator. 'He could have it tucked away in his suit, but that could create uncomfortable bulges if you're not careful!'

Eton-educated Danger Mouse is a fearless defender of justice who lives in a secret HQ in a red pillar-box in London's Baker Street. Just like the famous address's other celebrated crime-fighter, Sherlock Holmes, the mouse has a sidekick too. Unfortunately Penfold is no Dr. Watson. 'We desperately needed a sidekick for Danger Mouse and we were really up against it,' recalls Cosgrove. 'We had a meeting with Thames to show them our characters but we still didn't know what Penfold was going to look like. Mark and I were waiting in reception and I just started sketching a little figure. Mark turned to me and said: "You know what you've done? You've done a caricature of your brother." He was right!' Thames liked Penfold, a tubby, myopic, balding hamster in an-ill fitting suit. 'My brother was then the chief sub-editor of the *Daily Express*,' says Cosgrove, a little guiltily. 'All his colleagues called him Penfold when the series first aired, but he always smiled about it.'

Brian Cosgrove believes that the characters of Danger Mouse and Penfold would have been nothing without the comic interplay of the two actors who brought them to life – a pre-*Only Fools and Horses* David Jason and *Terry and June* sitcom star Terry Scott. However, the search to find the perfect rodent partnership was fraught with problems. Initially William Franklyn, a silky smooth actor best known for the 'Schweppes – you know who' TV commercials was drafted in to play *Danger Mouse*. Penfold was, alarmingly, voiced in Welsh. It was not a success. ('William Franklyn can't be anybody but William Franklyn,' quips Cosgrove.) Finding the right chemistry between two performers takes time and when David Jason was paired up with Benny Hill's stooge Bod Todd, the results were even more disastrous. 'I'd never met David before and he came into the studio hobbling,' remembers Cosgrove. 'His leg was in plaster after a lawn mower accident. Then Bob Todd arrived. He was always plastered and he took over completely. He totally swamped the recording and it wasn't very good. But after I let them go I knew David had something. I stuck with him, and then hired Terry Scott, and the magic was there!'

'Terry Scott was not the most responsive actor,' says Cosgrove, 'but when you got him doing the Penfold voice he was perfect every time. That relationship between Danger Mouse and Penfold was completely invented by David and Terry. You'd give them the script, but how they played it was up to them. I'd sit in the recording studio and watch them through the glass. I'd just be falling about laughing. If they ad-libbed something hilarious I'd mouth: 'Don't stop!' I never interrupted them. They were having a party in there!' Cosgrove judged the quality of the *Danger Mouse* episodes by how much he'd cry with laughter. On occasions his glasses would even steam up.

Cool, casual Danger Mouse ('Good grief!') and his gibbering wreck of an assistant, Penfold ('Ooh crumbs! Ooh crikey!') were the first major child-adult crossover successes of the 1980s. The series' sophisticated humour and anarchic plotlines were soon attracting audiences of over 20 million. Each episode would see the tiny duo fighting a rasping, asthmatic toad called Baron Silas Greenback, his fluffy caterpillar, Nero, and two Italian crow henchmen. Occasionally other villains would appear, including a vegetarian vampire duck, which was given his own spin-off series – *Duckula* – in 1988. Most of the time, however, the formula stayed the same and audiences across the

globe adored it. 'We sold the series to the States in 1984,' recalls Brian Cosgrove. 'It was beamed into 18 million homes or something at the time on Nickelodeon. It became their number two show on a Saturday morning. When Ed Koch, the mayor of New York, decided to address the city he used the *Danger Mouse* slot and the city was in uproar. There were newspaper columnists condemning Mayor Koch. It was wonderful to have that sort of impact. We only made the series for fun!'

DEPUTY DAWG

BBC TV / Produced 1960 / A Terrytoons Production / Produced by Bill Weis / Written by Larz Bourne / Music by Philip Scheib / Featuring the voice of Dayton Allen / 102 episodes / First broadcast (UK) 31 August 1963

In the deepest recesses of America's Deep South is a long forgotten Mississippi bayou inhabited by slack-jawed animals that talk. Well, it's a sort of 'talk'. They greet each other with a holler of 'Hey boi' and scream 'dagnabbit' when iron anvils fall on their toes. Most of the time their speech is so incomprehensible that they sound totally inebriated. Must be all that that moonshine. This is *Deputy Dawg* country, or should I say 'Dep-ty Dow-ag', a fanciful place where you can spend 30 days in jail for filling your shorts with nuts at that thar peanut plantation. The world of *Deputy Dawg* is about as far removed from the suburban sitting rooms of Britain as is geographically possible. When I was a boy I didn't understand what the characters were saying. And I still don't, but then again half of America probably doesn't have a clue either.

As one of the best-remembered imported cartoons of the sixties and seventies, *Deputy Dawg* was also one of the BBC's perennial repeats. For nearly 20 years children attempted to unravel the mysteries of the Deep South drawl. What was a 'pesky varmint' and a 'cotton-pickin' rascal' anyhow? This show was full of them, that's for sure. The plot? An overweight, dim-witted bulldog is the human sheriff's unlikely deputy, assigned to keep the pesky varmints from

raiding eggs from the hen house, fruit from the melon patch and catfish from the lake. The main varmints are the myopic Vincent van Gopher, Ty Coon the raccoon and, most famously of all, Muskie, the muskrat. Do you know what a muskrat is? A school friend told me it was a rat that smelt particularly bad.

The dippy Deputy is a 'good ole boi', a mentally retarded, toothless canine with a hint of Tourette's Syndrome who attempts, and usually fails, in his running battles with Muskie and his reprehensible pals. 'You shud know Muskie,' he drawls through his jowls, 'you can't outsmart Deputy Dawg!' Oh, the poor misguided fool. Mr Dawg's distinctive voice is almost beyond description; suffice to say that his tongue is probably too big for his mouth and his demented laughter sounds like he's hiccupping on speed. New York comedian Dayton Allen made his fortune providing the voices for this series, but it also kept Eddie Large, Britain's number one *Deputy Dawg* impersonator, busy during those interminable *Seaside Specials* that the BBC foisted upon us during the 1970s.

FINGERBOBS

BBC TV / Produced 1971 / A Q3 London Production / Created and Produced by Michael Cole / Written and Designed by Michael and Joanne Cole / Directed by Michael Grafton-Robinson / Animation by Maureen Lonergan / Music by Michael Jessett / Starring Rick Jones as Yoffy / 13 episodes / First broadcast 14 February 1972

Yoffy lifts a finger and something quite incredible happens. Not since Captain Birdseye have fingers been so much fun. The flexible fingers in question belong to former *Play School* presenter Rick Jones, a hirsute hippy from Canada with a nice line in roll-necks. Jones's relaxing psychiatrist-like voice and mellifluous manner had made him a favourite with Big Ted and Humpty, but in 1971 he was given his own starring vehicle. *Fingerbobs* was the brainchild of the late Michael Cole, one-time producer and writer of *Play School* and the creator of Britain's most famous boy philosopher, *Bod*. '*Fingerbobs* is a very typical name my father would have thought of,' explains his son Lo Cole, with a smile. 'It's a funny, meaningless sort of word, but it just sounds so good. He loved playing around with words and expressions and *Fingerbobs* gave him space to develop his ideas. If you look back at the series now, it's actually quite avant-garde in a way. I'm amazed that the BBC took it on!'

Fingerbobs is all about puppets on Rick Jones' dextrous digits. Jones plays Yoffy, a balding beatnik in a ribbed sweater and a paisley neckerchief. It wasn't a difficult part to play as Jones looked like this all the time in real life. Few kids' presenters could boast that they played in a heavy metal band, but Jones did just that, playing guitar and keyboards for a rock group called Meal Ticket. Signed to EMI, the band recorded several LPs but never troubled the British charts with their progressive rock sound. Even the novelty of having a *Play School* presenter on stage just wasn't enough. Nonetheless, there's certainly no denying Jones is one hip dude. Giving new meaning to the word

'mellow', the straggly-haired Canadian has an aura of calming benevolence absent from *Fingerbob*'s childish contemporaries.

Jones brought a quiet sensuality to the *Watch with Mother* slot. His outward purpose was to entertain and educate under-fives, but his devilish smile, knowing looks to camera and unnerving habit of winking was enough to give stay-at-home mothers flushed cheeks and a quickening heartbeat. He's hardly Robert Redford, but his subtle sexuality is shockingly transparent. While 1970s mums were wetting their knickers listening to Jones' smooth mid-Atlantic tones their offspring were filling their nappies watching his hands. Yoffy's hands are the centrepieces of *Fingerbobs*, as the series' theme tune asserts: 'His hands were made for making and making's what they'll do!' It's almost like he has no physical control over them. 'Rick was just brilliant at it,' says Lo Cole. 'He was incredibly clever with his hands. It was all part of the illusion – to show the hand attached to the puppet. Children totally believed in those puppets and Dad desperately wanted to show the simplicity of them.' With Yoffy's help, an energetic ensemble of simplistic puppet characters, each with their own distinct personalities, would appear each week.

'Yoffy lifts a finger and a mouse is there.
Puts his hands together and a seagull takes the air…'

I'd rather not dwell on tortoise heads peeping out, because it doesn't sound very nice, but Yoffy's eight fingers and two thumbs became an inspiration to British children everywhere. Unlike, say, *The Muppet Show* where the puppeteers are safely hidden, in *Fingerbobs* Rick Jones rejoices in blatant puppetry. Jones 'orders' his hands to do his bidding – scampering across the table or soaring through the air, whilst always maintaining his 'separateness' from them. For the duration of each episode his hands are not, strictly, his own. He's often nodding off at his desk or yawning, blithely unaware of what his fingers are doing are up to. The illusion, and Jones' ability to make it so believable, is pure genius.

The programme's best-loved star is Fingermouse, the grey pest with the paper-cone nose and big flappy ears. Arrogant to say the least, he describes himself as 'a sort of wonder mouse' who revels in his

taunting of the local moggy. 'I am the mouse called Fingermouse,' he wails. 'The mouse with guts and nerve. I get past cats so easily with my famous body swerve.' He's a shameless show-off, completely unlike Flash the tortoise ('They call me Flash. I won't dash!'), who has an unpleasant habit of detaching his shell and filling it with pinecones. I wonder how many children tried to do that to their pet tortoises? Best of the puppets is Gulliver the appalling operatic seagull with delusions of grandeur. (Yoffy's white gloves make for perfect wings.) There's also Scampi, the pink shrimp – in many ways the Liberace of the *Fingerbobs* world. His fondness for jewellery, regular cries of 'Coo-eee!' and his misogynist attitude to the lady shellfish lets him down badly. He confused me terribly when I was a kid. He looked nothing like the scampi I used to eat at The Berni Inn, chopped into bits and fried in breadcrumbs.

For those readers with long memories there were other Fingerbobs too, but they only made cameo appearances. Scaredy the crow, Louise the squirrel (who looked freaky), Enoch the woodpecker, 'Mole' the mole, Prickly the hedgehog and the worms – Herbert, George and Alistair – never achieved the same heights of fame as the others. Fingermouse always stole the limelight; he was given a glamorous mouse friend called Gloria and even had his own spin-off series, *Fingermouse*, in 1985.

The puppets were designed to be simple, so that tiny viewers could copy them at home. (Gulliver was the most difficult character to reproduce because his head was created using a ping-pong ball.) Predominantly made of paper, the characters often fell foul of Yoffy's RADA-trained fingers. 'Fingermouse's nose used to get bent regularly,' recalls Lo, who himself made a cameo appearance in one episode as a pair of footballer's legs. 'My poor Mum had to make multiples of the characters. We were living in a flat in Marylebone at the time and I can remember my parents' bed covered in duplicate mice and tortoises. My parents had a very hands-on approach to toys. My Dad, in particular, wanted to produce a programme which was an intelligent alternative to what was already out there; a show where the characters could be copied at home.'

Fingerbobs has a definite folksy, rustic feel. From the opening title sequence superimposed over a raffia tablemat, to the knit of Yoffy's jumper and the whimsy of the accompanying music, the series has Steeleye Span written all the way through it. Each show has a naturalistic theme, concentrating on the shapes, textures or sounds of natural materials: shells, seeds, feathers, twigs or water. Yoffy's animal friends are despatched to the countryside or to the beach to collect him a bit of bark or a sea sponge so he can use them for a story, beautifully illustrated by Michael Cole's wife Joanne. However, Fingermouse begins to get really cheesed off persuading passing sheep to donate their hair to holly bushes, and by the penultimate episode he's ready to scuttle back to a hole in the skirting. 'Don't think me unwilling,' moans the paper rodent. 'I enjoy helping you Yoffy, but sometimes it's hard work!' Just a barely perceptible glance from Yoffy is all it takes to get Fingermouse motivated again. It's that easy. In every way the series has a simple beauty to it, full of homespun wisdom, good humour and an appreciation for nature. 'My Dad's entire philosophy is in that show,' explains Lo. And what's more, watching just one episode of *Fingerbobs* is the perfect mellow hangover cure.

THE FLINTSTONES

ITV / Produced 1960-1966 / A Hanna-Barbera Production / Produced and Directed by William Hanna and Joseph Barbera / Music by Hoyt S Curtin / Featuring the voices of Alan Reed (Fred Flintstone), Jean Vander (Wilma Flintstone), Mel Blanc (Barney Rubble), Bea Benaderet (Betty Rubble) and John Stephenson (Mr Slate) / 166 episodes / First broadcast (US) 30 September 1960

British-made animation of the 1960s and 1970s is best categorised by string puppets (*Cloppa Castle*), cut-outs (*Captain Pugwash* and *Ludwig*), stop-motion figures (*Morph* and *Noddy*) and hand puppets (Zippy and George in *Rainbow*). Actual cartoons were few and far between, although the ones we did produce, like *Roobarb* and *Jamie and the Magic Torch*, were incomparable. Harassed children's TV schedulers had to look to the US to fill teatime slots with cartoon tomfoolery, and one studio in particular – Hanna-Barbera. The words

'A Hanna-Barbera Production' at the beginning of a series meant only two things to pre-pubescent armchair critics in Britain: inspired excellence or utter dross. For three decades Hanna-Barbera was the televisual equivalent of Walt Disney (that is until the 1990s, when Uncle Walt began to muscle in on TV production too). Once upon a time nobody could touch HB in terms of sheer quantity of product. The studio operated a cut-price factory cartoon conveyor belt, churning out hundreds of animated series and over 2,000 individual characters – some awesome, others instantly forgettable.

William Denby Hanna and Joseph Roland Barbera founded the company in 1957. Born in 1910 and 1911 respectively, both men worked for other movie studios before teaming up to establish their own. Hanna had worked for MGM since 1929 (he directed his first short film in 1936) and Terrytoons had employed Barbera. New York-born Barbera impressed the studio so much that he was soon being headhunted by their competitors. Whisked away to MGM, Hanna and Barbera finally met, became great friends, and began fooling around on new cartoon ideas. Their first collaboration was a chase movie called *Puss Gets the Boot* (1940), featuring a cat called Jasper and a mouse named Jerry. Later re-christening the cat Tom, the cartoon marked the beginning of a classic partnership, not only for Hanna and Barbera, but also for Tom and Jerry. Over the next 12 years no fewer than 13 Tom and Jerry films, all released theatrically, were nominated for Academy Awards, seven of which actually won. *The Cat Concerto* (1946) and *The Two Mousketeers* (1951) are two of the best and prove, beyond all shadow of a paintbrush, just how the animators had reached the pinnacle of perfection.

However, throughout the 1950s television's insatiable demand for kids' cartoons began to erode the stranglehold cinema had on animated shorts. In 1957 MGM closed its animation studio and Messers Hanna and Barbera were out of a job. Instead of taking their talents to Disney they set up their own company and within months had produced their first cartoon series for NBC television. *The Huckleberry Hound Show* (1958), about a dog with a laconic drawl, was their first small screen success and thereafter the hits just kept coming: *Quick Draw McGraw* (1959), *The Yogi Bear Show* (1960), *Snagglepuss* (1960), *The Flintstones* (1960), *Top Cat* (1961), *The Jetsons* (1962) and

Secret Squirrel (1965). Relying heavily on talking animals stealing food and solving wrongdoings, the series all became firm favourites on American TV and within months the BBC and ITV were bidding to bring the characters to British shores. Many of these ancient old shows are still showing on Saturday morning television across the world.

Whilst *Yogi Bear* was Hanna-Barbera's first genuine superstar, it was *The Flintstones* who really cemented the studio's reputation for witty quality animation. The series started out as *The Flagstones*, and then reverted to *The Gladstones*, before finally settling on the family name we are all now familiar with. As the very first primetime cartoon, *The Flintstones* debuted on US television on the ABC network in September 1960 at 8.30 pm. It was a brave move for a channel that had never experimented with 'adult' animation before. Perhaps fearing that audiences would find the show hard to stomach, it's amusing to note that the first season was sponsored by Alka-Seltzer. Over here in the UK the show was always going to be kiddie fare and was immediately dropped into a Saturday morning slot.

Luckily for Hanna-Barbera the show was a runaway hit with grown-ups and children alike and has since secured a place as one of US television's all-time classics. Spoken about in the same reverential tones as *The Lucy Show* or *Sergeant Bilko, The Flintstones'* rise was meteoric and is reflected in the fact that a colossal 166 episodes of the series were produced over the space of just six years. The series, America's very first animated situation comedy, centres on two next-door neighbours: loudmouthed leopard skin-wearing Fred Flintstone and dim-witted Barney Rubble. It was a tale of intense rivalry and silly one-upmanship, but also of lasting friendship and loyalty. Watching from the sidelines were Fred's sceptical wife Wilma (the one with the smoker's voice) and Barney's missus Betty (the one with the squeaky voice). Their domestic trials and tribulations were no different from any other American sitcom of the era, except that these suburbanites lived in a prehistoric town, co-existing with 30ft high dinosaurs. Bedrock, population 2,500, is like no other town you've ever seen; the locals live in cave dwellings, but with all mod cons. The innovative home designs of the 'modern stone-age family' and way-out caricatures of twentieth-century conveniences are actually more appealing

than the lead characters. Fred's car is a wooden construction with hefty stone rollers for wheels. Unfortunately, there's no engine so Fred pedals it with his feet, which rather defeats the object . Back at the cave Wilma loves to catch up on all the local gossip with Betty on a telephone made of ram's horn whilst listening to a gramophone record played by a bird's beak. When he arrives home Fred keeps abreast of national events in *The Daily Slab* – a heavy stone tablet carved with news. But the poor caveman can't even read in peace. His irascible pet 'dog' (Dino the snorkasaurus) invariably disturbs him and turfs him out of his granite armchair.

Throughout each episode *The Flintstones* managed to seamlessly mix social comment and gentle satire, although much of the battle-of-the-sexes humour was lost on kids. The only thing that struck me as a child was why two such glamorous, leggy women as Wilma and Betty would agree to marry such intellectual inferiors. Fred's brash, overwrought personality was partly based on American sitcom actor Jackie Gleason (who allegedly threatened to sue, then backtracked when he saw how funny the show was). Ex-radio actor Alan Reed originally provided Fred's famously raucous tones, and coined the phrase 'Yabba-dabba-doo!' Allegedly, Reed asked to change a 'yahoo' in the script to his own phrase, in memory of his mother. As a child Reed's mother would put ointment on his grazed knees with the cheery saying, 'A little dab'll do ya!' (The classic Brylcreem advertising slogan.) It's a nice story, but perhaps a bit too cute to be true. While Fred Flintstone took all the vocal glory it was his stupid sidekick who enjoyed a better pedigree of intonation. Mel Blanc, the man behind a host of Warner Bros cinema characters like Bugs Bunny, Daffy Duck and Tweety Pie and Sylvester, lent his tones to TV for the first time as Barney Rubble.

As with all long-running sitcoms *The Flintstones* evolved over time and new characters were introduced. In 1962 Fred and Wilma produced a pretty baby girl named Pebbles (instead of a bow in her hair, she had a stegosaurus bone) and Barney and Betty had a little boy. However, little Bamm Bamm Rubble (a prize-fighting forerunner to Scrappy-Doo) turned up on his adoptive parents' doorstep only after they prayed for a son. Perhaps Barney was just too dim to know how to have sex. The junior members of the family were popular with kids, but by the fifth season of the show, ratings had begun to dip and ABC consulted with Hanna-Barbera, hoping that a new twist could be introduced into the tired formula. Typically they came up with the most bizarre plot device yet – a visitor from outer space. In episode 145 The Great Gazoo made his first appearance. This diminutive green spaceman was a political exile from the planet Zetox, banished for eternity to prehistoric Earth. Executives at the ABC channel touted Gazoo as 'the man who will save *The Flintstones*.' He didn't. After 21 further episodes of caveman versus alien antics the network cancelled the show.

In 1966, the show was given the send-off it deserved with the theatrical release of a spin-off movie *A Man Called Flintstone* but, for the time being, that was that. After concentrating on the wonderful *Wacky Races* (1968), and *Scooby Doo, Where Are You!* (1969) Hanna-Barbera returned to fertile dinosaur droppings in a spin-off series called *Pebbles and Bamm Bamm* (1971), which concentrated on the junior rock-breakers. Unfortunately the series lacked its prehistoric predecessor's wit and adult humour and duly flopped. Sadly its lack of success was a signpost of worse to come. Throughout the 1970s Hanna-Barbera's output was marked by derisive attempts to create mass appeal shows at the expense of real quality. Only four original shows made any impact worldwide – *Help! It's the Hair Bear Bunch* (1971), *Inch High Private Eye* (1973), *Hong Kong Phooey* (1974) and *Captain Caveman and the Teen Angels* (1977). The rest of the studio's output was marred by cynical series featuring recycled characters from the fifties and sixties and rehashes of old ideas. Did anyone *really* like *Goober and the Ghost Chasers* (1973) or *Dynomutt – Dog Wonder* (1978)?

As for *The Flintstones*, poor Fred and Barney were insultingly paired up with a big white blob of ectoplasm in a crime-busting caper called *Fred and Barney Meet the New Shmoo* (1979). Little heard of in this country, the Shmoo is a shape-changing entity (not unlike *Barbapapa*) from an American comic strip called *Li'l Abner*, drawn by a crazy one-legged artist called Al Capp. Able to reproduce at will, the Shmoo can lay eggs and give milk and adores being eaten. Yes, you read right. Hanna-Barbera made a sub-*Flintstones* series featuring two cavemen and a character that yearns to be fried in butter and served up with

tartare sauce. Having quite obviously lost their grip on children's television, Hanna-Barbera continued their downward spiral into cartoon hell throughout the 1980s. Scores of animated atrocities like *Dirty Dawg* (1981), *Pac-Man* (1982) and *The Snorks* (1984) curled up and died one after another. There was even a disastrous attempt to mix *The Flintstones* with *The Addams Family* in 1980's *The Frankenstones* (featuring a character called Rockula – heaven help us).

In the 40 years or so since *The Flintstones* first appearance on TV there have been over 30 TV and cinema Stone Age spin-offs, varying from the bearable to the really awful. The live-action *Flintstones* movie, released in 1994, is the only film I've ever fallen asleep to in a cinema and its belated sequel *The Flintstones in Viva Rock Vegas* (2000) is just steaming dinosaur dung. It's probably best to remember Fred and Barney during their early 1960s heyday. Only then will you be assured of having a 'Yabba-doo time. A dabba-doo time. You'll have a gay old time.'

THE FLUMPS

BBC TV / Produced 1976 / A David Yates Production / Created and Written by Julie Holder / Produced by David Yates / Puppets and Animation by David Kellehar / Set Design by Ruth Collier / Music by Paul Reade / Trombone by George Chisholm (uncredited) / Narration and songs by Gay Soper / 13 episodes / First broadcast 14 February 1977

You can look at *The Flumps* in two ways. It could be set in a post-nuclear apocalyptic world, where the human race has been wiped out, and the only survivors are small fluffy balls eking out an existence amongst the rubble and desolation. *Or* it's set in a post-World War II Leeds allotment where small fluffy balls secretly grow cabbages in a bomb crater. Both scenarios sound pretty bleak, but then so are set designer Ruth Collier's bizarrely barren landscapes of broken bricks, rotting planks of wood and brown vegetation. All the same the Flumps choose to call this derelict building site home. Smashed masonry, dirt and twisted roots are very chic in the 3D puppet world, don't you know. *The Flumps* themselves aren't much

more attractive than their surroundings, either. They look like fur balls coughed up by a suburban pussy or the sort of stuff swirling round a Dyson vacuum cleaner. They have arms and legs of course and facial features, but they still look a bit, well, dirty. Keen-eyed viewers will notice that the Flump family's limbs get gradually filthier as the series progresses. Continual handling by mucky-fingered animators and standing around in a muddy vegetable patch is not conducive to good Flump hygiene.

Writer Julie Holder created the spherical fluffy Flump family. She wrote the original stories for her children and one fateful day her youngest child took a Flump tale to read at school. His teacher was so impressed with the characters that she immediately told her husband, who just so happened to be a BBC producer. And, as luck would have it, the BBC were looking for a new series to fill the lunchtime *Watch with Mother* slot. David Yates, the man who breathed cartoon life into *Bod* the previous year, was commissioned to bring Holder's creations to life. The resulting stop-motion animation enjoyed huge success on TV for nearly ten years, which isn't bad going since only 13 episodes were ever made. The non-stop repeats etched the puppets' broad Yorkshire accents onto millions of children's memories, yet interestingly *The Flumps* was the first BBC series for under-fives to experiment with regional dialects. Odd then, that the show's narrator hailed from Surrey. 'They wanted June Whitfield,' explains actress Gay Soper, 'she's brilliant at voices, but for some reason she had to pull out at the last moment. My agent put me forward, but they desperately did not want my Surrey voice, or a cultured voice, for want of a better expression.' Gay has been a star of musicals, television and film since the late 1960s. Just ten weeks after graduating from drama school she was playing Eliza Doolittle in *My Fair Lady*, before appearing in other stage productions as diverse as *Canterbury Tales* and *Godspell* (opposite David Essex). On TV she's appeared with Sid James in *Bless this House* and just prior to *The Flumps* she even had the lead female role in a naughty X-rated movie entitled *The Ups and Downs of a Handyman*. She's best known for her amazing voice, which has graced the stage throughout the world. This is just as well because the Flumps have to sing and I'm not aware that June Whitfield has ever been famous as a chanteuse. 'They asked me to use a regional accent,' she recalls, 'so

I tried a Scottish voice, then an Irish one, but they weren't right. Eventually we settled on a Northern voice and it just fitted. It had some earthiness and warmth about it.'

There are six different Flumps and Gay provided the voices for all of them. 'It could be tricky,' she says. 'At the beginning we had to stop the recording because one character's voice lapsed into the other, but it got easier and quicker as I got more sure of the characters as I went along.' The Flump family is unashamedly traditional and the division of labour is clearly defined. Mother Flump in her unflattering headscarf is a champion cake baker and knows her way around vegetable soup like no other. Aside from cooking, she's incredibly adept at laying the table and mopping the floor. She does this endlessly. Her husband, Father Flump, is practically minded. He builds 'things' in his workshop and invariably has a spanner in his hand. There are three kids: Perkin the eldest son is fractious and excitable, his sister Posie is inquisitive, girlie and terribly proud of the big bow she wears in her hair. (Well, she wears it in her fluff, actually.) The baby of the family is Pootle, the one with the perpetually blocked nose. 'It's not a cold,' interjects Gay, 'it's adenoids. He just hasn't had them removed yet.' Ah! At last the truth is out. Julie Covington (the singer who had a number one with 'Don't Cry for Me Argentina' in 1976) was the real inspiration behind Pootle's muffled tones. She often did silly voices on stage during the rehearsals of *Godspell*, which co-starred Gay. 'Julie was always making us laugh with a funny little voice. It was really cute so I immortalised it in *The Flumps*.' Pootle is the Flump everybody loves, probably because he gets his words confused. His questions about 'hodgehegs' and 'extraplorers' are met with wails of 'Oh, Pootle!' from his family, but to be honest, Flumpspeak is full of oddities. Have you ever gone bulgering, been flupp or had a nasty bout of the fududdles? Who can forget the occasion when Perkin got all umpty? In *The Flumps'* most infamous episode a foul-tempered Perkin stomps around his forsaken garden followed about by a big black cloud. 'Scat. Hop it. Go away!' he screams and even Gay's singing doesn't make his bad mood shift:

'He's an umpty Flump. He just isn't flumping.
Growly and grumpy. Down in the dumps!'

Thankfully Gay didn't have to sing in the Yorkshire accent. She was able to use her real singing voice for the many lullabies which fill the episodes with a certain class absent from so many of the series' contemporaries. Her silky, seductive voice is a world away from the 'If You're Happy and You Know It' type caterwauling that tended to epitomise series like *Play Away*. One of Gay's songs in particular – 'No Summertime on the Moon' – is surprisingly sensitive and mature for a pre-school programme. Each week, in addition to the Flumps warbling, viewers were treated to Gay's sexy voice purring over an animated insert straight out of Mother Flump's storybook, whether it was dreamy moonscapes, spinning wheels or floating balloons. Yet, some of the most comedic tunes emanated from a musical instrument owned by the oldest Flump. Grandfather Flump likes to nap a lot, and when he's not napping he's thinking about having 40 winks. Apart from dozing, Grandfather's hobby is tootling on his flumpet – a strange metal instrument that looks like a cross between a kettle and an exhaust pipe. He just loves his 'quiet, after-breakfast tunes.' Oh hell! Comedian and jazz musician, George Chisholm, a regular fixture on children's TV during the 1970s, was the uncredited trombone player behind Grandfather's parping.

Because *The Flumps* were so popular, the BBC had intended to re-commission the fluffy squatters for a second and third series. However, author Julie Holder was allegedly appalled at the amount of money she was offered and refused to let the BBC make any more. Thus the original 13 episodes were repeated endlessly until they finally disappeared off screen in the late 1980s, but their legacy lives on through the music of Gay Soper. Between 1988 and 1991 Gay played the role of Madame Thenardier in the London production of *Les Miserables*. Considered by many critics to be the definitive performer of the role, Gay was often besieged by fans at the stage door clamouring for autographs. 'Particularly after matinees there would be queues of fans waiting to meet the cast,' she recalls. 'It was mainly autographs, but one day back in 1989 a young man tapped me on the shoulder and said: "Could you do me a big favour? Would you do a Flump voice for me?" I was totally floored. Actually I had to think about it for a moment and then the Pootle voice just came out! It soon caught on and every week hoards of 20 year olds would ask me

to do Grandfather or Perkin and so on. It was very strange.' It got even stranger when Gay started doing cabaret performances in the early 1990s. 'I had a very young pianist at the time and when he discovered I was the voice of the Flumps he was so in awe of me. This is true. It is so funny. He said to me that I had to put some Flump voices into the show. So now alongside Noel Coward, Cole Porter and Stephen Sondheim I sometimes add a bit of Pootle. People cheer and get very excited. The reaction I get is nothing less than astounding!'

FRED BASSET

BBC TV / Produced 1976 / A Bill Melendez Production / Created by Alex Graham / Produced by Graeme Spurway / Directed by Dick Horn / Edited by Steven Melendez / Written by Nick Spargo and Hitch Hitchins / Featuring the voices of Lionel Jeffries, Victor Spinnetti and Ann Beach / 26 Episodes / First broadcast 25 April 1977

Fred Basset is a very old dog indeed. Created by Scots cartoonist Alex Graham, he made his debut on the comic strip page of the *Daily Mail* on 8 July 1963 and after 40 years is still residing there, making wry observations about current affairs and the state of the nation, but mainly about digging up bones, barking at cats and stealing sausages from the kitchen table. As well as gracing the pages of the *Daily Mail* for nearly half a century, the strip has been syndicated throughout the world and is incredibly popular in the US where they assume Fred's heritage is probably more upstate New York than downtown Glasgow. In 1972 animation producer Graeme Spurway made a ten minute theatrical short (directed by Jacques Vasseur) chronicling the life and times of Britain's best loved basset and was encouraged by its success to go ahead with a fully-fledged series for the BBC. Producing the eventual series was the Bill Melendez Company. Mexico-born Melendez was a legendary animator in the US, having worked on Disney's *Dumbo*, *Bambi* and *Pinocchio* before moving over to Warner Bros to help create Bugs Bunny and Daffy Duck. He gained excellent notices in 1965 when he directed the

very first Charlie Brown TV special – *A Charlie Brown Christmas*. Melendez worked on all the subsequent specials, even providing the distinct, but unintelligible voice of Snoopy. The Charlie Brown character had evolved from Charles Schultz's *Peanuts* cartoon so Melendez knew everything about translating four-frame black-and-white strips into full colour television animation.

Melendez set up a studio in London in 1970 and his first major European production was *Dick Deadeye, Or Duty Done* (1975), based on the music of Gilbert and Sullivan. The film was a critical success and paved the way for the *Fred Basset* TV adventures, made in conjunction with Graeme Spurway. The job of directing the 20 episodes was given to experienced animator Dick Horn, a veteran of such films as *Yellow Submarine* (1968) and the *Dick Deadeye* project. He recalls making the doggie chronicles with mixed feelings. 'We were working on adrenaline making *Fred Basset*,' chuckles Horn. 'We were on a very tight budget and it felt like everything was rushed. We completed each episode within just three weeks, which is pretty incredible when you think about it. I can't say I was too pleased with the outcome. Half a dozen episodes are bearable.'

The series follows the relatively humdrum existence of a suburban dog. Fred styles himself as 'the hound that's almost human' and shares his cynical views on a variety of subjects, including women drivers, package holidays and cats. But mainly cats. He's definitely got a bark louder than his bite since he's actually more terrified of felines than they are of him. And as for the bulldog around the corner... 'I'm not scared,' pleads Fred, scampering from the marauding mutt. 'I'm just careful!' As in the original cartoon strip, he doesn't talk but just conveys his mischievous views via the 'think bubble'. The granddaddy voice provided by comedy actor Lionel Jeffries expresses his disgust for mundane living perfectly.

Fred is owned by a dreary middle-aged couple who dote on their canine companion. 'We made a conscious decision not to change the way Fred's owners looked,' explains Horn. 'They're a commonplace couple who still live in the never-never land of the 1940s or 1950s.' The only time Mr and Mrs ever do get excited is when Fred attempts to destroy the lawn again. If he's not digging enormous holes to hide garden gnomes (a pet hate of his) he's retrieving humungous bones

from the perfectly manicured flowerbeds. The series abounds with nicely observed sequences like Fred circling the carpet before sitting down and digging gigantic holes in the grass, accompanied by the sound of a circular saw.

Fred's creator Alex Graham died in the mid 1990s, apparently having left some 18 months worth of unpublished cartoon strips. But Fred did not die with him and the cartoon still appears, albeit drawn by a new artist. A few years after Graham's death Fred was all set for a comeback in a series of half-hour programmes aimed squarely at the US market. 'They tried to modernise him,' comments Dick Horn, 'but it just wouldn't work. You can't Americanise Fred and take him into the new millennium because it's not right. They made a pilot but it was all wrong. The thing with Fred is that he's timeless and you can't go tampering with something which works perfectly well already.'

GRANGE HILL

BBC TV / Produced 1978 - / A BBC-Mersey TV Production / Devised by Phil Redmond / Originally produced by Anna Home / Originally directed by Colin Cant / Starring Todd Carty (Tucker Jenkins), George Armstrong (Alan Hargreaves) Terry Sue Patt (Benny Green), Michelle Herbert (Trisha Yates), Peter Moran (Pogo Patterson), Gwyneth Powell (Mrs McClusky), Susan Tully (Suzanne Ross), Mark Burdis (Stewpot Stewart), Mark Savage (Gripper Stebson), Lee MacDonald (Zammo McGuire), Erkan Mustafa (Roland Browning), Alison Bettles (Fay Lucas), Simone Nylander (Janet St Clair) and Michael Sheard (Mr Bronson) / Over 500 episodes so far / First broadcast 8 February 1978

Back in the late 1970s and early 1980s *Grange Hill* was hated by grown-ups everywhere who considered it to be a thoroughly 'bad influence' The first soap opera for children relished its reputation for an unflinching portrayal of the realities of secondary school life, but just how realistic was it? I started watching *Grange Hill* from the very beginning. My dad loathed it, of course. He didn't like my sister and I watching 12-year-old children smoking, cheeking teachers and swearing at one another. Well, when I say 'swearing' I mean cockney kids using the vernacular tolerated by the controllers of BBC teatime. 'Oh flippin' 'eck Tucker,' screamed Trisha Yates. 'You gotta be messin' me abart!'

I honestly thought, aged seven, that 'flippin' 'eck' was the very rudest thing you could ever say. It was disgusting language, perpetrated by common alley children from London's East End. And fat Alan Hargreaves enjoyed a crafty smoke too. *Still wearing his school uniform* no less. Until then the only people I'd seen smoking were Tarragon the dragon from *The Herbs* and Irish comedian Dave Allen (the one with the funny finger). This really was an eye-opener to secondary school. The smoking and the swearing I could handle, but the head flushing I could not. Children at 'big school' regularly had their heads stuffed down the toilets and flushed by big bullies with names like

'Gripper'! Really? This was an absolute outrage. The headmaster at my primary school even called a 'special assembly' the day after that episode was shown to allay any fears that it would ever happen to us when we turned 11. Teachers detested *Grange Hill*, parents were terrified by it, but naturally kids loved its rebellious streak and ensuing tabloid controversy.

The series was devised by Phil Redmond, a Liverpudlian writer, who would later go on to create the soap opera *Brookside* (1982-2003). He had first come up with the idea for a school-based drama in 1976, but his script about a Liverpool comprehensive was turned down by every regional ITV company. He turned to the BBC, expecting a rejection too, but they signed him up for a one-off series, but on one condition: the action had to move to East London. It was Redmond's first big TV project, and although it enjoyed modest success during its first run, it received scathing criticism from inner city kids who felt that it just wasn't 'tough enough'. The BBC recommissioned the series in 1979 and, changing tack slightly, Redmond beefed up the show's storylines. As a result he catapulted *Grange Hill* into TV lore. By the second series viewers had witnessed the infamous 'canteen riot' started by a sour-faced troublemaker called Jessica Samuels (played by Sara Sugarman) and her band of militants stamping up and down on the tables. Then there was the incident involving several pupils barricading themselves in the school secretary's office because they didn't want to wear school uniforms anymore. Angry parents swamped the BBC's *Points of View* with complaints, the Women's Institute campaigned to have the show axed and questions were raised in Parliament as to whether children should be exposed to this kind of 'filth'. Thankfully, for the BBC, children *did* love it and nine million viewers a week were soon watching *Grange Hill*.

It wasn't just the fantastical storylines that appealed to kids (although starting a school riot was a secret fantasy for most children) it was also the strong characters. A trio of likeable working class lads dominated the show's formative years: cheeky anti-hero Tucker Jenkins (played by Todd Carty), tubby Alan Hargreaves (George Armstrong) and football crazy Benny Green (Terry Sue Patt). Tucker initially became the focus for the series. He was incredibly popular with boys because he displayed great loyalty to his mates and a

swaggering disobedience to his teachers. And girl viewers just fancied the blazer off him. Carty regularly appeared as the centrefold in magazines like *Blue Jeans* and *Patches*, losing count of how many times he was asked what his favourite colour was. On screen Tucker was always up to tricks with his two best mates and together they experimented with fags, booze and the opposite sex. Carty's heart-throb bad-boy character was always the ringleader for most of the show's dramatic storylines, but he was never naughty just for the sake of it. He always remained true to himself. Terry Sue Patt, the first black actor to star in a children's serial for the BBC, also gave a poignant performance as the council house kid who dreamt of becoming a footballer, but was held back by prejudice and his impoverished family. Redmond's scripts did not flinch from showing the realities of inner city youth, but to many viewers in the provinces *Grange Hill* was almost too exciting to be true.

When the time came for Todd Carty to walk out through the school gates for the last time his character was rewarded with a short-lived spin-off called *Tucker's Luck* (1983-1985) in which the eponymous hero goes to college. Inarticulate as ever, Tucker shed a little light on why he failed all his 'O' levels: 'You see at school I couldn't be bothered,' he explains earnestly. 'I mean I couldn't see much point in passing exams in subjects that were forced on you. That's why I haven't got any qualifications.' He instantly gave hope to time-wasters everywhere. The series tried hard to be grittier than its predecessor (scripts even allowed the open discussion of tampons) and there was a lot more snogging if my memory serves me right, but it failed partly because of its scheduling on BBC2 (it was up against the national news) and because Tucker no longer had an apoplectic teacher in a tweed jacket to lock horns with.

The secret of *Grange Hill*'s success has always been its counter-clash moments: pupils having volcanic rows with their teachers and rioting in the classrooms. The head teacher everyone remembers is Mrs McClusky (or 'Bridget the midget' as she was fondly nicknamed). Played with steely reserve by actress Gwenyth Powell, McClusky was firm but fair, patiently listening to pupil's grievances, and occasionally meeting them half way. There was a Mr Starling and a Mr Llewelyn in charge before her, but McClusky firmly stamped her foot of

autocracy on the school for a decade, that is until a certain Mr Bronson arrived.

French teacher Maurice Bronson was never elevated to headmaster status, but his grandiose presence has made him an iconic figure in *Grange Hill* history. Michael Sheard, who played the character for five years, was blessed with naturally terrifying looks. His imposing height, expansive forehead and Hitler-style moustache, coupled with an unblinking stare, has, for decades, made him a favourite of movie producers looking to cast cruel Nazi generals and sadistic Gestapo officers. The actor brought a sense of blood-curdling horror to *Grange Hill* not seen since Pogo Patterson started spitting every time he spoke. Sheard based his character on one of his own childhood teachers – a man who was incredibly strict and liked nothing more than hurling lumps of chalk at his unruly pupils, but Bronson was far, far scarier. There was always an air of palpable insanity about him; that if pushed too far he would totally lose all of that cool calculated control he tried so hard to maintain. Who can blame the old dinosaur? Bronson was a Latin teacher, forced into teaching French when his grammar school was merged with a comprehensive full of little toe rags who mocked his ill-fitting toupee. Things went rather badly for Britain's most despotic schoolmaster. Bronson's teenage nemesis was Danny Kendall (played by Jonathan March), who ended up dead in the teacher's car. After the ensuing scandal the teacher everybody loved to loathe was pensioned off. Sheard believes he stayed in the series two years too many, but nearly 20 years after his departure no other actor has elevated *Grange Hill* to such heights of camp notoriety.

Talking of notoriety, if there ever was a pupil who generated most outraged letters from *Radio Times* readers then it was Lee MacDonald. The Tucker Jenkins of his day, MacDonald played Zammo Maguire, the new teenage centrepiece of the show, after Carty, Armstrong and Patt left in 1982. A naive kid who mixed with the wrong crowd, Zammo found himself addicted to heroin in *Grange Hill*'s most infamous storyline of all. Drug abuse hadn't been a centrepiece of much adult drama, let alone kids' series, so naturally when *Grange Hill* introduced the controversial storyline the BBC was inundated with complaints. National newspapers asked whether such scenes should be broadcast at teatime, but *Grange Hill* forced a national debate on drug addiction and brought the series a slew of prestigious awards. However, it wasn't all doom and gloom in the classrooms; there was still a strong comedy element to the series too. First-time actor Erkan Mustafa was drafted in to play one of Zammo's classmates, Roland Browning, but his character became a butt of jokes for years to come. Browning, an obese, bespectacled loser with a fondness for Milky Ways, was hardly pin-up material compared to some of his contemporaries. Whilst schoolgirls had lusted after Tucker, all Browning lusted after was the school tuck shop. Yet, surprisingly, the chubby loner became a source of obsession to a sugary-voiced black girl called Janet St Clair (played by Simone Nylander) who eagerly pursued him down the school corridors flatly wailing 'Come back Ro-land! I love you Ro-land!' Janet and Roly never got it together. He got bullied and was sent to a child psychologist and she, presumably, found some other fattie to stalk.

The heroin storyline dominated the series throughout the mid-1980s, culminating in an anti-drugs charity record sung, rather horribly, by the cast. The song, 'Just Say No', had worthy lyrics, but was a musically worthless piece of pap. Nevertheless, the tune was popular enough to get to number five in the charts and earned the young actors an all-expenses paid trip to visit First Lady Nancy Reagan in the USA. All good stuff, yes, but the experience was somewhat tarnished years later when Erkan Mustafa sensationally revealed that many of the cast were actually high on drugs when they shot the song's video. An accompanying cast album featured such memorable classics as the heartbreaking 'School Love', the rebel-rousing 'No Supervision at Break' and the ambiguously-titled 'Girls Like to Do it Too!'

Grange Hill has yet to return to a big drugs storyline since, preferring to concentrate on more homely issues like accidental death, teenage pregnancy, arson, rape and lesbianism. It continues to shock and educate in equal measure, but has seen its viewing figures fall alarmingly since the late-1980s. In a bid to reverse the downward trend, creator Phil Redmond's television company, Mersey TV, has taken over production of the series since 2002, moving the entire production, lock, stock and cockney barrel from BBC Estree (also the

home of *EastEnders*) to Liverpool. Few parents would let their kids commute that far out of London, so it will come as no shock if Scousers begin increasingly to populate *Grange Hill*. It seems rather a shame to so dramatically change the East End character of Britain's premier kids' soap, but one has to remember that *Grange Hill* has still run for far longer than any of ITV's best efforts including *Murphy's Mob* (1983-1988) and *Children's Ward* (1989-2001). *Grange Hill* is a different kind of show now and today's sophisticated kids would laugh at heads-down-toilet-bowl bullying techniques, but if any readers have actually experienced bog-flushing I'd be fascinated to hear about it.

HECTOR'S HOUSE

BBC TV / Produced 1966-1967 / A Europe 1-Telecomagnie Production / Created by Regine Artarit and Georges Croses / Produced by Peggy Miller / Directed by Georges Croses / Music by Francis Lai / 78 episodes / First broadcast (UK) 9 September 1968

The greatest soap opera of all time is not, as many would have you believe, *Dallas* or *Dynasty*. It was, in fact, a Anglo-French concoction about a sulky dog, a simpering cat and a mentally unstable frog which played in four-and-a-half minute chunks at 5.45 pm. You mean you've forgotten about the sexual tension, the jealousy, the backstabbing, and the odd sleeping arrangements, the lesbian undertones and the voyeurism? You've obviously not visited the grand theatrics of *Hector's House* then.

Hector's House started life as the more romantic sounding *La Maison de Toutou,* first screened in France in 1967. It told the story of three eccentric animals who lived in happy disharmony in a luscious walled garden, somewhere in the beautiful countryside. The dog was an obsessive-compulsive DIY addict and his constant companion was an air-headed pussy. They were both continually spied on by a bug-eyed frog who clandestinely watched their volatile domestic arrangements from the top of a ladder, propped against the wall. The series became a French institution, thanks to the clever writing and irascible puppets created by husband and wife team Regine Artarit and Georges Croses. The characters originated when Croses was working away from home. He would write to his wife using the affectionate term 'my little frog' and always signed his letters using a sketch of a dog. The cat, modelled on Artarit's own pet, then started making appearances too Their correspondence brought them so much laughter that Croses, a puppeteer, suggested they turn their letters into a TV programme. Between 1966 and 1967 the couple made 78 episodes of bestial domestic bliss, usually filming at such a

rapid pace that each episode took no longer than a day to be shot. The dog was called Toutou (French slang for 'doggie'), the cat Zouzou and the frog Kiki. Zouzou, the ditsy feline, was originally christened Pompon, but, after two weeks of filming, a man from the French government visited the set and asked her name be changed. He claimed that having a silly puppet pussy called Pompon would seriously undermine the credibility of the then-French premier Georges Pompidou! Those crazy Frenchies!

The show was exported to Germany, Switzerland, Belgium, Italy and Canada, but made its biggest impact in the UK. Acquired by the BBC in 1968, the show was promptly re-voiced by British actors. Toutou was considered to be an unacceptably sissy name for a grumpy old dog, so the titular character was re-named Hector. Zouzou became Zsazsa, after Hungarian actress Zsazsa Gabor, but Kiki remained untouched. Broadcast immediately before the news the show's influence was immediate. Suddenly playgrounds and offices around the UK echoed with the mercurial sayings and twisted philosophy of hot-headed Hector, delivered at the conclusion to each instalment. 'Oh, I'm a great big silly old Hector!' was the catchphrase everybody remembers, but Hector's moods were so prone to change that the word silly was often interchangeable with 'ugly', 'easy-going', 'stingy', 'cautious' or 'generous'.

The secret to the programme's lasting appeal is its reliance on the OTT personality traits of its three main stars and their frequently fickle relationship with each other. Hector, an orange beagle in dungarees, lives in an elegant thatched-roof house with his constant companion 'Miss Zsazsa', a mealy-mouthed grey cat, keen on knitting and wearing flowery aprons. They have separate bedrooms, but seem closer than 'just friends'. Zsazsa dotes on Hector and hangs on his every word whilst he likes to act macho and show off to her. He chops the wood and catches the fish. She picks the pansies and bakes the cakes and everything is just fine. Despite his love for his fluffy feline, sexist old Hector likes to assert his dominance and point-blank refuses to allow her to set foot into his beloved workshop. 'Once I let a cat inside my workshop I know I'll never find anything again!' he screams hysterically at her. 'A junk heap, a shambles, a bear garden. I'm very tidy, tidy, tidy, tidy, tidy, tidy!'

Their unbalanced, yet bizarrely idyllic, relationship – based upon alfresco eating, weeding the borders and dressing up as firemen – is shattered by the sudden arrival of a new next-door neighbour: Kiki the frog. Kiki, who claims to work for the Weather Forecasting Bureau in London, but never actually goes to her office, is a mentally disturbed voyeur who spends every minute of the day or night standing at the top of a ladder eagerly watching Hector and Zsazsa's domestic arrangements. Earwigging their every conversation, neurotic Hector is initially furious that she is invading his personal space, but then decides, rather patronisingly, that he might like the slimy amphibian to move in with him and Zsazsa. 'I think I'll tame her,' he muses. 'It would be nice to have a little tame frog about the house.'

When Kiki reveals she's actually 'tame' already, she manages to befriend the dog-cat couple and is soon a regular fixture in their garden. Kiki, a right manipulative little minx, does all she can to undermine Hector's authority, creating rows and getting rather too close to Zsazsa for comfort. The frog encourages the cat to climb trees and drop apples on Hector's head. It's all too much for the dog and Hector and Zsazsa's relationship rapidly deteriorates ('Shut up alley cat,' he chides her. 'You horrid cat, be quiet!'). Weary of Kiki's constant interruptions, Hector blocks up the hole in the wall, from which she always appears. Yet, his affection for 'Mrs Frog' is blooming too, ('She's very sweet,' he confides to a piqued Zsazsa. 'I am very fond of Kiki'). At the same time he bitterly complains when skittish Kiki doesn't show her face until 2.30 in the afternoon. And so it goes on: a love-hate *ménage a trios* – full of bitching and adulation, tantrums and tenderness, infatuation and fury. The manic interaction between the puppets, coupled with some obvious ad-libbing, makes for one of the most hysterically funny kids shows ever to grace British TV.

Hector's House continued to be repeated throughout the 1970s, whereas the original *La Maison de Toutou* made a brief return to Gallic screens in 1987 when the series enjoyed a repeat run. Thereafter the puppets were consigned to a cardboard box in creator Regine Artarit's house, just outside Paris. For 15 years Hector's preposterous barkings were silenced, but then in 2002 The Royal Bank of Scotland bizarrely decided their customers might like to have him back. The bank enlisted the service of an advertising agency in the hope of relaunching their One Account serv-

ice, aimed primarily at 30 to 40-something homeowners. And what does this age group love more than anything? Well, apparently the answer is *Hector's House*. Artarit was contacted to ask whether she had any objections to her old beagle being shamelessly exploited to advertise mortgage repayments and she did not. Unfortunately, she told them, the puppets were now 'unavailable'. 'We were told that the originals had been chucked out,' explains Mark Wood from Asylum Models & Effects Ltd in London, the company responsible for making the new puppets. 'It was really annoying as we had to get the *Hector's House* DVD and take stills from it. Using these stills as a sort of template we had to completely remake everything – the puppets, the house and the garden.' The new Hector, Zsazsa and Kiki were made in hard fibreglass shells, but Regine was not impressed with the millennium edition Kiki and her flip-top bin gob. 'We had real trouble with that frog,' says an exasperated Wood. 'We had to keep adjusting her face until Madame Artarit was satisfied. Then one week before we were due to start filming, she contacted us to say she'd suddenly found the original puppets in her loft. It was a real pain!'

Four 30-second commercials were made featuring the most famous French threesome since Brigitte Bardot and her perky breasts. They finally debuted on British TV in the spring of 2003. Directed by Danny Kleinman, the most recent creator of the opening titles to the James Bond series, Hector's world has evolved over the past 35 years since he first hit British screens and he now has a satellite dish on his roof, wears a baseball cap and uses a mobile phone. Kiki, still as insane as ever, hides behind her Oakley sunglasses and gets pissed on cocktails, whilst naughty kitty Zsazsa hangs her saucy Agent Provocateur knickers on the washing line. As our favourite old dog might say: 'I'm a great big modern old Hector!'

THE HERBS

BBC TV / Produced 1967 / A FilmFair Production / Executive Producer Graham Clutterbuck / Directed by Ivor Wood / Written by Michael Bond / Narrated by Gordon Rollings / Music by Tony Russell and Brenda Johnson / 13 episodes / First broadcast 12 February 1968

In medieval times herbs were reputed to have magical powers. They were excellent for healing the pox, improving one's sex life and repelling the odd wart-encrusted witch who had been hanging around the neighbourhood. *The Herbs* are also magical, but this being kids' telly the pox is best ignored, although a dreadful old sorceress does make a fleeting appearance, before departing with her broom between her legs. The series' quirky stories come from the expert pen of Berkshire-born author Michael Bond, he of the wonderful Paddington books. Despite the first Paddington story being published in the late 1950s, it was his other famous creation, *The Herbs*, which made it to television first.

Inside a radiant walled garden, somewhere in a pre-war England where the sun always shines, the birds always sing and people laze about eating cucumber sandwiches and drinking homemade lemonade, magic thrives amongst the flowers, vegetables and plants. Owned by the aristocratic Sir Basil and his stuffy wife Lady Rosemary, the garden can only be accessed through a large oak door, and it won't just open for anybody either. You have to know the password. If you happen to utter the phrase 'Herbi-dacious!' very loudly the door will miraculously swing open, leading you to the one of the most marvellous treats in British kids' telly. On the face of it, a children's series centred on a herb garden doesn't sound the most exciting setting for laughter and music, but *The Herbs'* strengths lie in its prestigious storytelling and ambivalent cast of crazy characters. It might help if we get reacquainted with the inhabitants of this ornate idyll. Sir Basil's head gardener is Bayleaf, who keeps the flowerbeds weeded, the topiary trimmed and the grand dome-topped glasshouse sparkling. Probably a ex-member of The Worzels, Bayleaf dispenses his words of wisdom with a broad Somerset burr: 'Oooh Arrr! 'Tis a terrible thing to behold, 'tis that!' Constable Knapweed, the local officer of the law, keeps a steely eye on the garden's comings and goings, particularly those of Tarragon the smoke-breathing dragon (although on screen it looks suspiciously like cotton wool), Sage the bad-tempered owl, who rarely leaves his nest, Dill the hyperactive dog and Parsley the sensitive lion. Few National Trust properties can boast a dragon *and* a free-roaming lion, but this is no ordinary garden.

Other characters who make their presence felt include Mr Onion, who runs the adjacent primary school, the pupils of which are

pasty-faced chives, his wife, naturally Mrs Onion, and old maid Aunt Mint who likes to knit continually. Lying on a bed of nails by the fence is Pashana Bedi, the Indian fakir. He's old-school Indian with a 'Goodness, Gracious me' kind of attitude, and a habit for losing his charming snake, but is lovely nonetheless. Belladonna (the polite name for 'deadly nightshade'), the malevolent country witch, likes to stir up trouble too, but when she loses her broom her perfidious powers are sapped.

The undisputed king of the herb jungle is Parsley the cordial lion and he, like the rest of the cast, always appears on screen singing his own individual theme tune. 'I'm a very friendly lion called Parsley,' he croons. 'I am always very glad to see you wave, but please don't shout or speak too harshly. Because I'm not particularly brave.' Parsley isn't the slightest bit frightening, he's without teeth and his mane is made of herbaceous leaves. He's also obsessed with his tail. If he doesn't stop fiddling with it, he'll go blind. You can imagine how Parsley feels when the huntin', shootin', fishin'-fanatic Sir Basil accidentally shoots his pride and joy off with his shotgun.

The Herbs rivalled *The Magic Roundabout* in the popularity stakes, so it's little surprise to learn then that Ivor Wood, the uncredited co-creator of Brian the Snail and company, animated this series too. Master-animator Wood managed to translate much of the surreal charisma of *The Magic Roundabout* into his new series and the beautiful puppet figures, their jerky stop-motion movements and even the background trees and flowers all flagrantly display their French roots. In particular, my favourite character, Dill the dog, looks like the little brother of Dougal. Dill is actually the real comedy focus of the show with his manic scampering, incessant panting and pink tongue hanging out of his mouth, like he's overdosed on too many 'E' numbers. Strange then, that *The Herbs* begat a spin-off series called *The Adventures of Parsley* (first broadcast 6 April 1970) when it should have been called 'The Adventures of Parsley and Dill'. In fact the new show was really a two-hander for the unlikely friends. The opening titles alternated each episode from Parsley roaring through a laurel wreath (in a mickey-take of the MGM movie logo), and frenzied Dill jumping through it.

The Adventures of Parsley was shown in five minute chunks in the fabled BBC teatime slot (as opposed to the 14-minute *Herbs* episodes, which were shown in the lunchtime *Watch with Mother* slot) and emphasised the Morecambe and Wise-type relationship between the puppy and the big cat. Parsley is cautious and alert, whereas Dill is downright reckless, throwing all his energies into his latest money-making scheme; whether it's becoming a car salesman, starting a pop group or, eccentrically, opening his kennel to the general public. *The Adventures of Parsley* enjoyed seven consecutive years of repeats until finally being dropped from the schedules in the late 1970s. A decade later, when DJ Simon Mayo was presenting the Radio 1 Breakfast Show, he and his crew introduced a segment where they reminisced about their favourite childhood TV programmes. *The Herbs* invariably became the focus of the discussion with Mayo singing along to Parsley's song each morning. FilmFair, the programme's production company, noticed this bizarre resurgence in interest and in 1989 brought out a video – *The Herbs' Timeless Classics* – featuring old episodes interspersed with new linking material. Mayo was filmed at Ivor Woods' London mews house where the original (very youthful-looking) puppets lived on a shelf. In a nice twist *The Herbs* came back to life, invaded the lounge, and, with Dill sitting on the remote control, played back some of their favourite moments.

HONG KONG PHOOEY

BBC TV / Produced 1974 / A Hanna-Barbera Production / Executive Produced by William Hanna and Joseph Barbera / Directed by Charles A Nichols / Music by Hoyt S Curtin / Featuring the voices of Scatman Crothers (Hong Kong Phooey), Joe E Ross (Sarge), Kathy Gori (Rosemary) and Don Messick (Spot) / 16 episodes / First Broadcast (UK) 17 March 1975

Think about the greatest innovations of the 1970s – duvets, Ski yoghurts (in a pot infuriatingly narrow at the top and wide at the bottom, if you recall), Victor Kiam and his razors, the sexy rabbit from the Cadbury's Caramel adverts and Kung Fu. Ah, happy days! Bruce Lee was dead, but so what? The world still went martial arts crazy. And the massive appeal of 1973's *Enter the Dragon* was just the

start of it. American telly waded in with David Carradine, in inappropriate make-up, as a Shaolin master in *Kung Fu* (1972-1975) and the irrepressibly eccentric Carl Douglas scored a worldwide number-one hit with 'Kung Fu Fighting'. (Mr Douglas rather over-egged the pudding with the follow-up, 'Dance the Kung Fu.' It stalled at number 35, bless him.) Long before the scary Japanese series *Monkey* hit BBC2 screens, children were happily practising lethal karate chops on each other, and their terrified teachers, in playgrounds across the land. And the latest, most violent, craze since conkers, was not overlooked by children's television either. In 1974 American TV premiered one of the most cheerfully demented kids' series in history. It told the saga of a stupid dog, pretty useless at Kung Fu as a matter of fact, who solved devious crimes with the help of a striped cat called Spot.

'But who is this super hero?' is the question posed at the start of each episode of Hanna-Barbera's classic cartoon *Hong Kong Phooey*. Is it dimwit Sergeant 'Sarge' Flint (catchphrase 'Ooh-Ooh!'), ditzy telephone operator Rosemary (catchphrase 'Hello! Hello!'), or the 'mild-mannered janitor' Penry? Vain, clueless Penry is the canine cleaner for the New York Police Department HQ who, inadvertently, receives inside information from his stupid superiors. Sarge is a bumbling, stuttering buffoon with a low-slung arse who couldn't solve the case of a stolen paperclip if it was stuck on the end of his hooter. He regularly turns to advice from glamorous blonde telephonist Rosemary (with ear-splitting flat, squeaky vowels in the Julie 'Marge Simpson' Kavner mould), but it is Penry who takes on the mantle of crime fighter *extraordinaire*. Using the office filing cabinet to the same effect as Superman's telephone booth, Penry transforms himself into 'number one super-guy' Hong Kong Phooey. And this is no mean feat either, as he dives into the bottom drawer wearing his grey smock and emerges, unruffled, from the top drawer in a resplendent red silk dressing gown. If only super heroes dressed like this today.

I must re-iterate that Hong Kong Phooey is a complete and utter doofus. For all his high kicking, karate-chopping action and unique threats ('And a rinky-dinky do to you!') he is *totally useless* at catching the baddies. He certainly looks the part, driving around New York's 42nd Street in his Phooeymobile (a miniature version of the Chinese Theatre on wheels – built for comfort rather than speed). The

resourceful Phooeymobile can convert, at the bang of a gong, into a wide variety of other vehicles – the Phooey-Copter, the Phooey-Hovercraft, even the Phooey-Pogo stick. But it is Penry's feline side-kick, Spot, who is the real brains of the operation. Never seeking to embellish his own crime-busting reputation, Spot allows Phooey to take full credit at the end of each episode.

Certainly Mr Phooey has no authentic Oriental credentials. He's not even a Shih-Zsu, for God's sake. He's more of a neighbourhood spaniel and has learnt all he knows from the 'Hong Kong Book of Kung Fu' (a correspondence course, no less), which he refers to on a regular basis. The wisecracking, jive-talking dog can't even boast an oriental voice either, since the actor approached to bring him to life was black singer-comedian Scatman Crothers. The 65-year-old Crothers was the first Afro-American actor to be employed for a principal role by the Hanna-Barbera studios, but it seems ironic that he was asked to play a pseudo-oriental, rather than somebody of his own race. It goes without saying that Phooey's vocal characterisation owes more to Antonio Fargas's Huggy Bear in *Starsky and Hutch* than it ever did to Bruce Lee in *Fist of Fury*. *Hong Kong Phooey* also has more of its roots embedded in the slew of gritty police shows which littered the 1970s schedules, like *Kojak* and *The Streets of San Francisco*, than in low budget Hong Kong cinema. But even if the Eastern philosophy is diluted for the kids, *Hong Kong Phooey* is still superior chop-socky entertainment. It is, in the words of the titular character, just 'pan-rific!'

HOW

ITV / Produced 1966–1981 / A Southern Television Production / Created by Jack Hargreaves / Programme organiser – Kevin Goldstein-Jackson / Presented by Jack Hargreaves, Fred Dinenage, Bunty James, Jon Miller and Marion Davies / First broadcast 1966

No doubt you were like me as a child and regularly woke up in a hot sweat at 3.00 am pondering the great questions of the day. How did the skull and crossbones become the symbol of the pirates?

How did the Pearly Kings and Queens get their name? How heavy is the human brain? And how do you separate a mixture of salt and sand? It was a tortuous burden to carry alone. Thankfully for little children everywhere help was at hand. And it was called *How*.

The symbol, and catchphrase of *How*, was an open palm held up whilst reciting, in a very, very, low and artificial voice 'Hooooowwww', just like a Native American. It became quite a playground craze during the 1970s and could be used to make friends and influence people, as well as infuriate teachers. I absolutely loathed scientific baloney when I was a kid. My highly practical father encouraged me to watch *Tomorrow's World* with Raymond Baxter every Wednesday evening and, apart from the odd item about robots in Japanese car factories, the show left me cold with anxiety. And how come the automatons at Japanese car factories never ever looked like C3PO anyway? You can imagine my horror when I stumbled upon *How*, billed as 'TV's fun with science programme.' The words 'fun' and 'science' had never been easy bedfellows at the best of times.

Thankfully, *How* successfully combined some funny stuff with more intellectual matters so the mix was quite palatable. It also provided much-needed answers to soothe my inquiring mind. The series began in 1966, the brainchild of self confessed salt-of-the-earth, Jack Hargreaves – a grizzled old pipe smoker with a white beard and lover of traditional 'country ways'. His co-presenters were John Miller, a marine biologist and self confessed 'fish collector', TV continuity announcer Bunty James and football pundit Fred Dinenage, but Yorkshireman Hargreaves always took the lead by answering any question beginning with 'How?'. The producers stretched it a bit actually, because some of the questions posed were 'How and why..?' or 'How and when..?' type quandaries. I always thought it was a bit of a cheat. Initially the series was only broadcast in the Southern Television region, but it proved so successful that the ITV network leapt on the idea and broadcast it throughout the land. Suddenly everybody could finally learn how to hiccup for five hours solidly or how flies could walk on ceilings. It was, quite simply, revolutionary.

Although the ancient Hargreaves was the show's anchor, the real star of the set-up was Fred Dinenage (he sported a rogue 'n' in his surname) whose embarrassing comb-over, extravagant side-burns and flowery shirts made him a teatime demigod. Dinenage, a newsreader and sports presenter since 1964, was invariably called upon to provide the answers to the more comical questions like 'How do you get an egg into a matchbox?' or 'How can you have fun with fruit?'.He happily obliged, whilst the other male team members (who got to explain more difficult stuff) sat patiently behind their kidney-shaped desk as Bunty's eyes glazed over. Loveable and avuncular, Dinenage grinned cheerfully behind his big specs, got on with the task in hand, and gained the respect of an entire generation of grateful children.

The series – which was initially broadcast live – was massively popular and ran, largely unchanged, for the best part of 16 years. In the mid-1970s batty Bunty James left the show after several awkward table-top stunts went wrong. It took her five weeks to get a grape into a wine bottle, and only at the fifth attempt was she successful. But it was too late. Glamour puss Marion Davies (a saucy singer from Benny Hill's band, The Ladybirds) was swiftly drafted in to replace her. In contrast to Bunty's misfortune, Jack Hargreaves was awarded an OBE for providing clever answers to very difficult questions. In 1981 the show was suddenly dropped (along with *Worzel Gummidge*) when Southern Television lost its ITV franchise and fruity Fred returned to his news reading roots and life as a genial game show host. For the next decade *How* remained just a wistful 'fun with science' memory but in 1990 the show was reborn when TV producer Nick Pickard demanded a reprise, cleverly entitled *How 2* Fred, by then stirring up controversy by writing a biography of the Kray brothers and befriending the twins, was invited back into the fold – but now rightly placed as the show's main presenter. The psychedelic shirts and bushy sideburns had disappeared, but the glorious TV-shaped specs persevered. *Countdown*'s resident brain-box Carol Vorderman, and ex-spiky-top Gareth 'Gaz Top' Jones, initially helped out.

The jovial presenting style of *How* has been much spoofed over the years and in 2003 the show provided the inspiration for a new TV advertising campaign for Lil-lets sanitary products. The 1970s-styled commercial showed a programme called *Well I Never!* featuring two excitable presenters, sitting behind a desk, explaining how tampons worked. Starchy-knickered viewers were not amused and flooded the

Independent Television Commission with nearly 100 complaints saying it was 'disgusting, inappropriate and distasteful.' There's no pleasing some people.

How, in both its incarnations, has been a whimsical highpoint of British kids' telly and has let millions of children enjoy a good night's sleep, free from intrusive questioning. And for those of you reading this *still* wondering 'How do you separate a mixture of salt and sand?' here's the ingenious answer. Dissolve the salt in water. Filter off the sand using a tea strainer and then boil the water away to reveal the salt once more. Thanks, Fred!

IVOR THE ENGINE

BBC TV / Produced 1975 (colour version) / A Smallfilms Production / Written and Produced by Oliver Postgate / Pictures by Peter Firmin / Music by Vernon Elliott / Voices by Olwen Griffiths, Anthony Jackson and Oliver Postgate / 40 episodes / First broadcast (colour version) 26 January 1976

Children love things with wheels, don't they? Boys especially are totally obsessed with cars, tractors, trains, fire engines and lorries, or basically any vehicle that chugs, trundles and blows. Over the decades canny programme makers have realised that where there's truck, there's brass. Today's generation of under-fives are well served with an animated diet of *Fireman Sam, Tractor Tom, Bob the Builder* (he even has a cement mixer on wheels!) and the sublime *Diggers and Dumpers*. Each one is slightly more cynical than the last, but they have, nonetheless, managed to ensnare the attention of budding blue-collar workers everywhere. Biggest of the lot is *Thomas the Tank Engine*, the publishing-television-toy-crossover phenomenon of the 1980s and 1990s. Thomas, a kind hearted loco who attracts trouble wherever he goes is adored by millions worldwide, but his slightly sinister grinning plastic face and deadpan Ringo Starr voice is not to everybody's taste. Nearly 30 years before Thomas was shunting his buffers on kids' television, a far more genteel and charming steam-powered star was making his debut. *Ivor the Engine* doesn't have a silly face. He doesn't have altercations with his pre-menstrual trucks, or have run-ins with a fat controller in a top hat. Ivor is a far more intelligent, cultured locomotive: he keeps a dragon in his boiler, sings in the local choral society and, most of all, yearns to be human.

The star of *Ivor the Engine* is a handsome green-painted train operated by the Merioneth and Llantisilly Rail Traction Company Limited, based in the top left-hand corner of Wales. His engine driver is Edwin Jones (aka 'Jones the Steam'), a kindly, ginger-haired

man in specs and a blue cap. Jones decided to call his train Ivor because referring to him as 'the locomotive of the Merionith and Llantisilly Rail Traction Company Limited', was too much of a mouthful, even for the Welsh, who are used to talking fast. Ivor is a cerebral little engine. He loves the cold weather, when he can get his steam up, and enjoys nothing more than gazing down over the verdant countryside from atop the viaduct. He's also probably the most generous engine you'll ever meet. His most important job is delivering coal to Grumbly Gasworks, but he prefers taking parcels of fish to the local chippy, new boots to Meredith Dinwiddy (the local hermit) or fancy hats for the latest Women's Institute Social Event. When called upon to take the local choir to the Eisteddfod he doesn't miss a puff. He's at the heart of the Llaniog town community and the children run to meet him when they hear his familiar *pss-t-koff, pss-t-koff* coming down the line.

Oliver Postgate and Peter Firmin's reassuringly cosy series is all about the importance of community; of looking out for your neighbour, cosying up with a hot pot of tea straight from Ivor's boiler and getting together for a steaming bag of chips after choir practice. It's safe, homely stuff; a gentle triumph which, peculiarly, always reminds you of Christmas, no matter what time of the year you watch an episode. Firmin's animated illustrations are the nearest you'll ever see to a moving storybook; engaging characters float across chilly looking landscapes and Ivor's smoke is soothing wisps of cotton wool which drift upwards out of shot. The muted, rustic colours of the series also give it an unforgettably charming, bygone feel, which is interesting since the series was originally made in black-and-white.

The very first monochrome series of *Ivor the Engine* was screened on ITV over Christmas in 1959. A further 26 instalments, shown from March 1962, followed these initial six episodes and the complete series was repeated in a lunchtime slot until the end of the decade. It was the first classic series to be made by Postgate's Smallfilms production company and was swiftly followed by the adventures of a little Norse prince in *The Saga of Noggin the Nog* (1959), also for ITV. After the meteoric success of *The Clangers* for the BBC, the head of children's television, Monica Simms, asked Postgate whether he might like to remake some of his ITV serials in colour. Associated Rediffusion (the first ITV franchise to broadcast in London between 1955 and 1968) owned the copyright, but Smallfilms were able to buy back their films and remake them for a brand new generation. Six new colour episodes of *The Saga of Noggin the Nog* were also made for BBC2 in 1981, but it was the new Ivor stories which really made the biggest impact on TV viewers.

The well-crafted chronicles of the little Welsh steam train seemed more at home at teatime on BBC1, but millions of new viewers were unaware that this was Ivor Mark II. The series had, without wishing to cheapen its appeal, an addictive soap opera quality about it. Many of the stories were self contained in individual episodes, others spilled over from day to day with a continuing narrative that instinctively drew the viewer back to its 5.40 pm slot. Ivor remains at the epicentre of the snug-fitting stories, but the comings and goings of the ingenious townsfolk make for compulsive viewing too. There's Evans the Song (as the name suggests he's the resident choirmaster), Owen the signalman, Eli the baker and fruity Mrs Porty, the haughty lady of the manor, whose wobbly voice sounds like she's been at the gin, and has a soft spot for donkeys. The English are portrayed as silly asses with buck teeth, keen on fox hunting, but the real anti-hero of the show is Dai the lugubrious station master, a stickler for rules and usually with his nose stuck in the *M&L LRTC Ltd Regulation Handbook*. Dai has much in common with miserable omnibus inspector Blakey from cheeky 1970s sitcom *On the Buses*, but I can't ever recall there being a specific rule about dragons living in the boiler.

Ivor the Engine's most captivating storyline, and the one that everybody seems to remember, involves a dragon called Idris. The little beast is hatched from an egg in the friendly loco's firebox and he becomes the talk of Llaniog after he jump-starts Mrs Thomas's deep fat fryer. The series is full of cosy fantasy like this, but it is not without its poignant moments too. Ivor adores singing in the choir and being the centre of attention – 'Not many choirs have a locomotive singing first bass,' we are told. 'It's not at all usual, even in Wales' – but he is also painfully aware of his mechanical limitations. In solemn moments he can sit alone on the embankment, deep in thought. Dirty tears well up in his windows and trickle onto the

sleepers. He wants to do the same things his friends do, but polished brass will never become flesh. Through sentimental storytelling and atmospheric illustrations, Postgate and Firmin succeeded in giving their lovely loco a real heartfelt personality and more than a little humanity.

JACKANORY

BBC TV / Produced 1965-1996 / A BBC Production / Created by Anna Home and Joanne Symons / Originally Produced by Joy Whitby / Over 3,500 episodes / First broadcast 13 December 1965

Are you sitting comfortably? Good! Then we'll begin... Well we weren't *always* sitting comfortably at 4.45 pm, especially if the dog was having a barking fit and making rude words out of spaghetti letters was more interesting than yet another laborious tale of 'Littlenose' the Scottish caveboy and his pet mammoth 'Two-Eyes'. Annoyingly, the 'Littlenose' stories cropped up on *Jackanory* too regularly for my liking, but at least you could always bank on Bernard Cribbins to liven things up a bit. All kids love a good rollicking read and I was no different. At school Mrs Bascombe regaled us with stories from the adventures of Professor Branestawm (he was the mad inventor), Pippi Longstocking (she was Scandinavian and had, erm, long stockings) and Mrs Pepperpot (she was the size of, you guessed it, a pepperpot, but worringly had a normal size husband – don't go there). For those of us hungry for more stories outside of school there was always mum or dad at bedtime, but they didn't always react favourably to the whine of 'Please, just one more chapter. Pleeease!' Mercifully, there was always *Jackanory*. And Kenneth Williams could do all the funny voices that parents couldn't do anyway, so he was better entertainment value. Second only to *Blue Peter* as the BBC's longest-running children's TV programme, *Jackanory* was 'inspired' (albeit *very* loosely) on ye olde English nursery rhyme which went something like this: 'I'll tell you a story about Jack-a-nory. And now my story's begun. I'll tell you another of Jack and his brother. And now my story is done.' Not terribly good is it? Hardly up there with 'Ding dong bell, pussy's down the well' or 'Old King Cole was a merry old soul' really, but all classic TV shows have to start somewhere I guess.

It could be argued that *Jackanory* was made on the cheap, since there was no cartoon animation, no furry bears or clown marionettes. There weren't even any songs to speak of. It was just a scholarly TV personality sitting in a comfy chair reading from a book. The camera would often glide over a few tasty Quentin Blake illustrations of the 'action', but that was about it. Locations varied from the storyteller's chair being placed in a bare studio, a leafy conservatory, or, if you were really lucky, they'd do it by the seaside or on top of a mountain. But it honestly didn't matter one jot. The most important thing was whether the story was up to much. And if you got a storyteller with a good fruity voice you'd be onto a winner.

The show made its debut in December 1965 with the story 'Cap of Rushes' read by Lee Montague. 'Cap of Rushes'? Lee Montague? Mmm, clearly not a classic episode that one. Dame Wendy Hillier was up next, so things did improve and thereafter a star-studded parade of the famous and infamous filed into BBC Television Centre to read from the storybook. During the 1960s such luminaries as Celia Johnson, James Robertson Justice (Lancelot Spratt in the *Doctor* movies), Ted Ray and Rodney Bewes came and went, each leaving an indelible imprint on the minds of small children. The wonderful Margaret Rutherford even reigned supreme in February 1966, reading tales from Beatrix Potter. Rutherford's ripe, resonant enunciation was an unforgettable aural treat.

Initially there was a story a day – Thora Hird did five Paddington Bear tales over the space of a week – but this meant certain stories had to be abridged just to fit them into the 15 minute slots. Eventually, entire sagas, like *The Hobbit*, were introduced, which meant the storyteller had to create daily cliff-hangers to encourage children to tune in day after day. *Jackanory* really hit its stride in the 1970s when the show, now shot in colour, was attracting the very *crème de la crème* of British talent. Willie Rushton, Peter Sellers, Judi Dench and Arthur Lowe queued up to appear, but the most familiar face to grace the studios was Bernard Cribbins, who notched up over 100 appearances. Despite Cribbins' huge popularity, Kenneth Williams was *the* king of *Jackanory* in my childhood eyes. Nobody could do silly voices or flare their nostrils better than he. His reading of Norman Hunter's sublime 'The Dribblesome Teapots' in December 1980 is one of the highpoints of the series. It's no surprise that the best storytellers all ended up narrating their own animated shows: Cribbins (*The Wombles*), Lowe (*The Mister Men*) and Williams (*Willo the Wisp*), and many stars such as Alan Bennett and Joanna Lumley cut their teeth on kids' telly via the *Jackanory* storybook.

Some of my favourite childhood books like *Stig of the Dump, Charlie and the Chocolate Factory, The Stranger at Green Knowe, Flat Stanley* and *The Borrowers* all made their TV debuts on *Jackanory*, each with a celebrity perfectly tailored to give the tale the correct amount of suspenseful drama and/or calamitous comedy. As a result, *Doctor Who* star Tom Baker's eccentric reading of Ted Hughes' *The Iron Man* was almost too terrifying for teatime. The programme was so popular that it spawned a bizarre playground craze at my school. Any child accused of lying or telling a tall tale (eg 'My Dad went to Mars at the weekend in a rocket' etc) was deftly humiliated with a cats' chorus of 'Jacka-noreee!' from his or her cruel contemporaries.

The programme made front-page news in September 1984 when HRH The Prince of Wales agreed to read his own story, *The Old Man of Lochnagar*. It's not a very good book to be honest, but it gave Britain's favourite fictional 15 minutes its highest viewing figures for a decade. Sadly, even with royal patronage, *Jackanory* was rather losing steam by the late 1980s, with less appealing stars like Su Pollard and Jonathan Morris (from TV's *Bread*) spread too thinly over a week. Rik Mayall even caused parental outrage with his manic interpretation of Roald Dahl's 'George's Marvellous Medicine'. Horrified Home Counties types flooded the BBC with letters of complaint, demanding the instant reinstatement of cuddly Bernard Cribbins. But not even trusty stalwart Cribbins could save the programme and in 1996 the BBC, seemingly bored with the format, axed the show after 31 years. Reading, they reasoned, was passé. How wrong they were; if only they'd hung on until Harry Potter came along.

JAMIE AND THE MAGIC TORCH

ITV / Produced 1977-1979 / A Cosgrove Hall Production for Thames Television / Produced by Brian Cosgrove and Mark Hall / Written and Narrated by Brian Trueman / Animation directed by Keith Scoble / Edited by Dave Street / Music by Joe Griffiths / 39 episodes / First broadcast 3 April 1978

My pulse is quickening, my heart is racing and I'm suddenly feeling far too excited for a boy of seven. I know what's coming and the anticipation is agonising. Picture the scene: a suburban street in Manchester, bathed in moonlight. Stars are twinkling in the night sky. An unseen cat meows and an owl hoots in the distance. All is peaceful as the camera pans to an illuminated bedroom window. 'Sleep well, Jamie,' says mum as she tucks her son into bed. She switches off the light and suddenly magic happens. The gentle tinkling of a piano immediately launches into a massive T-Rex guitar riff. Kapow! 'Jamie! JAMIE! Jamie and the Magic Torch! Down the helter skelter, faster and faster, Towards Cuckoo Land!'

Jamie climbs out of bed, is handed his magical torch by his shaggy dog and within seconds they're hurtling down a fairground ride, before being fired out of a tree onto a trampoline. Most little boys had a copy of *Whizzer and Chips* under their bed. One friend of mine even had a dead bat. But under Jamie's divan is another world, populated, in the words of the theme tune, by 'the strangest people you've ever seen.' This awe-inspiring cartoon is what childhood was made for. Can anything be as exciting as this?

Hot on the heels, or rather wheels, of *Chorlton and the Wheelies* came *Jamie and the Magic Torch*; in my view Cosgrove Hall's most wondrous animated series ever. 'That's extremely kind of you to say that,' says the series co-creator Brian Cosgrove. 'It was great fun to make because we thought up the most outrageous ideas and nobody said 'no' to us. Thames Television just let us get on with it. Cuckoo Land is full of crazy characters and we got more outrageous as we went on. I like cats that can walk backwards and huge, theatrical rab-

bits. We even had a character with a trumpet for a nose,' he pauses for a moment, then laughs. 'Mmm, it was a bit weird wasn't it?'

Weird *really* doesn't do the show justice. *Jamie and the Magic Torch* is beautifully, exhilaratingly insane and for that we can be forever thankful. Nobody knows where Jamie got his magic torch. That's not important. What's more interesting is what he does with it. With a deft twist of its clunky controls it shoots a sparkly beam to take him to Cuckoo Land, where funny peculiar and funny ha-ha drink from the same champagne glass. Under an orange sky grow purple trees, volcanoes spew pink candyfloss, plateaux are made of gateau and when snow falls it's fluffy and warm. Brian Cosgrove and Mark Hall, the Lewis Carrolls of their generation, created a cartoon world so utterly bizarre that children of the 1970s could barely comprehend what they were watching. All the best bits of *Alice in Wonderland, It's a Knockout, The Goodies* and even the *Complete Works of Oscar Wilde* were expertly combined to make a phantasmagoria of pure animated pleasure. 'It has lots of Monty Python-esque humour in it too,' says Cosgrove, 'but Brian Trueman's scripts were peppered with highbrow references too. I think we were always pushing the boundaries of children's television and we never played safe. You don't need to take drugs to create outrageous ideas. You just need very creative minds.' Cosgrove also recalls how relatively easy it was to make a series back then. 'It was a boom time for ITV, because there was no competition from other commercial stations,' he says. 'It was just ITV. After the first transmission of *Jamie* the costs would be completely covered.'

Some of *Jamie*'s unconventional influences came from an earlier series made by Messers Cosgrove and Hall called *The Magic Ball* (Granada Television 1971). Sam, the hero of that show, used a bewitched ball to transport himself to other worlds, but it is Jamie's adventures that really pushed the padded envelope. Who wouldn't adore a storyline about an entire mountain going missing, or the Cuckoo Land inhabitants adopting the physical characteristics of monkeys and chickens? How about an episode featuring a sperm whale burrowing underground or one set entirely inside a top hat, full of psychedelic geometric shapes? Nobody could ever accuse Cosgrove Hall of being predictable.

Jamie, with his big coiffured hair and yellow jimjams, wanders innocently around Cuckoo Land, stumbling upon one eccentric after another. He's unfazed by most things, but his Old English sheepdog, Wordsworth (based on animation director Keith Scoble's real life mutt), has a more cynical view. 'The people here are totally bonkers!' he growls in his West Country accent. Dogs can talk in Cuckoo Land, you see, but weirder is yet to come. Jamie's best friend is Mr Boo, a pedantic red-whiskered statistician who counts anything and floats – yes, floats – around in a submarine. If he has trouble with his machine he'll call upon Jo Jo Help, the work-shy odd-job man with verbal diarrhoea. Jo Jo has a lame excuse for everything. 'Sorry mate, I've left all me tools at 'ome!' or 'I'd love to 'elp, but I'm just cuttin' sandwiches for me pet hedgehog's tea!' are pretty representative.

The Cuckoo Land constabulary consists of the singular Officer Gotcha, a unicycling Keystone Cop with a brilliant investigative mind, and a penchant for eating his truncheon. 'Three suspects and two of them didn't do it,' he ponders. 'This is trickier than I thought.' Gotcha's adversary is the road running Yoo-Hoo bird (catchphrase: 'Yoo hoo!') who blows raspberries and is thoroughly annoying. However, Cuckoo Land's biggest villain is the erudite Bulli Bundy ('E Bullient Bundy to you!'), the showbiz rabbit with overweight feet and Lawrence Olivier diction. He talks rubbish too: 'That is TS Eliot,' he booms, pointing at a pot plant, 'the biggest aspidistra in the world!' Jamie's other freaky friends include Wellibob the backwards-walking Glaswegian cat, a drippy rag doll called Nutmeg and Strumpers Plunket, Cuckoo Land's resident hedonist. Strumpers, who has definitely tuned in, turned on and dropped out long ago, is a big orange beatnik with a trumpet for a snout. ('Hey man! If that ain't too much!')

Parents probably did not best appreciate *Jamie and the Magic Torch*'s radical storytelling and idiosyncratic cast, but kids loved it. 'Yes, it's crazy and mixed up,' says Brian Cosgrove, 'but we never wanted to be predictable. *Scooby-Doo* was the much the same every week, but our show was supposed to be outrageous.' As a kid I yearned to be Jamie. I even had a torch – well, a tin kaleidoscope you could look down – but the only thing I ever found under my bed was *Muppet Show* socks. As I continue in my search for Cuckoo Land, I salute Brian Cosgrove and Mark Hall. *Jamie and the Magic Torch* – you're still the best!

Above: Would you swap your game of Ker-Plunk for Cheggers? *Multi-Coloured Swap Shop* star Keith Chegwin in 1978.

Above:
The cast of *The Adventures of Black Beauty* (1972): (clockwise) Charlotte Mitchell (Amy), Roderick Shaw (Kevin), Judi Bowker (Vicky) and William Lucas (Dr Gordon).

Right:
Tiswas in 1977: Trevor East, Sally James and Chris Tarrant.

Below: Basil Brush meets Abba's Anni-Frid and Agnetha in 1976.

Above: Britain's number one plasticine hero in *The Amazing Adventures of Morph* (1980).

From John Noakes, Peter Purves and Lesley Judd (1976) to Simon Groom, Tina Heath and Christopher Wenner (1980). How was this allowed to happen to *Blue Peter*?

Jamie and his pet dog Wordsworth meet the erudite Bully Bundy in *Jamie and the Magic Torch*.

Miss Piggy ties herself up in knots over Kermit in a classic scene from *The Muppet Show*.

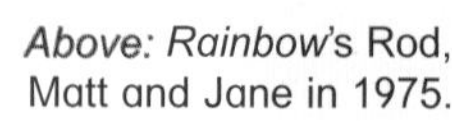

Above: Rainbow's Rod, Matt and Jane in 1975.

Left: One happy family. The *Rainbow* cast in 1980: Rod Burton, Freddy Marks, George, Jane Tucker, Bungle, Zippy and Geoffrey Hayes.

Above: Worzel Gummidge (1979): Geoffrey Bayldon (The Crowman), Jeremy Austin (John), Worzel Gummidge (Jon Pertwee) and Charlotte Coleman (Sue).

Below: Grange Hill ruled in 1980. Todd Carty (Tucker), George Armstrong (Alan) and Terry Sue Patt (Benny).

Above: As if by magic! *Mr Benn* live on stage in 2003.

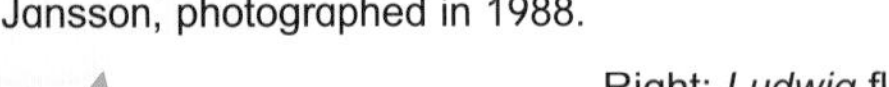

Above: The real 'Moominmamma', *Moomins* author Tove Jansson, photographed in 1988.

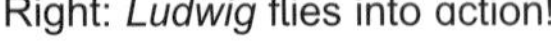

Right: *Ludwig* flies into action!

Above: Publicity material announcing the arrival of *The Perishers* in 1978.

Right: *Bod*'s Aunt Flo is batty about hats!

JOE

BBC TV / Produced 1966 / A Q3 London Production / Illustrated by Joan Hickson / Written by Alison Prince / Produced by Michael Grafton-Robinson / Narrated by Colin Jeavons / Music by Laurie Steele / 13 episodes / First broadcast 3 October 1966

Unlike other animated series in the BBC's *Watch with Mother* strand, *Joe* has tragically faded away. You won't find fluorescent *Joe* T-shirts in your local HMV or *Joe* mouse-mats in the WH Smith sale. Sadly, this underrated little character has slipped anonymously into broadcasting history as quickly as he first appeared in the late 1960s. Produced by the prolific Q3 Animation Company, who later brought the legendary *Fingerbobs* and *Crystal Tipps and Alistair* to life, *Joe* told the quietly understated, but refreshingly poignant, story of a little boy growing up and eagerly learning about life.

The character of Joe is a little dungaree-wearing pre-schooler with wide eyes and rosy cheeks. He's an inquisitive kid, who asks too many questions and can't get his words out quick enough; so keen is he to get to the bottom of the serious issues of the day. 'Are we nearly there yet?' is a regular squawk as he sits in the back of his Dad's VW Beetle. Joe's father is a working class 'cor blimey' sort of fellow with a dour expression, but so would you have been if you were the manager of a motorway transport café. Joe's mum is a drab, world-weary martyr, heavily pregnant with her second child. Over-tired, she thinks nothing of letting her eldest climb into the back of truckers' lorries or roam about unsupervised on a beach whilst playing with a baby elephant. This all sounds rather depressing doesn't it? Actually it's not. Despite looking like it was animated in the Czech Republic, the series brims over with beautiful burnished colours and a charming naivety.

Alison Prince, who subsequently composed the simple, but jolly, stories of Trumptonshire, wrote the series with Joan Hickson doing the exquisite illustrations. No, not *that* Joan Hickson of *Miss Marple* fame, but an artist of the same name who a decade later began

drawing the book adventures of *Postman Pat, Tots' TV* and *Rosie and Jim*. The 2D animation for *Joe* is completely static with the camera just scanning over and zooming in across particular scenes. Hickson paints with deep oranges, browns and ochres and her stylish line drawings are over-flowing with sexy curves, intricate hatching and solid squiggles. Believe me, nobody draws autumnal leaves better than Joan. The stunning visuals are offset by Laurie Steele's jazzy musical score, some of which would not be out of place in an early Brit porno flick. That's a compliment.

The series ran to the obligatory 13 episodes and, despite spawning some tie-in books, games and jigsaws, it subsequently quietly disappeared. There was no sequel and the final episode shows Joe embarking on his first day at nursery school. It's probably just as well we left him there, frozen in time. If he was alive now he'd be knocking 40 and probably considerably less rosy-cheeked after inheriting the family business. Poor grizzled old Joe, wearing a greasy string vest and churning out sausage, beans and egg at a truck stop on the A48.

LARRY THE LAMB IN TOYTOWN

ITV / Produced 1972-1974 / A Larry the Lamb Ltd Production / Created by SG Hulme Beaman / Directed and Adapted by Hendrik Baker / Animation by Robert Bura and John Hardwick / Music by Barry Cole / Voices by Patsy Blower, Peter Hawkins, Wilfred Babbage and Paul Bura / 26 episodes / First broadcast 18 September 1972

Hands up who likes *Larry the Lamb in Toytown*. What? Nobody at all? Is Larry really that disliked? The truthful answer is that he probably is. You look at Larry and think, mmm, well he's kind of weird-looking. Then you hear his voice and you *know* you actually really hate him. Naturally I understand that some series were madly popular in their prime, but not all classic kids' TV shows remain classics. And *Larry the Lamb in Toytown* is a case in point. We'll get onto the reasons why Larry is so unpalatable later, but it's important to see where the little woolly irritant came from originally.

Larry is older than *Muffin the Mule*, and that's saying something. He was created by Sandy George Hulme Beaman (1887-1932): a man with an aristocratic name and some considerable artistic flair. Hulme Beaman, a former theatre actor, began to expand his work into carving wooden animals of Noah and his animals. These figurines, with their very distinctive square faces and angular limbs, were to become his trademark, and his illustrative style followed suit. Beaman wrote his first Larry story in 1925 entitled 'The Road to Toyland'. Other Toyland storybooks followed, all detailing the misadventures of a well-intentioned, but innately stupid, lamb, his best friend Dennis the Dachshund, and the grumpy human inhabitants of their quaint little rural community. The books sold sufficiently well for Larry to get noticed by BBC radio. The long-running *Children's Hour* was looking for a new regular item and, in 1929, the Toytown folk debuted on the wireless. Suddenly, children everywhere were tormented by *that* voice. The segment ran on radio throughout the

war years and by 1947 had transferred to TV in a one-off black-and-white special featuring actors dressed up in animal costumes. A puppet series succeeded it in the 1950s – *The Toytown Story Adventures* – featuring three-dimensional characters, and voiced by, among others, Roy Skelton (later to become Zippy in *Rainbow*) and Derek Nimmo. A stage musical, based on the stories, was written in 1969, but to hear Larry singing must have been sheer torture. That should have been that, but tragically there was more to come.

Amazingly, a new colour television series was put into production in the early 1970s, but this time Larry had shamelessly defected to ITV. Robert Bura and John Hardwick, the formidable team behind Gordan Murray's Trumptonshire chronicles, animated the new-look *Larry the Lamb in Toytown*, but regrettably this series has little of the charm and grace of their earlier work. The animation, in essence, is beyond reproach, but the series' failure lies, yet again, at the heart of the production: the awful characters created by Hulme Beaman. Clumsy, pathetic Larry and his incessant 'Baa, I'm only a little lamb. Baa!' routine is ordeal enough to sit through without his despicable, shrieking, mean-spirited 'friends' joining in too.

The loathsome lamb lives in a quaint little chocolate box town (it looks like somewhere in Switzerland, but it's probably Bedford) populated by hideous, hateful characters, possessing not one ounce of vim or verve between them. There's the Worshipful Mayor – a plump, egotistical buffoon who shouts, 'This is an outrage! This is a disgrace!' at the top of his voice and is incandescent with rage whenever Larry upsets him. Bringing up the rear is the fat local bobby Earnest who, rather than dropping his aitches, positively collects them: 'H'im h'an h'officer h'of the law, I h'am!' he pompously proclaims. Toytown's very own scrooge, Mr Growser, is easily the nastiest, however. With his shrill, stuttering voice and regular unstable outbursts ('It ought not be allowed!' and 'You ought to be ash-amed of yourself!' etc) screamed across the town square, Mr Growser makes an enemy of everybody. Particularly young viewers.

However, my real contempt lies for Larry himself. I can't think of a more revolting children's creation than the pre-pubescent lamb, with the curiously vibrating head, who bleats, wails and whinges through every episode. His grating voice (this time performed by actress Patsy Blower) is so horrible it almost defies description. Think of a Bonnie Langford gargling with marbles, but attempting to speak at the same time, and you've almost got it. Larry means well, but he's just so incredibly thick. He doesn't mean to set fire to the Mayor's desk. He doesn't mean to smash up Mr Growser's house with a hammer. He doesn't mean to soak Arkville's mayor when he splashes around in the fountain. He doesn't mean to, but he still ends up being at the very epicentre of all Toytown's troubles. Everybody shouts at him and, in his defence, he can only bleat, 'Baa, I'm only a little lamb. Baa,' for the umpteenth time. *Larry the Lamb in Toyland* leaves you with an overwhelming feeling of despair and with one question firmly on the tip of your tongue: Why don't they just chuck him on the barbecue?

LUDWIG

BBC TV / Produced 1977 / A Mirek Lang Production / Created by Mirek and Peter Lang / Written by Jane Tann and Susan Kodicek / Post-Production by David Yates Ltd / Narrated by Jon Glover / Music by Ludwig Van Beethoven / 25 episodes / First broadcast 20 June 1977

Ludwig came as a bit of a shock for children more used to watching sedate fare like *The Wombles* or *Captain Pugwash* at teatime on BBC1. I recall my dad not liking it because 'it doesn't make sense' and, with hindsight, it was pretty avant-garde stuff compared to its more traditional contemporaries. After all, how can you love a cartoon character that hasn't even got a face? 'It was pretty weird wasn't it?' laughs *Ludwig*'s co-creator Peter Lang. 'It was improvisations on a basic idea. The fact that there wasn't much of a story didn't really seem to matter to us. In fact we never even decided what Ludwig was, anyway!'

Getting to the bottom of what exactly Ludwig was has perplexed a generation for over a quarter of a century. It is, perhaps, an even more unanswerable question than that of the meaning of life. It doesn't help matters that Ludwig wasn't really supposed to be called Ludwig

anyway. His real name is Kikiriki, which, apparently, is Czechoslovakian for Cock-a-doodle-doo. Perhaps we better go back to the beginning. Mirek Lang, a Czechoslovakian documentary film-maker, had been exposing political corruption in current affairs programmes in his home country for many years. Forced to leave, he brought his family to England in 1968. Finding that *Panorama* was a tough nut to crack, Lang changed direction for British TV via the trend-setting deaf children's series *Vision On*, for which he produced some animated inserts consisting of geometric shapes. Monica Simms, the head of children's programming at the BBC from 1968 to 1978, asked him whether he had any other ideas for a stand-alone series and *Ludwig* was born. Although of course at that stage he was still crowing like a cockerel.

Mirek asked his son Peter, who had just graduated from art school, to help create the series and together the two men came up with the most surreal, and baffling, piece of children's telly yet seen on Auntie Beeb. 'I can't remember where the idea came from, but we just came up with this... thing,' explains Peter. 'I don't think he's a robot. He's some sort of living creature, but I'm not sure what really. We never felt the need to explain it, but I'd say he does have a soul in there.'

'In there' is the appurtenant expression since what is *in* the lead character is far more important than what is actually outside. *Ludwig*, to be blunt, is a big crystalline egg with metal arms and legs and a predilection for opening hatches on his body and pulling out inanimate objects. Ludwig's body is actually akin to *Doctor Who*'s TARDIS as out pop objects that would not logically fit inside – out pokes a helicopter rota, a telescope, a horn and even a chemistry set. But mainly it's a violin, which he uses to play snatches of Beethoven's best. Where Ludwig has come from nobody knows, but in the first episode of 25 instalments his bejewelled form is deposited in a magpie's nest, much to the consternation of the local wildlife. Along with the thieving magpies, a family of hedgehogs, a daft squirrel and a shortsighted owl all fall foul of Ludwig's meddling. On the face of it he's a pretty nice guy (that is, if he is a 'guy') because he helps the woodland inhabitants out of all sorts of calamities. On any number of occasions he has to turn himself into an ambulance and it's 'Ludwig to the rescue' once more. However, the misfortunes that befall the indigenous wildlife – getting stuck in pots of glue, falling off faulty swings and getting swept off by kites, that sort of thing – are all Ludwig's fault anyway. He just can't stop pulling things out of his abdomen! Talk about polluting the natural environment. It would be no surprise if he pulled out a Burger King restaurant right there in the middle of the glade.

A mysterious man, lurking in the bushes, observes *Ludwig*'s increasingly erratic behaviour. Dressed in a coat and deerstalker, binoculars pressed firmly to his face, this spooky voyeur never seems to go home. He's there in all weathers, sunshine, rain and snow, always pondering the same question: 'What's Ludwig doing now?' (An old friend of mine says that this became quite a catchphrase in his household when he was a kid). If I saw a big gleaming egg walking around a forest I'd be straight onto the *News of the World*. This watcher-in-the-woods just prefers to hang about the undergrowth and narrate the bizarre proceedings. Actor Jon Glover provides the kinky observer's strangely disinterested voice, but the Langs originally wanted *Monty Python*'s Michael Palin. 'We did actually get him to narrate some episodes, but we showed it to the BBC and they thought it was a bit too much for the tea-time slot,' laughs Peter. 'We had to change him, but it's a shame because Michael was absolutely brilliant and the show was a bit like *Monty Python* anyway.'

Ludwig was certainly quite a risk for the safe pre-BBC News slot and throughout the country millions of puzzled children and infuriated parents attempted to unravel the mysteries of the sparkling egg. But even today we're none the wiser about this most peculiar of British programmes. 'If you ask me now what he is,' says Peter Lang, 'I still couldn't tell you!'

THE MAGIC ROUNDABOUT

BBC TV / Produced 1963-1967 / A Serge Danot Production / Produced by Serge Danot / Designed and Directed by Serge Danot and Ivor Wood / Music by Alain Legrand / English Narration and Scripts by Eric Thompson / 441 episodes (UK) / First broadcast (UK) 18 October 1965

You just can't keep a good spring coiled for long, as 2005's *Magic Roundabout Movie* should prove. After all, who wouldn't want to keep going back to a magical garden that boasts an enchanted Merry-Go-Round, a pink, maidenly cow and a thing that goes boinggg? Everybody loves *The Magic Roundabout* and all those crazy characters – Pollux the dog, Ambroise the snail, Flappy the Spanish rabbit and bouncy old Zebulan. What d'you mean you've never heard of any of them? Sad to say, Britain's very first 'cult' TV programme for children was not, contrary to first appearances, originally made in English. It was French and started life as *La Manége Enchanté*. Dougal was not Dougal. He was called Pollux. What a terrible name. And adding insult to injury he was a dopey dog who spoke very bad Français with an appalling English accent. The cheek of it!

A bigheaded French man called Serge Danot created the series in 1963. I don't mean he was a 'bighead'. I mean physically he had a big head. Huge. And with massive specs and masses of curly ginger hair. You've never seen anything like it. Danot was working for an advertising agency called La Comete on various animated commercials, but he was getting bored with the drudgery of it all. One day he came up with the idea for a children's series about a magic garden and a roundabout. Most of his colleagues thought he was too clever for his own good. However, one of his fellow animators thought it was a jolly good idea. Ivor Wood was born in Yorkshire to a French mother and an English father, but had spent much of his working life in Paris. With his French wife, Josiane, in tow, Wood set up partnership with Danot and they quit the agency to establish their own animation studio. Strange to think, but at the time nobody on the Continent believed that a stop-frame animated children's TV series was sustainable, long term. Danot and Wood proved everyone wrong. French television channel ORTF broadcast the very first episode of *La Manége Enchanté* on 6 October 1964 and it was immediately successful with viewers.

The first batch of over 200 episodes were shot in grainy black-and-white and offered for sale to the BBC. Portugal, Germany, Spain and Italy had already bought the series, but after the BBC had viewed a handful of episodes they rejected them, outright. 'They are charming,' the corporation wrote in a memo to Danot, 'but far too difficult to dub into English.' Undeterred Danot approached the BBC again in 1965. This time around Joy Whitby, the then-producer of *Play School,* was invited to cast her eye over them again and immediately saw the potential of a moustachioed man with a spring where his legs should be. Whitby offered the series to Eric Thompson, one of the *Play School* presenters, who was also a theatre actor, director and screenwriter. Thompson, the father of actress Emma, couldn't speak a word of French – his wife Phyllida Law claims he 'didn't much like the French' – so he just watched the episodes and wrote his own stories to match the visuals, using a pad and pencil balanced on his knees. Supremely eccentric, wickedly funny and, by all accounts, a very loveable man, Thompson was an inspired choice for the now re-named *Magic Roundabout.* Over the next 12 years he set about transforming over 400 episodes of a rather attractive, but dull, kids' TV series into a witty, sardonic cultural phenomenon.

It was an extremely time-consuming job for the actor. Thompson laboured over individual episodes, gradually anglicising the characters and injecting the visuals with absurd jokes for the kids and topical references for the adults. When the British version of the show debuted on BBC TV in October 1965 it became the very first kids' series to be stripped across the week from Monday to Friday. Those early monochrome episodes always finished with a cliffhanger which kept children and grown-ups hooked. The series first appeared immediately before the BBC News at 5.50 pm and adults, tickled by Thompson's hip references to the government, The Beatles, trade unions, Hollywood celebrities and even British Rail, couldn't get

home quick enough to watch the latest instalment. In 1966 the broadcaster foolhardily switched *The Magic Roundabout* to an earlier 4.55 pm slot. The BBC switchboard was instantly jammed with complaints and the duty office swamped with angry letters from adult viewers. After four notorious weeks the BBC relented and moved it back to its old timeslot.

Thompson used his own mellifluous voice to narrate the series, bringing new life to the original Gallic characters. The actor's delivery was virtually deadpan and he honed his calm, considered vocal style to perfection. Thompson totally transformed the asinine character of Pollux the dog, himself a late addition to the French series, into a pompous terrier called Dougal. Self-important and patronising, Dougal's newfound Britishness was based on comedian Tony Hancock, although his immodest characteristics were likened to other TV personalities. The *Daily Express* wrote that he looked like 'Alf Garnett's moustache out for a walk'. (In fact Dougal's long skirt-like hair was a trick used by Serge Danot, so that he didn't have to animate four legs.) Back in France the press was horrified at how Pollux had been made into an Anglo-Saxon. They inaccurately thought the name 'Dougal' to be a slur on their ex-president, De Gaulle.

Dougal's new English friends included Brian, the dim-witted, yet optimistic snail (dubbed a 'Pathetic little mollusc,' by the sniggering hound) and Ermintrude the theatrical, but graceless fat cow. Ermintrude is the campest cow ever, constantly chewing a daisy and coming out with pearls of twisted wisdom. 'Lying on the ground won't win the race, dear heart!' she wails. Florence is the programme's Christopher Robin character, an inquisitive little girl, with bunches of bananas for hands. She adores Mr Rusty's Merry-Go-Round, and has a Jack-out-of-the-Box as a faithful companion. Zebedee appears in the very first episode of *La Manége Enchanté* as a parcel delivered to Mr Rusty. He pops out of his box to grant the fairground owner a wish, namely to make children love his wooden horses again. In the early days Zebedee closed each episode with a 'Time for bed' speech for the toddlers but this disappeared in favour of him just going 'Boingggg!' and twitching his fetching black moustache. The cast was rounded off with a gardener called Mr MacHenry, a hormonal female locomotive and a spaced-out rabbit called Dylan.

It's all about drugs of course. Well, that's the persistent rumour, continually denied by Serge Danot, who died in 1990, and his collaborator Ivor Wood. Certainly the series' pop art set designs of vividly coloured trees and flowers on a stark white background have a peculiar hallucinogenic quality about them. The hypnotic organ music, which sounds like it was played backwards, doesn't help. Nor does Dougal's penchant for sugarlumps (a subtle reference to LSD abuse?). However, it is Dylan the rabbit who is most to blame for *The Magic Roundabout*'s trippy reputation. A laid-back bunny with hooded eyes, Dylan would probably be the cartoon equivalent of Robert Downey Jr. 'Yeah man,' he drawls. 'It's like, Wow!' The late Eric Thompson would probably be the first to admit that his wicked translation of the series probably encouraged some of the drug rumours. Why else would he write a scene in which Dylan falls asleep among fungi? 'I'm watching these crazy mushrooms grow,' he slurs. 'Like it's, er... very tiring. Like exhausting.'

By 1970, when the BBC finally caught up with the colour episodes, *The Magic Roundabout* was watched by eight million viewers a night. Danot had actually ceased production of the series in France three years earlier, after some 500 episodes were in the can. He and Wood parted company in 1967, but Danot's subsequent children's series did not take off as he had hoped, and the BBC did not want to buy them. In 1972 he returned to the fertile magic garden with a movie spin-off, released in Britain as *Dougal and the Blue Cat*. This sorely underrated film is a triumph of Thompson's anarchic scriptwriting skills ('The sugar was very tempting,' says Dougal, 'even GRANULATED!'), but children were scared away by the obsessively dark art direction and a disembodied female voice, courtesy of Fenella Fielding. The film introduces a feline nemesis for Dougal, a blue cat called Buxton. Menacing and manipulative, Buxton attempts to turn the garden royal blue and locks up the main cast in a dungeon. Despite the funny dialogue ('I'm touched,' sneers the cat. 'I'm overcome with touch...') children left the cinema in tears.

Sadly, Eric Thompson delivered his last batch of *Magic Roundabout* TV scripts in autumn 1976, and in January the following year, after 12 magnificent years, the BBC quietly dropped the series. Thompson died, aged just 53, in 1982. A decade later actor Nigel Planer adapted

52 previously unscreened episodes for Channel 4 and then 25 years after Thompson's series ended *The Magic Roundabout Movie* went into production at the Bolexbrothers' studio in Bristol, featuring the voices of Robbie Williams, Kylie Minogue and Tom Baker. It's not surprising that viewers and animators keep going back to Zebedee and company. The original series broke the kids' television mould and has been deeply influential in numerous other children's series including *The Herbs* (1967), *Hattytown Tales* (1980) and, most explicitly, the wonderful *Chorlton and the Wheelies* (1976). 'A lot of animators looked to *The Magic Roundabout* for inspiration,' believes *Chorlton*'s co-creator Brian Cosgrove. 'It set the benchmark by which other series followed, by its style and with its wit. I was lucky enough to have been a friend of Eric Thompson and I'm proud to say – and this is an exclusive – Brian the snail is named after me!' Mollusc immortality doesn't come easy. And nor does TV gold. 'What I like about this place, dear heart,' Ermintrude tells Florence, 'is that there's never a dull moment around here!'

MAGPIE

ITV / Produced 1968-1980 / A Thames Television Production / Executive Producer Lewis Rudd / Originally produced by Sue Turner / Presented by Susan Stranks, Tony Bastable, Pete Brady, Mick Robertson, Dougie Rae, Jenny Hanley and Tommy Boyd / 13 series / First broadcast 30 July 1968

'One for sorrow, two for joy. Three for a girl and four for a boy. Five for silver, six for gold. Seven for a secret never to be told. Eight for a wish, nine for a kiss. Ten for a bird you must not miss.' *A bird you must not miss*? Now what *bird* exactly are we talking about here? The feathered mascot of a children's magazine series, or one of its comely presenters? We'll come back to that question later.

The jolly rhyme above provided the baited hook by which Thames Television were able to launch their twice-weekly response to BBC1's *Blue Peter*. It was a tune that remained in teenagers' heads persistently throughout the 1970s and will no doubt follow some people to their

graves. *Blue Peter* had the kids' magazine format sewn up since 1958, but, finally, ten years later some bright spark at ITV thought that they could do better. For 12 years the two shows battled it out for the rapt attentions of children throughout Britain, but only one show could ever win. Sadly, it was to be *Blue Peter*. Apparently you were either a *Magpie* kid or a *Blue Peter* kid. One was for middle-class goody-two-shoes, the other was for naughty, working-class ne'er do wells. I actually rather liked both.

The executive producer of *Magpie* throughout its 12-year run was Lewis Rudd, who envisaged his programme as not only a serious competitor to the BBC's old workhorse, but also to be the antithesis of the chronically happy, safe and slightly stuffy style of kids' magazine programmes. From its echoey glam rock-esque theme tune through to its more relevant take on teenagers' issues and the trendy presenters, *Magpie* beat *Blue Peter* hands down every time. When I say trendy presenters I mean *most* of its presenters were trendy. The initial team consisted of former Radio 1 DJ Pete Brady, cravat-wearing Tony Bastable and stunning brunette Susan Stranks. Needless to say it was Stranks ('the bird you must not miss') who was the main focus of the show, both to teenage boys who felt the sap rising whenever she came on screen, and their dads who felt it even more. The secret of Stranks' kittenish appeal can be attributed to her inspired fashion sense. Tight satin trousers and billowing transparent shirts left little to the imagination. Valerie Singleton she was not. 'A vicar wrote in and complained that he could see my nipples once,' Stranks revealed in 1999, 'but that was the fashion then!'

Fashion or not, going bra-less on kids' TV was a winning formula. *Magpie* really hit its purple patch when Brady and Bastable finally left in 1972. Cheeky Dougie Rae and lanky Mick Robertson were drafted in to 'bookend' (so to speak) Ms Stranks and the show just flew. Corkscrew-permed Robertson, in particular, became an icon to teenagers everywhere. Alongside *Pipkins'* Wayne Laryea, he was the coolest-looking kids' presenter of the era and ITV realised that horny housewives were tuning-in in their droves to watch, even if they didn't have children.

Robertson presented *Magpie*'s weekly 'Pop Slot' (complete with low-budget screen effects) where the latest bands were allowed to promote

their new singles. Biddy Baxter would have had a coronary. ITV's golden boy was oft-compared to Marc Bolan himself and was somehow persuaded that a rock career would be a good idea. He predictably released an album in 1975 curiously entitled *When I Change Hands*. Robertson looks pretty smooth on the album sleeve – thumb casually linked into his belt hoop – but his singing was patchy to say the least. The public loved him, but seemingly not that much. The album, and its accompanying single, failed to reach even the lower reaches of the top 75.

Stranks quit the show in the mid-1970s and went off to do things with two fluffy spiders called Itsy and Bitsy in *Paper Play* (1974), but the sense of loss was only fleeting. Her replacement was a young lady with an even saucier pedigree, and an X-rated one at that. Bouncy blonde Jenny Hanley was the daughter of showbiz couple Dinah Sheridan and the late Jimmy Hanley. After doing a bit of modelling in her early 20s Hanley was snapped up for glamour roles in a string of adults-only cinema releases including *The Flesh and Blood Show* (1972), *Soft Beds, Hard Battles* and *Percy's Progress* (both 1974). The latter film was a comedy about a penis transplant and Hanley was just the sort of ding-dong *Magpie* was looking for. She was *Magpie*'s second unmissable bird.

The show went out live, just like its BBC counterpart, but the undisciplined presenting style and haphazard camera movements made *Magpie* pretty ragged around the edges. However, the programme was all the better for it. It was infinitely more fashionable to watch *Magpie* than *Blue Peter* and it proudly wore its trendiness on its feathered sleeves. Appealing very much to inner-city kids, the show highlighted disaffected teenagers' problems through a series of sporadic 'specials' including *Who Cares?*, *Kids About Town* and *My Brother David*. The latter – about living with a handicapped brother – won the Prix Jeunesse, an international prize for best children's TV programme. Presenter Dougie Rae disappeared in 1977 and in came another curly mop-top Tommy Boyd, whose incessant enthusiasm was not to everyone's taste. He was game for a laugh though, especially in the notorious episode where special guest Arnold Schwarzenegger instructed him how to pump iron. It was painful to watch.

Whilst *Magpie* was knowingly groovy, it still looked to *Blue Peter* for inspiration. Like TV's old-timer *Magpie* had a yearly charity appeal, occasionally broadcast items on less than thrilling themes like collecting old coins, origami boats and flour (yes, *flour*, so popular it seems, that it was featured twice!). The producers even had elephants stampeding the studio. There was also a *Magpie* badge, but unlike *Blue Peter*'s solitary prize there was more than one. In fact there were ten. Each variety was awarded to viewers if they performed a particular task and they echoed the series' hypnotic theme tune. The 'One for sorrow' badge showed a bleeding eyeball (yes, really) and was given to children who spent a night in hospital ('Ask your nurse or doctor to sign your letter to us'). The promising-sounding 'Seven for a secret never to be told' badge featured a pair of lips, but was only given to a lucky child secretly nominated by one of their friends. Sadly 'Nine for a kiss' did not entitle the badge-wearer to snog the lissom Ms Hanley. This one was given to any kid who'd learnt to swim since 1970. What a stitch up! Thames cashed in on *Magpie* chic by producing a wide range of merchandise including the yearly hardback annual, jigsaws of Jenny Hanley, bookends ('to prop up your books') and a kite illustrated with a cartoon of *Magpie*'s emblem – an overweight bird called Murgatroyd.

Brisk sales of Jenny jigsaws notwithstanding, ITV suddenly axed *Magpie* in June 1980, ironically at a time when *Blue Peter* was at its lowest ebb, thanks to a particularly unedifying bunch of presenters (Simon Groom, Tina Heath and Cristopher Wenner). Conspiracy theories abound, but somehow the BBC had finally nailed the competition. There was no more huge hair and razor sharp cheekbones from Mick, no more naughty Jenny dressing up as a policewoman, no more Tommy being, well, slightly annoying. It's a shame it had to come to an end and I recall the desperate sense of loss when the programme finally came off air. Over in the *Blue Peter* production office Biddy Baxter was probably drinking a Campari and lemonade and having a damn good laugh.

MARY, MUNGO AND MIDGE

BBC TV / Produced 1969 / A John Ryan Studios Production / Created and Drawn by John Ryan and Priscilla Ryan / Written by Daphne Jones / Filmed by Bob Bura and John Hardwick / Voices by Richard Baker and Isabel Ryan / Music by Johnny Pearson / 13 episodes / First broadcast 7 October 1969

'*A town is full of buildings. Some tall, some short, some wide and some narrow… Do you live in a town?*' Yes, I certainly did! But not one half as exciting as the town *Mary, Mungo and Midge* lived in. There were no red double-decker buses in my neighbourhood, and definitely no mice playing flutes, come to think of it. Mary's 'town' looks suspiciously like a London borough, but let's not split dog hairs. It's urban and concrete and choked full of delivery lorries and a world away from the fresh air and cornfields of *Camberwick Green*. 'When the BBC asked us to make the series the instruction was that it had to be utterly contemporary,' recalls *Mary, Mungo and Midge*'s creator John Ryan. 'It wasn't cosy like other *Watch with Mother* series, which had a fairytale cosiness about them. They wanted something totally bang up to date!'

Mary, Mungo and Midge, the 13-part saga of a pretty little girl in a pinafore dress, her languorous dog and gauche pet mouse, living on the top floor of a block of flats, was a huge departure for the BBC's lunchtime children's slot. 'It had to be modern,' says Ryan, 'and they wanted me to get away from *Captain Pugwash* and introduce more motor cars, buses, lifts, cranes, anything like that. They asked me to show high-rise life.' The only pirate galleons in evidence in this series are the ones in Mary's gigantic sunny playroom, where she seems to be completely unbothered by parental supervision. Mary lives on the eighth floor of a smart tower block (the one with the colourful window boxes) and gazes out of the windows over a town bustling with new adventures. This was an innocent era when apartment blocks were fun places to live in – with gleaming stairwells, pristine corridors and flowerbeds at the entrance. An era before the rot had set into city centre high-rises. In her beautiful flat, sweet little Mary is happy to play with her toy trains and model farmyards. Mungo tries to have a crafty snooze in the corner and Midge keeps playing 'Three Blind Mice' on his flute. 'I wish that mouse would learn another tune,' grumbles Mungo, his jowls quivering with disapproval. But it's pretty amazing that vermin can play any sort of tune on a musical instrument. 'Mungo was the establishment,' says Ryan. 'He was a touch stuffy and pompous. In fact, he lacked a sense of humour at times. Whereas the mouse was the one who enjoyed mischief and got into scrapes.'

The wise old dog and the cheeky mouse have a love/hate relationship. Midge never stops rushing about ('He could think as fast as he could run, which was quite fast!' says the narrator) and making an ass of himself. 'You mean the milk we drink comes from cows?' asks Midge incredulously. 'Your head is too small to know about such things,' berates his doggy friend. Each episode begins with Midge asking too many questions ('Gosh that looks interesting! What's a stamp?') and then disappearing into the wide world to find answers and cause chaos.

Mary allows her pets to travel around the town on their own. 'Don't be long boys!' she calls after them as they take the lift to the ground floor. The lift is the life-bringer of the series: it signifies the abundant excitement and pleasures to come. Mungo and Midge have their 'own special way' of calling the elevator. The rodent sits on the canine's nose, presses the button and they climb in. Inside, the lights methodically count down to the bottom floor. Midge can't wait to get out and while sensible Mungo makes sure the lift doors have closed after they depart, the mouse has already run off, cadging a lift on the bumper of a passing Mini Cooper. 'You silly mouse!' growls Mungo.

Midge just can't help himself. In his eagerness to find out what a postage stamp does he tumbles into a mail box, gets stuffed into the postman's sack, has a trip on a mail train and is delivered, unscathed might I add, to Mary's granny in Scotland. His other mishaps include: hanging onto helium balloons, climbing into hospital X-ray machines and operating a 150 tonne crane on a building site. 'Midge is the message you see,' says John Ryan. 'He finds things out for the children watching.' And risks his life doing so.

Mary, Mungo and Midge's magnificent cut-out animation even manages to surpass, if that is possible, John Ryan's achievements with *Captain Pugwash*. The ebullient colours and fluid shapes come together with Johnny Pearson's smooth, jazz-tinged musical score to make one of the loveliest *Watch with Mother* entries. 'They were beautifully put together,' says John Ryan's daughter Isabel. 'The quality of the imagery is amazing.' Isabel also provided the voice of Mary, alongside burnished narration from BBC newsreader Richard Baker. 'I think I was fairly precocious and well spoken as a child,' she recalls. 'Various BBC actresses were put forward to do voices of little girls in children's series, but my Pa recorded me speaking and the BBC chose me instead. They hadn't realised who I was. It was the most exciting thing in the world because I was only ten or 11 at the time. I was paid £4 per episode, but the most exciting thing was all the recording was done during school time. I was thrilled!'

THE MOOMINS

ITV / Produced 1979-1980 / A Semafor Studios Production for Film Polski-Jupiter Films (UK version adapted by FilmFair for Central Independent Television) / Created by Tove Jansson / Animated by Lucjan Dembinski, Krystyna Kulczycka, Dariusz Zawilski and Jadwiga Kudrzycka / Adapted and written by Anne Wood / Edited by Andi Sloss / Music by Steve Hill and Graeme Miller / Narrated by Richard Murdoch / 100 episodes (UK) / First broadcast (UK) 24 January 1983

Most 1970s children had literary heroes when they were growing up, maybe Willy Wonka or Caractacus Potts, perhaps Pippi Longstocking or Nancy Drew and the Hardy Boys even. Me, I idolised a short fat Finnish troll which looked like a baby hippo and who hung around with a tramp in a felt hat. But he was no ordinary run-of-the-mill troll though. Not a common fat hairy one with yellow teeth who abducted goats walking over his bridge, like in Grimm fairy tales. Moomintroll (for that's his name) was complex, single-minded and brave. And he loved his father's palm wine, although he probably shouldn't have drunk it because he was underage.

Moomintroll's adventures have been with me all my life ever since I first discovered him in *Comet in Moominland* in creased Puffin paperback in my school library when I was just seven and a half. His legendary creator was Tove Jansson (1914-2001), a native of Helsinki and the daughter of a famed cartoonist mother and a sculptor father. Jansson was working as a magazine illustrator when she started writing her first book. 1945's *The Little Trolls and the Great Flood* became the first of nine Moomin novels and marked the beginning of a very personal fantasy which has drawn in millions of readers, young and old, for over half a century.

Tove's imaginary world is centred on Moominvalley, a place of unbelievable beauty and calm. Under a rose pink sky indigo trees hang heavy with pears, silver poplars sway in the cool breeze and pretty flowerbeds filled with peonies are carefully marked out with seashells. A crystal clear river sweeps down from the faraway Lonely Mountains and loops itself around a slender blue-painted house and out to the ocean where the waves lap the golden sands, scattered with red dried seaweed. The house in question is the Moomin residence, built to resemble a porcelain wood stove with a pointed roof (as a tribute to the Moomin ancestors, who used to make their homes behind stoves). Often found sitting on the veranda, contemplating life from beneath his top hat, is Moominpappa. The head of the household is a dignified, but pompous man. Once a courageous young adventurer, he is now experiencing a mid-life crisis, becoming obsessed with writing his tortuous memoirs. His cuddly wife, Moominmamma, is practical and commonsensical. Her infallible household remedies and expertise in making lemonade is famous throughout the valley. Mamma's good at preserves, too, and her larder is stacked with more jams than a Women's Institute fete.

The Moomins have only one child, a sensitive boy called Moomintroll, who is struggling to adapt from boyhood to adulthood. Tove's books perfectly judge the abundant discoveries, as well as the hidden anxieties of childhood and speak to young readers around the globe. Moomintroll is *every* child, keen to make their mark in life, but inexorably drawn back to the cosiness and safety of home. Moomintroll idolises a tent-dwelling nomad named Snufkin. Fiercely independent and deep-thinking, Snufkin likes nothing better than

smoking raspberry leaves in his pipe and hiking southwards across Moominland from November until April (when the Moomins hibernate, after lining their bellies with pine needles). Snufkin hates authority figures, particularly park keepers, and it makes him feel uneasy that Moomintroll considers him a life mentor. It is this affectionate, sometimes strained, friendship between the carefree drifter and his young protégé which is at the heart of Jansson's amazingly sophisticated children's stories.

The Moomin house provides refuge to any number of waifs and strays, all of which are welcomed into Moominmamma's benevolent arms. Her adopted son is Sniff, a small cowardly creature full of bravado, but deeply insecure. There's also the Snork Maiden, who resembles a Moomin, but is slightly fluffier and prone to changing colour with her moods (green and mauve are popular). Despite her frivolous love of jewellery, hair combs and staring at her own reflection, Moomintroll experiences his first stirrings of love with her. Contemptuous of the friendship, and innately cynical about everything else, is Snufkin's half-sister, Little My. Brusque and hilariously obnoxious, My is the bad girl of Jansson's books (and allegedly partly based on the author herself). The raven-haired urchin is so small that she can hide in Snufkin's floppy hat and often sleeps in Mamma's sewing basket, but her shrill, obstreperous voice can fill any room.

Aside from her main ensemble of characters, Jansson created a fascinating world of backslapping, bombastic Hemulens, jittery Fillyjonks, crestfallen Whompers, headstrong Mymbles, vexed Gaffsies and innumerable Woodies, little creeps and tree spirits. The author manages to sustain a deeply intimate mood throughout her novels, filling them full of warmth and believability, but also of melancholy and loneliness. As Jansson's writing career progressed her work became more imbued with introspection and sadness, often with her characters hopelessly gazing out to sea, desperately searching for acceptance and spiritual freedom. It could be argued that her later books aren't even children's books at all; such is the subtle complexity of intricate novels like *Moominvalley in November* (1970). Because Jansson had lived in Finland during the Russian invasion of World War II, many of her books reflect the darkness and fear of the period. The allegories are obvious. In several of her stories the idyllic Moominvalley is threatened by natural disasters: a severe flood, the imminent arrival of a comet and the terrifying Lady of the Cold. All are eventually overcome, but only after her characters pull together and liberate their vulnerability.

Tove Jansson loved solitude and nature, due to her Bohemian upbringing. In 1947 she moved to an isolated island in the Gulf of Finland, and only reluctantly left after it became overcrowded with family and friends. From 1964 to 1991 she and her girlfriend Tuulikki Pietila lived on a nearby scrap of grey rock, barely big enough to build a house, until a torrential storm wrecked their boat and they were forced to retire to Helsinki. Jansson gave up writing Moomin novels in 1970, reasoning that she was unwilling to take Moomintroll through the trials and tribulations of puberty. Happily, several Moomin picture books followed, including *The Dangerous Journey* (1977) and, finally, *An Unwanted Guest* (1980), each one beautifully illustrated by the author. Her beguiling creations had been previously adapted for the stage, operas and Scandinavian television, but it was an exquisite 1979 TV series which really allowed her loveable trolls to blossom into three dimensions.

Jansson and Pietila travelled the world with the royalties from the Moomin books (by the mid-1970s her books had been translated into 30 languages) and in 1978 an animation studio called Semafor, based in Poland's central city of Lodz, approached the author's publishers with a view to adapting her novels for TV. Poland has always had a strong tradition of animated films, although many of the cartoons were barely-disguised critiques of the country's communist rule. At the time all Polish animation studios were state owned, but were pretty much allowed to do what they wanted, provided they adhered to the strict bureaucratic guidelines. Studio Semafor was famous for its esoteric children's animation, something that Tove had admired for some time. After agreeing to let Semafor adapt her books, as well as some stories from the Moomin cartoon strip, which had appeared in the London *Evening Standard* from the mid-1950s, the author travelled to Poland to oversee the project.

The original Polish productions were nearly an hour long, but throughout the world the animation was adapted for different

television channels. In 1981 Lewis Rudd, the then-head of children's programmes for ITV, bought the series in its original format and offered it to producer and writer Anne Wood, hoping that she could Anglicise it for a UK audience. 'I was thrilled to be asked,' recalls Anne, now better known as the creator of *Rosie and Jim*, *The Teletubbies* and *Boohbah*. 'I knew Tove Jansson's work very well since I'd worked in children's publishing and on a magazine called *Books for Your Children*. Her work was just brilliant. It transcends age and culture and I had long recognised her as a very great writer.'

Anne had no doubts that she could adapt the series. 'I felt a great affinity to Tove's work and, because she had personally visited Studio Semafor when it was being made, I knew it would be good stuff,' she says. 'It was distributed by a German company back then and I seem to recall we cut it down from half hour chunks. ITV wanted it in five minute long episodes so Andi Sloss, the editor, and I got to work on it. All-in-all, it probably took us about two years to complete.'

Anne recalls her determination to not lose a single second of footage for her adaptation. 'I saw the series and was amazed at how beautiful it was,' she remembers. 'I didn't waste one scrap of film, although creating 100 episodes out of it was quite a task. Poland has produced some wonderful animation in the past and the visual quality of *The Moomins* was second to none. The Studio Semafor was the best in Europe and the total opposite of Disney's productions in the US. The thing about *The Moomins* was that it had such great depths and lushness, something you just can't capture using cell animation.'

The Polish animators used a stop-motion technique to bring Jansson's imaginary world to life. Three-dimensional felt characters gracefully glide over delicately painted backgrounds – the series has been dubbed by aficionados as 'The fuzzy-felt Moomins', to distinguish it from an inferior Japanese cartoon version from 1991. In addition to the cuddly warm shapes of the Moomins, there is a vibrant use of textures (sand, glitter, flowers, buttons, feathers) and fabrics (corduroy, gingham and woollen skeins). By creating layers of exotic colour and interesting weaves the series' fastidious animation style is completely unlike any British series of the era.

'I totally revered Tove's original books,' admits Wood, 'so when I was writing the scripts for my version of the series I constantly referred to the Puffin paperbacks, marked up in pen with all the relevant dialogue.' However, Wood was surprised when some of the Polish visuals had no connection with the novels. 'Andi Sloss and I would be watching the episodes and we'd stumble on subliminal political messages! It would be like: "Oh, what's this then? This isn't in the book!"' Although careful to remain faithful to the text of the novels, Wood still managed to cleverly inject some of her own dry humour into the storytelling. Snufkin, for instance, becomes an out-and-out hippy, affixing a 'Far out, man!' to the end of much of his dialogue and slipping in the odd line never seen in any of Tove's novels. 'Cocktail parties are not my scene,' he drawls in one particularly droll episode. Even Moomintroll gets to laugh at himself. 'I'm not a hippo,' he explains. 'I'm a Moomin!'

The job of voicing the Moomin characters was awarded to veteran actor Richard Murdoch. He brings a befuddled tension to the stories – on occasion it sounds like he's ad-libbing – yet he still flits between the numerous, crumbly voices with great aplomb. Murdoch, who was 78 at the time of recording, created some minor headaches for the British production. 'We had a discussion, early on, as to who we wanted to do the narration,' explains Wood, 'and we came up with Richard's name. I was always there when he did the dubbing, and although he was excellent, I did have to coax him through it. He was always late to the recording sessions too and because it was a period when so many great actors had suddenly died, like Peter Sellers and Arthur Lowe, I was always worried that he'd never make it back!'

The breath-taking Polish animation perfectly captures the melancholy spirit of Jansson's illustrations. It's like watching the highly decorated lid of a chocolate box, just after the Christmas holiday: there are still so many delights, but you can't help but feel slightly sad. The series is imbued with a certain amount of dark horror too. The menacing Hattifatteners, long white sock-like creatures with pale eyes and sharp paws, spookily crackle with electricity across the screen. Worse still is the Groke – the dread spirit of winter, who glides across the grass, freezing everything she touches. The latter creature, animated with flashing eyes and dubbed with slow, heaving breathing, is

enough to give any four-year-old nightmares for a month. 'It's very difficult to pull off tension and horror in a children's serial,' explains Anne Wood. 'There's a definite fear factor in *The Moomins*. I mean there's that scene where Moomintroll climbs into the Hobgoblin's hat and then emerges as a monster. That is really frightening for little children. But the stop-frame animation and the cuddly, toy-like characters help children to accept these terrifying concepts.'

Also adding to the melancholy is the series' haunting incidental music, composed by two young British performers, Steve Shill and Graeme Miller. 'We did the music in three batches, I think,' says Miller, 'and we supplied individual themes for each character or situation. We had to be very specific when writing music for creatures like the Hattifatteners because so much of Jansson's writing is quirky and ironic. There's a kind of nostalgic quality to her books and we tried to reflect that in the music.' The pair's music, performed on synthesizers, is some of the saddest ever to make its way onto kids' TV. 'We were very influenced by the sad theme to *Robinson Crusoe* [an imported black-and-white series, screened by the BBC during the sixties and seventies], but also by Kraftwerk, so there's a bit of both in there,' he laughs. 'You must remember that we were only in our early twenties when we wrote the music, so it was such a thrill when, at 4.15 pm, we'd hear our tunes on the telly. Writing a theme for a children's TV series is like writing an ice cream van jingle in a way; it is injected right into people's consciousnesses.'

Miller and Shill's enchanting music captures the Eastern European flavour of the animation, and the wistful penny whistle-like theme tune is eerily memorable. This emotive music, coupled with the whimsical dreamlike quality of the animation, creates a deeply affecting atmosphere of dark forebodings in the Moominvalley shadows. Despite the stories not being in chronological order, the Polish production is undoubtedly the definitive accompaniment to the novels. *The Moomins* is consistently dazzling and you'd be hard pressed to find a more beautiful image in classic kids' TV than the shimmering, bejewelled seahorses leaping out of the ocean in the series' adaptation of *Moominpappa at Sea*. It is quite simply breathtaking.

'I was really proud to have been associated with *The Moomins*,' says Anne Wood. 'People forget that creating a children's series is actually

an art form, but it really is. In general terms children's TV is not given serious attention, and this is a tragedy. I later met some of the animators from Studio Semafor and used them on my own series, *Tots TV*, because you don't get animators of their calibre very often. The important thing about *The Moomins* is that it was a children's series made with great skill, with great respect to Tove Jansson and ultimately made with a lot of love.'

THE MISTER MEN

BBC TV / Produced 1974-1976 / A Mister Films Production / Created and Written by Roger Hargreaves / Directed and Produced by Terry Ward and Trevor Bond / Narrated by Arthur Lowe / 28 episodes / First broadcast 13 December 1974

The Mister Men books were a big part of my early childhood, and obviously quite a lot of other people's too, as over 100 million copies have been sold since they were first published in 1971. Their late author, Roger Hargreaves, is second only to Harry Potter creator JK Rowling as the world's best-selling children's author. The little five inch by five-and-a-half inch books with staples in the middle became a publishing phenomenon and all because Hargreaves' son Adam asked him what a 'tickle looked like'.

Yorkshire-born Hargreaves was working as a copywriter in the advertising industry when his son posed that awkward question. It had always been Hargreaves' ambition to be a cartoonist, so he set about working on a comedy character to explain how tickles were made. The resulting character – unsurprisingly called Mr Tickle – was a fat orange creation with long bendy arms, a little blue hat and a mischievous grin. Initially published to great acclaim by Fabbri Books, Hargreaves followed up Tickle's touchy-feely antics with a further 38 characters over the next 17 years, including Mr Happy, Mr Noisy, Mr Worry and Mr Slow. Each was a brightly coloured, simply drawn symmetrical figure occasionally donning a trilby or pair of clunky Oxford brogues.

The books were required reading for trendy toddlers everywhere. My personal favourite, and the one I still have on my bookshelf with my name scrawled in the back from the mid-1970s, is Mr Daydream – a fluffy blue concoction who looks like a cumulous cloud and encourages naughty boys to drift off into flights of fancy. Hargreaves' drawings were done with clunky felt-tips and the beauty of his work was that you could see all the haphazard pen marks and the bits he'd inadvertently left out. This style of artistry gave me confidence that my own felt-tip masterpieces weren't all bad. The success of the books meant a TV series adaptation beckoned, and in 1974 London-based animators Terry Ward and Trevor Bond began working closely with Hargreaves on a series. The first set of 13 episodes debuted on BBC1 in the 1.30 pm *Watch with Mother* slot in December 1974 and was an immediate hit with pre-schoolers already familiar with the classic books. The episodes remained pretty faithful to the original tales, but I must take umbrage with the cartoon Mr Snow, who bore scant resemblance to his original book version. To a five-year-old Mr Men expert like myself I could clearly identify that Mr Snow had a totally out of proportion nose and hat. He also had fingers. The original Mr Snow does not have fingers! He wears mittens!

To see, in the 'flesh' so to speak, my heroes like Mr Silly actually 'driving' around Nonsenseland in a shoe and popping back to his teapot house to 'drink' a piece of cake was simply sensational. The hideous flowery wallpaper and bed linen, which adorned every self-respecting Mr Man's home, was there too, in vivid colour and it was reassuring to see the prevalence of smiling worms (a Hargreaves trademark) poking out of manicured lawns everywhere. The characters are mostly insane and the episodes full of beautifully surreal moments. Mr Forgetful has a look of resolute dismay on his face every morning when he hard boils his egg and burns his toast for the millionth time. And don't ask him to remember an important message. 'There's a sheep lose in the lane,' Farmer Fields tells him anxiously. By the time Mr Forgetful has found an officer of the law to report the mishap there's 'a goose asleep in the rain.'

The man who helped bring the hysterical stories to life was actor Arthur Lowe, apparently a bit of a Mr Grumpy himself. Lowe, best known for playing the pernickety Captain Mainwaring in *Dad's Army*,

happily blunders through the story-telling duties, even going so far as to absent-mindledly hum along to the series' dotty theme tune. Lowe's gruff tones fit perfectly with the characters' eerily exaggerated mouth movements, although he does sound suspiciously inebriated throughout. However, this only adds to the high drama. Will Mr Messy ever get clean? Will Mr Greedy ever shed those extra pounds? A second series, this time of 15 episodes, debuted on BBC1 in 1976 and told all of the Mr Men stories written up to this point.

The Mr Men weren't Hargreaves' only literary creations, far from it. His bibliography of crazy characters also includes the *John Mouse* books (1973), *Count Worm* (1976), *Grand Father Clock* (1977), *Albert the Alphabetical Elephant* (1977) and the *Timbuctoo* series (1978), which consisted of humungous-headed animals with tiny feet having adventures rather similar to the Mr Men. They included Roar the lion, Neigh the horse and, rather oddly, Puff the panda. The 1980s brought the Little Miss series (1981, and turned into a cartoon series the following year), *Once Upon a Worm* (1982) and the melancholy one-off *Mr Nobody* (1985) featuring a transparent character. Tragically, Hargreaves died following a stroke in 1988 and his final Mr Men stories (Messers Brave, Grumble, Perfect and Cheerful) were completed posthumously. His son Adam has now taken over the mantle of chief Mr Man and in 2001 wrote and illustrated *Mr Cheeky*, the first completely new addition to the series for 13 years. Mr Cheeky has subsequently led to *Mr Christmas, Mr Rude, Mr Good* and, the very millennium sounding, *Mr Cool*.

The TV cartoons have continued since Hargreaves' death too. Terry Ward produced a gigantic 104 *Mr Men and Little Miss* episodes for cable television in 1995, as well as *Timbuctoo* (ITV 1997-1999) with Ronnie Corbett pretending to be various pigs, frogs and monkeys. In January 2003 an oddball collection of strictly unofficial Mr Men also made their debut in the British media. The *Sun* got into trouble with the Press Complaints Commission for printing spoof cartoons of the sort of Mr Men 'flourishing under New Labour'. They included Mr Asylum Seeker, Mr Albanian Gangster and Mr Yardie – a black, gun-toting Rasta, smoking a joint. Mr Tickle was not tickled-pink.

MR BENN

BBC TV / Produced 1970 / A Zephyr Film Production / Created by David McKee / Directed by Pat Kirby / Produced and Written by David McKee / Illustrations by David McKee and Ian Lawless / Narrated by Ray Brooks / Music by Don Warren / 13 episodes / First broadcast 4 March 1971

Now the Mister Men are something special, but *Mr Benn* is a colossus among his TV contemporaries. Here is your everyday Englishman, happily minding his own business in suburbia, but, unknown to his neighbours, he leads a secret double life, which involves dressing up in weird clothes, travelling through time and space, and soothing the frantic lives of those he meets with his own personal brand of love and friendship. And not only that, he's also reputed to hold the BBC record for most repeat showings. More than *Fawlty Towers, The Good Life* and *Dad's Army* put together. That is some achievement.

But just who is this mysterious enigma? Mr Benn – no first name is ever specified – is a very ordinary type of chap of indeterminable age, who goes about his everyday life with a smile on his face and a skip in his step. A traditional, old fashioned gentleman, he insists on always looking his best in a dark grey suit, crisp white shirt, stripy old school tie and, most distinctively, his black bowler hat. He lives at 52 Festive Road, a terraced Victorian property in south London and keeps his home meticulously spic and span. The back garden is neatly trimmed and cared for. He'll stop for a chat over the garden fence and chuckle along with the children who happily play in the street. He likes his neighbours. They like him. The sun shines and everything is wonderful. Unremarkable? Absolutely not! Mr Benn has the sort of adventures we can only dream of. His life is like no other, and somehow he has managed to touch the consciences of millions of children, and adults alike. But exactly who is he?

Perhaps Mr Benn's creator can shed some life on this mystery. Could Mr Benn really be the alter ego of author and artist David McKee? 'Oh, everybody asks me that!' says McKee cheerfully. 'No, I

wasn't, am not, Mr Benn. He lived at number 52 you see, and I lived at 54.' Ah! So there is a real Festive Road then? 'No, there's not,' replies McKee. 'I lived at Festing Road. My next door neighbours were an elderly couple.' This is getting a bit confusing.

David McKee was born and raised in Devon. After his grammar school education he went onto Plymouth Art College, where he indulged in his passion for painting and drawing. He began selling his illustrations and cartoons to national newspapers and magazines, including *Reader's Digest* and *Punch*. He also discovered he had a knack for telling stories and in 1964 Abelard-Schulman published his first children's book *Two Can Toucan*. The book, with a captivating storyline and bright illustrations, was a massive success and was suitably brought to the attention of the BBC. 'They loved the book,' explains McKee, 'and asked to use it for *Jackanory*. I was extremely pleased, because the story lent itself so well to television.' Around the same time McKee had been working on a new character, a certain Mr Benn of 52 Festive Road. Dobson Books originally published the first Mr Benn book in 1967. It was called *Red Knight* and told the story of a suburban gent, who, after being handed an invitation to a fancy dress party by the local postman, seeks out a costume hire shop. He sets off to the shops but everywhere he looks is just the same old everyday attire. At this rate he may as well just go to the party dressed as himself. Then, as he is walking back home, rather dejected, he comes across a little lane he's never noticed before. And there is an ordinary little shop with very extraordinary costumes hanging in the window. He particularly takes a shine to the suit of red armour and, on entering the funny store, is approached by the shopkeeper – a tubby chap in a striped waistcoat, bow tie and Tommy Cooper fez. The man invites Mr Benn to try on the outfit in the changing room. However, when he does he notices a secret door at the back of the cubicle – a door that leads to incredible adventures. We'll leave it there for a moment, but suffice to say that the secret portal is reminiscent of the one at the back of the old wardrobe in CS Lewis' *The Lion, the Witch and the Wardrobe*.

Red Knight was successful enough to spawn a sequel in 1970 called, rather obliquely, *123456789 Benn*, which saw Mr Benn being sent to jail and stripped of his identity. Just as this jolly prisoner lark was

flying off the bookshelves, the BBC approached McKee again, and asked whether he had any ideas for a potential TV series of his own. 'We had this meeting,' explains the author, 'and knocked around one or two ideas. At the time I really liked Gordon Murray's *Trumpton* series and had had the idea of a programme about life in a fort. It was to be a period setting with lots of soldiers, but made simplistically and with lots of references to real life. Well, anyway the BBC saw it and rejected it outright. It was very disappointing, but when I happened to show them Mr Benn they couldn't accept it quick enough. They virtually bit off my hand to get it.'

The BBC commissioned a pilot, followed by a set of new stories, but there was a problem. McKee had no idea what he was supposed to do. 'I knew nothing about making films to be brutally honest,' he explains, cheerily. 'I was really thrown into the deep end with the *Mr Benn* series. I actually talked to John Ryan, who had made *Captain Pugwash* and *Mary, Mungo and Midge*, and asked for his advice. He was extremely helpful and very encouraging, so I got to work.' At the time McKee, alongside his writing and illustrating work, was spending one day a week teaching at the London College of Printing. There he had met a student named Ian Lawless. The two men became great friends and McKee enlisted Lawless help to make the 13 *Mr Benn* episodes. 'It was a crazy time. We had about a year to make all the *Mr Benns*,' McKee says. 'I was doing all the drawings and Ian was doing the colouring. It was extremely hard work, especially since I was working on books, magazines and advertising projects too. But all my money was thrown into *Mr Benn*.'

Around the same time McKee was also providing the illustrations for other children's classics like the *Paddington* books and *Hector's House* annuals, but there was little time for distractions. 'I had to write 12 new stories for the Mr Benn series, apart from *Red Knight*,' recounts McKee. 'The first book was always to be the starting point, but the BBC would not let me adapt *123456789 Benn* for television. They told me it would be too controversial for the *Watch with Mother* age group. I thought they were being over-sensitive, but I had to go away and write another story to replace it.'

The eventual 13 episodes of the *Mr Benn* TV series are as follows: 'Red Knight'; 'Hunter'; 'Diver'; 'Spaceman'; 'Cook'; 'Pirate'; 'Magic

Carpet'; 'Caveman'; 'Wizard'; 'Cowboy'; 'Clown'; 'Zoo Keeper'; and 'Balloonist'. Each episode title is indicative of the sort of costume Mr Benn tries on in the weird little shop, but what motivates the character to keep going back for, potentially death-defying, escapades? 'He's just an ordinary guy,' explains David McKee. 'He's a quiet neighbour who minds his own business and I like people like that. But he seeks some sort of excitement out of suburban living.' Mr Benn certainly is the archetypal English gentleman who lives a decent, well-meaning life in the sprawling outer edges of a big city; '52 Festive Road does actually exist you know,' says McKee, 'but it's really called Festing Road, in Putney SW15. I used to live there in the late 1960s and always thought how nice it would be to have a neighbour like Mr Benn.' In fact, in 'Red Knight' McKee's face can be seen peeping out of the window of number 54, keeping a watchful eye on the comings and goings. 'Whilst I wanted to have Mr Benn living in my road, I did have to change the name to Festive. After all, Festing sounds rather too much like 'festering' doesn't it?'

Apart from identifying Mr Benn's real-life residence, another thing that has puzzled the series' fans over the years is what the character actually does for a living. Does he even have a job at all? He's always smartly dressed, whatever the weather, or time of day, and his bowler suggests that he might work in the City. Perhaps Mr Benn is unemployed, but likes to pretend to his neighbours that he has a very important job somewhere, but in reality just sits in the park all day (one of his hobbies, anyway). Is he a deluded fantasist? Or a harmless, child-like dreamer? 'I don't think it's too important what he does really,' admits McKee, who is perplexed by fans' continual analysis of his famous creation. 'I want him to be intriguing, but of course in the American translation of the books he has to be a banker because they don't understand it otherwise.' The way Benn dresses is central to the stories, but in this instance McKee made him smart and dapper for a specific purpose. 'I wanted him to be correct and proper. Not sloppy,' he recalls. 'Having him in a suit and bowler emphasises the freedom he later experiences when he visits the costume shop. It just confirms his feelings of release. But on the other hand bowler hats were very common in London at that time. I just drew what I saw in Putney.' McKee happily admits that he was influenced by the work of Belgian

painter Rene Magritte, whose avant-garde works, like the famous 'Golconda', which shows bowler-hatted gents raining down over a suburban (and very Festive Road-looking) street. 'My art education did have a bearing on my later work,' he says.

Back at the costume shop, Mr Benn makes a startling discovery. After dressing up as the red knight he uses the door in the back of the cubicle and is whisked away to a mythical universe of fire-breathing dragons and medieval banquets. Most customers would be understandably terrified by such a worrying experience, but not Mr Benn. He thrives upon it. Once transported, he meets a big green miserable dragon, which has been living in hiding ever since being driven out of the city by an evil match-seller. The tradesman has convinced the people that the dragon caused the local barn fires and matches are a much safer option. What they don't know is that the match-seller is the true arsonist. Mr Benn, showing characteristic compassion, explains to the truth to the king and, with the villain thrown in the dungeon, the dragon is reinstated as the chief royal firelighter. Benn returns home to London, his job done. Having once discovered the secret delights of the costume shop Mr Benn just can't stop going back there, day after day, week after week. It almost becomes an addiction.

The central theme to McKee's beautiful stories is Benn's altruism. He sees goodness in everyone and everything and spreads his simple, yet effective philosophy to all he meets. The grass is not always greener on the other side. Beauty is only skin deep. We learn by doing, not by watching. His loving, peaceful, non-malevolent attitude to life makes him a role model children can really aspire to. 'The series is escapist entertainment,' believes David McKee, 'but I want there to be strong stories with real meaning. *Mr Benn* was a show watched by children and adults in that *Watch with Mother* slot and I was very conscious of having to do a good job.'

Over the 13 episodes Mr Benn displays his knack for peaceful mediation, the importance of showing compassion and explaining the value of friendship. His motto in life could be: 'Freedom is life's greatest luxury, don't waste your life arguing or being unhappy.' The children he sees playing in the street outside his house usually inspire his incredible adventures. The boys and girls might be playing with

juggling balls, dressing up as Red Indians or walking with helium balloons. Whatever they seem to be doing triggers off a fantasy in Mr Benn's daydreamer's mind and off he goes to the costume shop once more. 'Mr Benn suddenly tingled with excitement,' wrote McKee, 'as he entered the door that always led to adventures.'

Whatever world Mr Benn visits, problems are solved and people are made happier than before he arrived. Perhaps that's why the kindly shopkeeper keeps letting him try on costumes at his store, without ever asking for any sort of payment. The charismatic shopkeeper is, on reflection, more mysterious a character than his most regular client. He looks exotic, maybe even Moroccan and his bow tie, little 'tache and purple Fez give him an aura of hocus-pocus. The soothing *Mr Benn* narration, by actor Ray Brooks, explains that the shopkeeper always appears 'As if by magic!' and after Mr Benn has done his good deeds the proprietor is always the person to gently drag him back to reality. 'I wanted the shopkeeper to be as mysterious as humanly possible,' explains McKee. 'He's maybe not Moroccan, but he's certainly from overseas. If I were starting the series again now he'd definitely be more Arabian than he was then. I originally was going to have him wearing a pith helmet too, but chose the Fez instead. It's funny how these things evolve.' What's more surprising to discover is that the costume shop did *really* exist. Sort of. 'When I was an art student in Plymouth there was this mysterious old costume-cum-antiques shop in the centre of the city,' McKee remembers. 'The window display never, ever changed and the old owner never sold the bric-a-brac he had in the shop. He was pretty eccentric and his place inspired me to create the shop in *Mr Benn*.'

Mr Benn debuted at lunchtime on 4 March 1971 and not even years of repeats have diluted his refreshing appeal. If anything they have strengthened the legend. David McKee adapted two of the television adventures into books, *Big Game Benn* (1979) and *Big Top Benn* (1980), but sadly threw most of his original TV artwork into a skip in the 1970s, never realising that it would have any historical or cultural value one day. As well as Mr Benn he also devised the character King Rollo in 1979 – a young-at-heart royal who rules his kingdom with charming naivety. The books about the diminutive monarch were made into a 13-part TV series for the BBC in 1985 and also provide

the name of TV McKee's animation company, King Rollo Films, which he founded with friends Clive Juster and Leo Nielson. Mr Benn still attracts a lot of attention from fans and, although McKee now lives most of the year in France, the author still receives mail from his devotees. As a response McKee wrote the first new Mr Benn adventure for over 20 years, *Gladiator*, in 2001. And *Mr Benn – The Movie* has been on the cards for some time now, too, with actors as diverse as Michael Palin, John Hannah and even Johnny Depp lined up to take the starring role of Britain's most famous suburbanite. A thoughtful, modest man, McKee prefers not to over-analyse his work, but Mr Benn continues to follow him wherever he goes. 'I've enjoyed all the characters I created, but what is done just lives its life,' he says philosophically. 'Mr Benn continues to live his life too and I'm very happy to let him do that.'

MULTI-COLOURED SWAP SHOP

BBC TV / Produced 1976-1982 / A BBC Production / Series Editor - Rosemary Gill / Originally Produced by Crispin Evans / 'Swaparama' produced by John Lane / Designed by Philip Lindley / Music by Mike Batt and BA Robertson / Presented by Noel Edmonds, Keith Chegwin, John Craven and Maggie Philbin / 6 series / First broadcast 2 October 1976

There's far too much old tat on British television nowadays. I don't just mean crappy programmes; I mean crappy programmes *about* old tat. Flogging old junk on TV has become a staple of the terrestrial channels. Take your pick from *Bargain Hunt, Flog It, Cash in the Attic, Everything Must Go* and the supremely downmarket *Car Boot Challenge*. It would be no exaggeration to say junk has never had it so good. Back in my youth there was only one place you could get shot of your dog-eared set of Top Trumps cards and that was the *Multi-Coloured Swap Shop*. It's a stupid name for a series I know, but kids loved it.

Here's the deal. Leanne from Solihull wants to swap her Girl's World for a ballerina Sindy doll. Kevin from Halifax has a battered Ker-Plunk game (box held together with sellotape) and wants to exchange it for

a Millennium Falcon. Meanwhile Scott from Portishead has a punctured Space Hopper, which he wants to swap for a Raleigh bike (some hope). In the era before car boots and Ebay how can you make these miserable children's dreams come true? Easy. Get on the blower to 01-811 8055 and Noel Edmonds will sort you out. The 'swapping' concept of the series is not, on the face of it, the most promising idea for Saturday morning kids' telly. Not only that, it's a logistical nightmare matching up kids with the correct items. Just as well Noel had a team of middle-aged telephonists in cardigans sitting in a glass booth behind him fielding thousands of calls from anxious schoolchildren.

Swap Shop, as it was more commonly abbreviated, was the BBC's first attempt at a feature-length kids' magazine programme. Created by producer Rosemary Gill to cash in on the so-called 'swapping craze' that was allegedly sweeping the country (I must have missed that one), it was more likely a rapid response to ITV's *Tiswas* and *Our Show*. Noel, famous for his hilarious 'wind-up' calls on Radio 1's *Breakfast Show*, had previously transferred to kids' television in June 1975 in a short-lived Wednesday afternoon show called *Z-Shed*. A live, issue-led programme, *Z-Shed* aimed to address youngsters' personal problems – fights with siblings, lack of pocket money, school conflict etc. What set *Z-Shed* apart from other BBC series was that it encouraged worried children to phone in with their opinions on each topic. Weekly guests offered advice and the first episode, entitled 'Problems with Appearance', rather cruelly invited moon-faced actor Rodney Bewes on to take questions! It was not a resounding success, but proved popular enough for the DJ to be considered for the BBC's new interactive Saturday morning flagship series. *Swap Shop* was originally envisaged for a run of 12 weeks, but Edmonds' cheerful marketability, bouffant hair and funky beard lifted the series and it eventually ran for six years.

Edmonds, a showbiz veteran since the days of pirate radio, was the anchorman of the show, but his merry band of smiley co-hosts and static puppets gave *Swap Shop* a happy family feel which appealed to younger viewers as well as their parents. Apart from Edmonds, the only instantly recognisable face belonged to John Craven. Looking like a university-educated uncle in a sensible pullover Craven had

been the steely-faced king of the autocue for several years in *John Craven's Newsround* (from 1972). That ground-breaking show was Britain's very first current affairs programme for the under-10s and getting Craven on board the good ship *Swap Shop* gave the show some much needed intellectual kudos. Maggie Philbin, a shaggy-haired brunette with a stiff smile, provided *Swap Shop*'s glamour. It was Philbin's first TV job, having just graduated from Manchester University. She saw an advert asking 'Could you be a top TV personality?' in luvvies' newspaper the *Stage* and applied. She couldn't sing and she couldn't dance and she looked like she'd just stepped out of a convent, but the BBC liked her and gave her the job. *Swap Shop*'s foursome was completed by a cheeky, giggling ex-stage school kid called Keith Chegwin. 'Cheggers', as he preferred to be addressed, excelled in being relentlessly perky and good-natured. It sometimes got to the stage where it was exhausting just watching him. A former actor and musician, Cheggers had the perfect temperament for standing in a stupid bobble hat and rainbow-coloured overcoat on a freezing windswept Blackpool beach encouraging weather-beaten kids to 'get your swaps out!' You see, *Swap Shop* wasn't just studio based. Viewers had the opportunity, like the mythologized Radio 1 Roadshow, to get out and be part of the show.

Each week Cheggers would arrive to set up the next 'Swaparama' at some rainy, god-forsaken rugby field, beach or sports stadium, erect a stage and get rosy-cheeked kids swapping Action Man tanks and Escape from Colditz board games. From behind his cosy studio-based desk Edmonds would turn to his TV monitor and shriek 'Keith, where are you?' A crescendo of screaming children would then attempt to drown out the ever-smiling Chegwin as he explained that 'Hi Noelie! Ha ha! This week we're in, ha ha, cloudy Scarborough! Ha ha!' It was always cold because each *Swap Shop* series only broadcast from October to Spring, so poor Cheggers never got the chance to strip down to his Bermuda shorts. Over the years the swapping element of *Swap Shop* became less the *raison d'etre* of the show and more a source of extreme irritation.

Whilst viewers everywhere gained some sort of cruel satisfaction from the chirpy Liverpudlian's chilly misadventures, it was Edmonds who was really the series' main attraction. Incredibly popular during his 1970s and 1980s heyday, blue-eyed boy Edmonds rapidly rose up through the ranks of the BBC's most enduring radio and TV stars. He was television's good guy; the very antithesis of bad lad Chris Tarrant and for several glorious years *Swap Shop* and *Tiswas* endured the same light-hearted 'battle royale' as *Blue Peter* and *Magpie* did. One was seen to be innovative, all-round family entertainment. The other was evil, insidious stuff that corrupted children's minds. It's up to you to decide which was which. *Tiswas* certainly loved any opportunity to have a lighthearted dig at Noel and his team. One of the most popular placards standing in the background of the ITV show read: 'We'll swap Chegwin for a set of Lego!'

Noel's desk was, geographically, the cornerstone of the series. Sitting on his swivel chair Noel could spin round to look at Keith's TV screen, the *Swap Shop* clock, viewers' 'art works' (a-hem!) and Posh Paws. Yes! Posh Paws the purple dinosaur puppet (with felt teeth), *which did not move*. He certainly wasn't posh either and his so-called paws were claws. This stuffed toy got almost as much fan mail (which, incredibly, topped 75,000 letters and cards per week) as the human presenters, and the introduction of a fake rubber hairy hand called Igor created even more apoplectic adulation from excited viewers. Guests were invited to sit at Noel's desk and get a grilling from the bearded-one and take calls from the public via a trim phone. (I was going to mention the time when pop group Five Star came on the show and some youngster shouted down the phone 'You're a bunch of wankers!' but that was on *Saturday Superstore*. It also happened to Matt Bianco too, if my memory serves me right. Mike Read just didn't have the same control as Noel.) *Swap Shop* always seemed to attract a better class of guests than *Tiswas*, and the great and good queued up to answer questions from 'Katie from Northampton' such as 'What is your favourite animal?' Penelope Keith, Cliff Richard, Isla St Clair, Mike Yarwood, Barbara Windsor, Darth Vader and Delia Smith all just grinned and bore it with professional élan. Delia Smith, in particular, must have really loved *Swap Shop*, since she became the series' resident cookery expert. The programme was also famous for its silly skits and humorous hi-jinks. Edmonds, an inveterate giggler, needed no encouragement to dress up as Captain Kirk in *Swap Shop*'s infamous *Star Trek* parody (with

Craven looking uncannily like a Vulcan) or sing lead vocals on their record 'I Wanna be a Winner' released under the moniker of 'Brown Sauce', an unexpected number 15 hit in December 1981.

The rivalry between *Swap Shop* and *Tiswas* continued into the 1980s, but tellingly, by both series' final seasons much of the oomph had departed. It was only right that both shows bowed out at the same time in 1982, only to be replaced by far inferior productions. *Swap Shop* made way for *Saturday Superstore* (1982-1987), set in a fake department store, funnily enough, and Noel and his co-stars went their separate ways. Philbin obviously found Chegwin's non-stop hyperactivity highly desirable because she married him, but after his battle with alcoholism and rubber inflatables in *Cheggers Plays Pop* (1978-1983) they parted company. Craven carried on reading kiddies' news until he found his earthy roots presenting the ecologically sound *Countryfile* on Sunday mornings (a show we've all sat through bleary-eyed after a Saturday night bender). But it is Noel Edmonds who has seen the most dramatic downturn in his show business career. After a seamless transfer to 'grown up' television in *The Late Late Breakfast Show* (1982-1986) and *Noel's House Party* (1991-1998) the public apparently tired of his awful puns and practical jokes. Edmonds, the boy who once could do no wrong, found himself, very unfairly, dubbed the most vilified entertainer in Britain.

THE MUPPET SHOW

ITV / Produced 1976-1981 / An ITC-Henson Associates Inc Production / Devised and Produced by Jim Henson / Executive Producer - David Lazer / Directed by Peter Harris and Philip Casson / Chief Writer - Jerry Juhl / Theme tune by Sam Pottle / Featuring the voice and puppetry talents of Jim Henson, Frank Oz, Dave Goelz, Jerry Nelson, Richard Hunt, Louise Gold and Steve Whitmore / 120 episodes / First broadcast (UK) 5 September 1976

I was Muppet-obsessed as a kid. I'd been there, done that, and worn the T-shirt. Actually I *really* did have the T-shirt. My school did away with grey pullovers and shorts so we could wear what we liked to

class. That Muppet T-shirt never came off. It must have been glued on. There's a photo of me wearing it at my tenth birthday party and all my friends have Muppet gear on too, and it wasn't even a theme party either. I read the Muppet annuals too, did the Muppet jigsaws and my grandmother made me a Kermit the Frog out of fake fur, corduroy and two ping pong balls. For about 12 months I thought I'd make a career for myself as an underage ventriloquist, but I could throw up school semolina better than I could throw my voice.

My Kermit puppet's modest beginnings weren't that far removed from the real one. The original was made from one of Jim Henson's mum's old coats in 1956, but initially looked more like a lizard than a frog. Henson, a native of Greenville, Mississippi jokingly named the puppet after one of his old school friends, unaware that the little green one would eventually elevate him to the Walt Disney of puppetry. A sensitive and optimistic man, Henson believed that he could educate and entertain adults through puppets, and in 1954 he got his first break into television at his local station in Washington DC. The resulting series *Sam and Friends* (1955-1961) introduced Kermit and his chums to a wider audience and led to the word 'Muppet' (a conflation of marionette and puppet) being coined. The show's success brought Henson's furry creations to the attention of other up-and-coming talents including Herefordshire-born puppeteer Frank Oz and American comedy writer Jerry Juhl.

The expanding Henson organisation eventually moved to New York where Rowlf, the piano playing dog, made his paw mark on the country music series *The Jimmy Dean Show.* Muppets started popping up everywhere: in TV commercials, and as guests on the top-rated *Tonight Show* and *Ed Sullivan Show* Rowlf, all floppy ears and unfeasibly wide mouth, was Henson's biggest star of the 1960s. He graduated to his own show in 1967 and then moved to a supporting role in the most celebrated American TV show of all time, *Sesame Street.* Premiering in November 1969, *Sesame Street* was a production of the Children's Television Workshop and aimed to educate pre-schoolers in the rudiments of numbers, alphabet and good manners. It was Henson's first foray into children's television, and it was a hard decision for him to make. He never envisaged his characters as children's pin-ups, but nonetheless created some of the most

enduring puppet neighbours ever to live in a tough inner city New York zip code. Old timers Kermit and Rowlf were joined by Oscar the Grouch (who lived in a trash can), feuding friends Bert and Ernie, an eight-foot-tall yellow bird, called Big Bird oddly enough, and the biscuit-obsessed Cookie Monster. Everybody loved safe, happy *Sesame Street*: the kids, their parents, their teachers, even President Nixon, but for Henson it wasn't enough.

The Muppet's daddy didn't want to be typecast solely as a safe children's entertainer. He wanted his puppets to be appreciated by a more sophisticated audience too, a mature audience who liked more zaniness in their comedy. While Henson made two Muppet kids' specials in 1972, *The Frog Prince* (starring you know who) and *The Muppet Musicians of Bremen*, he was guest starring his puppets on the late night satirical sketch show *Saturday Night Live*. In 1973, and again in 1975, Henson's company made pilots for what would be later christened *The Muppet Show*. The latter show, called *Sex and Violence*, touched on subjects disallowed on *Sesame Street*, but not one American TV network would touch it.

Frustrated and disappointed by the rejection of US television executives, Henson was approached by corpulent British impresario Sir Lew Grade, and this is where it gets really interesting. Sir Lew was the chairman of ATV television, ITV's regional broadcaster for the Midlands during the week, and London at the weekends. He was also the man behind the ITC production company who had enjoyed smash hits with *Fireball XL5*, *Space:1999*, *The Saint* and *The Adventures of Rupert*. Grade saw the potential in the Muppets and invited Henson to make a series for him, on one condition: that the entire Muppet organisation was brought lock, stock and barrel from America to ATV's studios at Borehamwood, just north of London. It was a mighty risk for Henson, but by early 1976 *The Muppet Show* was producing the first of 120 episodes on British soil. It's easy to think that the series is American through and through, but aside from the performers, the show was designed, directed, and co-written by Brits.

The Muppet Show is, to all intents and purposes, an old time variety show with slapstick humour, risqué jokes and some singing and dancing. Its true Vaudeville roots are exposed by many of the special guest stars who agreed to come to Britain to film their contributions. Milton Berle, Bob Hope, Victor Borge and Danny Kaye all trod the boards of the Muppet theatre and enjoyed making absolute fools of themselves with bug-eyed puppets. It was Burlesque, but with added fur, felt and Velcro. Desperately trying to hold things together backstage is the theatre's MC, Kermit the Frog. Graduating from his role as *Sesame Street*'s roving reporter, Kermit became a harassed stage manager, vainly attempting to keep a tight reign on the crazy Muppet performers and the diva-like demands of his human guest stars. The show's first season started slowly, with Henson's showbiz acquaintances agreeing to travel from the US to co-star, but as *The Muppet Show* rose in popularity bigger and bigger names fought to appear: Liza Minnelli, Diana Ross, Glenda Jackson, George Burns, Alice Cooper, Steve Martin, Vincent Price, Mark Hamill, Elke Sommer, Leo Sayer, Liberace, Sylvester Stallone and Shirley Bassey, to name but a few. Although made in Britain, Lew Grade cannily managed to sell the show back to the Americans at a huge profit, and by the end of the second series over 100 countries were broadcasting it. In 1979 it was the number one TV series worldwide.

In our household *The Muppet Show* reigned supreme at the weekend. Sunday nights would usually be a time to dread, because it was back to school the next day, as well as being bath night. But the sense of excitement as Sunday at 5.35 pm came around was almost electric. The show's opening titles – big velvet drapes pulling apart revealing the Muppets marching on stage and taking their positions under ever-expanding illuminated arches – was the best tonic for a cold winter's evening. As soon as they started singing 'It's time to play the music. It's time to light the lights' you knew you were in for a treat. Of course, we didn't always like the guest stars. You couldn't have C-3PO or Spike Milligan every week, and the feeling of slight disappointment when a nameless performer appeared was palpable. We all loved Peter Sellers, John Cleese and Bruce Forsyth, but outside of the US did anyone really know who Teresa Brewer, Roy Clark or Wally Boeg were?

Kermit treats all his guests with the respect they deserve, even Wally Boeg, but it is the furry, feathered Muppet performers who usually cause him the most trouble. The theatre's resident comic is

Fozzie Bear, a fuzzy coated idiot in a pork-pie hat whose jokes are even worse than Basil Brush's. 'I had a dream last night that I was eating a giant marshmallow. When I woke up my pillow had gone' sets the standard. Statler and Waldorf, a couple of curmudgeonly geriatrics, sitting in the royal box, continually heckle Fozzie but the comedian perseveres with his lousy material. Fozzie's act is supposed to be embarrassing, but it's just so awful it's irredeemable. Much more watchable is Sam, an overly patriotic American eagle and the guardian of the Muppets' morals. 'Stop that, this instant,' he moans, 'it's un-American!' My mother loved Sam because his eyebrows were just like my father's.

The Muppet Show's biggest failure is The Great Gonzo, a scrawny, buzzard-like creature of unidentifiable species whose daring-dos should be daring don'ts. If his trumpet isn't exploding in his face, he's being fired out of cannons backwards, careering through the air on an Evel Knievel motorbike or juggling precariously with sticks of TNT. Things never go the way he wants ('Once again, I'll defy death and good taste!') and it's left to Kermit to pick up the pieces, sometimes quite literally. Thankfully Gonzo has his beloved chickens for company, dozens of which cluck around him. 'How come there are so many chickens on this show?' asks Statler. 'Well chickens thrive on corn!' comes Waldorf's honest reply. Kermit's factotum is Scooter the gopher. That's not strictly true, really. He's actually a go-fer. That is he'll 'go-fer coffee, go-fer sandwiches, go-fer anything!' Scooter tries too hard and his childlike exuberance gets on everybody's nerves. He's tolerated, however, because his rich uncle just so happens to own the Muppet theatre. That'll be Lew Grade, then.

Apart from Kermit, the real puppet star of the series is Miss Piggy. The most famous porker since Pinky or Perky, Miss Piggy initially styled herself as 'the most beautiful pig in the world.' Piggy is a voluptuous prima donna who worked her way up from a chorus line pig with a deep voice, in the early shows, to the most celebrated 'It Pig' of her generation. The public's adoration of the talentless sow helped *The Muppet Show* scale even loftier heights of worldwide exposure. Her porcine features graced the covers of *People Weekly*, *Variety* and *TV Times* and she was even interviewed on the *Parkinson* show, where she flirted outrageously with the host. But then again,

Piggy flirted with anyone under the age of 50, regardless of their species. She was Princess Leia to Mark Hamill's Luke Skywalker and Holly Goodhead to Roger Moore's James Bond, but to Kermit she was everything. Piggy so wanted to marry her froggy friend, but whilst she was eminently dateable, she was never going to be wife material. Her numerous neuroses and violent temper usually let her down. A self-taught martial arts expert, Piggy has the most wicked karate (pork) chop in the business: 'Hy-aahhh!' and although she loves her 'little Kermy', her staunch refusal to live with him in the swamp where he was born or eat anything other than swill stroganoff has been her downfall. And anyway, what would their kids be like? The thought of a pinky-green baby prog or even a greeny-pink frig, is just too horrible to contemplate.

The backstage Muppet melodrama was ably matched by the on-stage shenanigans of the regular cast. Each week viewers would be treated to the latest instalments of *Veterinarian's Hospital* ('The continuing story of the quack who's gone to the dogs!'), the insane Swedish Chef waving his chopper about on the cookery spot, the hilarious *Pigs in Space*, aboard the interplanetary *Swine Trek* and, best of all, *Muppet Labs*, easily the most violent segment of the show. Mad scientist Dr Bunson Honeydew (he had no eyes, just glasses – it freaked me out) enjoyed testing his latest experiments on his subservient assistant, Beaker. Poor Beaker ('Meep! Meep!') with his toilet-roll tube head and gloriously gloomy mouth endured years of being shrunk, blown-up, mutilated, squashed and force-fed paperclips. Cruel, yes, but very funny!

The Muppet Show had the biggest episode budget of any series in this book, and it was all up there on screen. Jim Henson and Frank Oz's finely-tuned puppetry and vocal performances where at the very centre of the show, but the extravagant sets, elaborate stunts and taut direction glued everything neatly together. Some of the individual musical sketches like Hell's Angels pigs riding motorbikes across the stage to the accompaniment of 'I Get Around' by The Beach Boys or Viking Pigs (Jim Henson *loved* pigs) singing 'In the Navy' whilst steering a vast longboat are stunning in their complexity. Guest star Julie Andrews even performed in a lush parody of *The Sound of Music* on a hillside scattered with bleating Muppet goats and Elton John

had a whale of a time performing 'Crocodile Rock' in a flooded bayou filled with life-sized foam crocodiles.

The series owed a lot of its success to celebrities looking daft on screen. Musical numbers afforded most puppet-human crossovers, and the Muppet house band was called upon regularly to supply the tunes. Dr Teeth's Electric Mayhem Orchestra is glammer than Gary Glitter and more tumultuous than T.Rex, with an extra liberal sprinkling of sequins and feathers for good measure. Dr Teeth himself is pretty scary. His teeth are huge, admittedly, but his arms must be five feet long. On drums is one Muppet who can be called upon to, literally, chew up the scenery with his performance. Animal is a seething, panting mass of pure testosterone. He doesn't say much, but when he does it's to the point: 'WO-MAN!' (His totally unhinged, unpredictable behaviour coupled with his big hooded eyes and flash smile is based upon the late Keith Moon, the eccentric drummer with The Who.) Not surprisingly the Muppets had hit records across the globe. Kermit's squashy, hunchbacked (did anybody else notice this?) nephew Robin was bizarrely introduced by Noel Edmonds on *Top of the Pops* in May 1977 when his song 'Halfway down the Stairs' hit number seven. Even better was the Muppet's rendition of 'Mnah, Mnah'. You must remember this. It was the one that went 'Mnah, Mnah. Do-do, do-do-do!' and everybody shouted it at each other in the school playground for weeks afterwards.

In 1981 *The Muppet Show* closed its doors after five tremendous years. Henson wanted to concentrate on the movie side of the business, capitalising on the successes of *The Muppet Movie* (1979) and *The Great Muppet Caper* (1981). Other films followed, as did new Muppet TV series including *Fraggle Rock* (1983-1987) and *The Muppet Babies* (1984-1992). Sadly, just when Jim Henson was attempting to get a new series of *The Muppet Show* back into production he died suddenly from a lung infection, just hours after admitting himself into hospital upon feeling ill. His death, aged just 53, was mourned throughout the world. A brand new Muppet series did finally emerge in 1996, but *Muppets Tonight!* lost all of its previous incarnation's magic and foolishly sidelined Kermit in favour of a more politically correct, street-talking, dread-locked Muppet named Clifford. The show was cancelled after just 22 episodes. The original, and best, Muppet series is still repeated throughout the world and the more recent big screen spin-offs, like *Muppets from Space* (1999) in which The Great Gonzo finally uncovers his extraterrestrial origins, are back on top form. *The Muppet Show* continues to make millions laugh out loud today because, in the words of the theme song, it's 'sensational, inspirational, celebrational, muppetational' and is still probably the best TV series the world has ever known.

NOAH AND NELLY IN SKYLARK

BBC TV / Produced 1976 / A Roobarb Enterprises Production / Created and Written by Grange Calveley / Produced and Directed by Bob Godfrey / Featuring the voices of Richard Briers and Peter Hawkins / Music by Peter Gosling / 30 episodes / First broadcast 13 September 1976

It would be true to say that the cult success of *Roobarb* has rather overshadowed animator Bob Godfrey's other brilliant creations. On the big screen he won an Oscar for his wonderful film *GREAT Isambard Kingdom Brunel* (1975) and has been nominated on four other occasions. His quirky adult cartoons (or 'sextoons' as he prefers to call them) have also won critical plaudits. Two of his best, *Henry 9 Till 5* (1970) and *Kama Sutra Rides Again* (1971), are well worth tracking down on late night Channel 4 and give a revealing insight into the psyche of one of Britain's foremost cartoonists. However, it will probably always be kids' telly for which Godfrey is best remembered. Godfrey's second series for children's BBC is easily his most extreme televisual work. Combining the anarchic story-telling qualities of *Roobarb* with the more subdued animation style of 1983's *Henry's Cat, Noah and Nelly in Skylark* falls somewhere between the stools of cult classic and untamed hysteria. Excitable narrator Richard Briers seems to salivate over each demented episode, egged on by fellow voice-over star Peter Hawkins in full *Captain Pugwash* mode.

Written by *Roobarb*'s creator Grange Calveley, *Noah and Nelly* perverts the much-loved Bible story and turns it into a wickedly esoteric animated adventure, much akin to The Beatles' lunatic odyssey *Yellow Submarine* (1968). Mr Nutty Noah and his wife Niggly Nelly steer their own version of the ark to every corner of the comedy globe. Using a completely blank map to navigate, they're mostly all at sea when it comes to knowing where they're going to, and where they've come from, but it doesn't really seem to matter. The ark itself is a vast spot-covered boat, or more like a giant rubber dinghy, with a giant head at each end. It can travel over the oceans with a stripy sail, traverse mountains with wheels, float over valleys hoisted by an immense pink party balloon or dip below the water as a submarine. It's a versatile vehicle certainly, but what makes this ark so unique is its ludicrously odd occupants.

The original Noah saved the earth's animals in breeding pairs; Bob Godfrey's Noah saves valuable space below deck by having two-headed animals. That's to say a head at each end, which in the case of a snake isn't a very nice concept. Despite having two heads, the animals have one consciousness, therefore we have Rose the elephants, Cedric the crocodiles, Achmed the camels and William the hippos. They're plural, but actually singular if you follow me. The animals have split personalities too – one end is cheerful the other downright miserable, which can lead to some friction. Continually arguing, the animals' ends can never make up their minds where they want to go. 'Let's stay at home,' says Brian the lions. 'No, lets go on holiday!' he disagrees. This barmy, twitching, glassy-eyed menagerie of freaks talks in almost-rhyme, as do their sou'wester-wearing guardians. Calveley's witty word play is full of tongue twisters and annoyingly articulate alliteration like 'Niggly Nelly knitted knowingly....'

Nelly is a champion knitter and there's nothing she can't magically needle, whether it be a ship's anchor, a piggybank, a piano, even a petrol driven mower. Her hobby is called upon regularly, especially when the ark lands in foreign parts. 'All aboard the Skylark, all aboard the Skylark,' shouts Noah, forgetting that they are *already* aboard as there's nowhere else to go. The off-the-wall script gives free reign to Godfrey's cartoon artistry as the curious critters are transported to various crazy situations, where obsessive compulsives abound. Strange continents are littered with toffee apple trees and candy canes, and skies heave under the weight of dribbling watering cans, but that's just the ordinary stuff. There's Televisionland where all the unhappy TV sets blast out news bulletins day and night (this was long before *Sky News*, of course); Cuckooland populated by shrieking Swiss clocks and a beach full of miserable Toby Jugs with missing handles.

The most seriously deranged episode, and the one most recalled to mind when I was watching the series again recently, is when Noah and Nelly visit the quaint town of Newhaven. This English backwater

has no streets, just rows upon rows of front doors feverishly clacking their brass knockers. The noise is deafening so Nelly knits each knocker a woollen crash helmet and peace resumes. It's an absurd episode typifying an even more surreal show. Full of lunatics in landscapes Salvador Dali would have been proud of; *Noah and Nelly in Skylark* is best appreciated with a big glass of Blue Nun.

NODDY

ITV / Produced 1974-1975 / A CPL-Stop Frame Production / Created by Enid Blyton / Produced and Directed by Brian Cosgrove and Mark Hall / Puppets Designed by Brian Cosgrove / Written by Ruth Boswell / Music by Mike McNaught / Narrated by Richard Briers / 26 episodes / First broadcast 24 March 1975

Ah, Noddy! The little pixie boy in a tinkling hat, famous for recklessly driving his car around Toytown with little care or thought for pedestrians. Happily this is a more colourful, joyous Toytown than the one *Larry the Lamb* inhabits. Noddy's Toytown is full of brightly painted houses built with alphabet bricks, white-washed picket fences, giant toadstools (non-poisonous, naturally) and a merry-go-round in the market square. It is a place where plastic elephant and clockwork mouse can walk hand in hand and feel no shame. This is the definitive Toytown and don't you forget it. Forever-youthful Noddy with his little round face and rosy cheeks has become one of the most instantly recognisable, and omnipresent, figures in children's entertainment – first in book form, then on stage, as a TV puppet, as a computer generated star of DVD and video and gracing thousands of pairs of slippers, socks and dressing gowns. He is, without doubt, a true British icon. Even so, not many people realise just how ancient Noddy actually is, and forget who his famous mummy was.

Formidable children's author Enid Blyton (1897-1968) had been a mainstay of British publishing since the 1930s, famed for her jolly hockey sticks and lashing of ginger beer adventures of 'The Famous Five'. In 1949 her publishers commissioned her to write a new series

of books for much younger children. They wanted to cash in on the success of Walt Disney's characters, like Mickey Mouse, and envisaged a new British creation, which could rival Hollywood's best. Central to this plot was the search for a new illustrator who could bring Blyton's words to life. The publishers had been very impressed with the advertising work of a Dutch painter called – a bit of a mouthful this – Eelco Martinus Harmsen van der Beek. Beek was duly summoned to England to take tea with the literary giant and, over the space of an afternoon, the pair, despite not speaking each other's languages, had thrashed out the ideas for a new character. Within months Blyton's words and Beek's pictures were married together in the very first Noddy book, *Noddy goes to Toyland* in November 1949. The success of the first book surpassed even Blyton's expectations and over the next 20 years nearly 150 Noddy books were published, selling an incredible 120 million copies.

The loveable little boy with the constantly nodding head (hence the name) was beloved by post-war children everywhere, appearing in pantomimes, on the radio and in doll form in toy shops across Britain. In 1955 Noddy finally made his debut on the newly formed ITV, in *The Adventures of Noddy*, but initially television did not serve him well. Noddy was a mischievous, fast-moving, vibrant little boy, used to frightening teddy bears on pedestrian crossings, but the TV series' string puppets only made him sluggish and plodding. It would be another 20 years before he finally came to life in the way Blyton had envisaged him.

Redoubtable British animators Brian Cosgrove and Mark Hall were set the task of creating a new streamlined *Noddy* for the 1970s. It's testament to Cosgrove's incredible model-making skills that he was able to keep the look of Noddy and his chums faithful to Beek's original 1950s drawings, whilst at the same time giving them a makeover. It was no mean feat, either. 'My enduring memory from that series is the length of time I spent carving the characters' heads,' says Cosgrove ruefully. 'It seemed like a never-ending task.' Indeed it was, because Blyton's Toytown books are bursting full of weird and wonderful playthings, straight out of a post-war English nursery. Next to an army of wooden soldiers, pink cats, blonde-haired dollies and ladybugs there are the better-known inhabitants of Toytown. Noddy's

best chum is Big Ears, a slightly crotchety gnome easily identified by, you've guessed it, his big lugholes. Also present and correct are Bumpy the excitable dog, Mr Tubby Bear, Mr Plod the policeman, Jumbo the elephant, the ever-expanding Skittle family and last, but not least, Mr Wobbly Man. The latter character was always my favourite because a big ball had replaced his legs, so – as his name suggests – he wobbled, rather than walked. This was pretty debilitating when Bert the kleptomaniac monkey was stealing from his shop and Wobbly Man wanted to catch him.

The *Noddy* series is narrated by Richard Briers who does the job splendidly, especially since earning his wibbly wobbly stripes providing the voices for *Roobarb* on the BBC. Briers manages to create just the right amount of childhood insubordination for the title character as well as giving Jumbo an Asian accent (he's an Indian elephant, naturally) and Mr Plod an air of failed superiority when handing out parking tickets. Big Ears is a grumpy old sod, initially, who likes to lord it over his fairy chum. 'You are ignorant aren't you?' he chides Noddy when he's knocked off his bike. Full of grovelling apologies, Noddy explains he's run away from his toy maker in the next village because 'He made a lion. I don't like lions. They frighten me!' Thereafter the two become inseparable friends.

Unfortunately even pre-pubescent pixies aren't immune to controversy. Over the years poor Noddy has been continually dogged by rumour, innuendo and barefaced lies. Noddy's close relationship with his gnome mentor has always been a source of mirth with British comedians. They've been known to share a bed, of course, and some people think that's amusing. But then again so did Morecambe and Wise and that *was* funny. Noddy and Big Ears' double act has been the staple of many a comic over the years. Just by donning a pixie hat and a pair of huge plastic ears comedians have been known to reduce a seaside theatre audience to uncontrollable guffawing. At the other end of the scale, Noddy has been accused of promoting unfavourable racial stereotypes. Blyton and Beek filled Toytown with gallivanting golliwogs back in the 1950s, but 20 years later they were forcibly ejected and replaced by naughty goblins. Oddly, in the era of *Love Thy Neighbour*, gollies still couldn't be seen on kids' TV. Blyton purists were furious, but the debate has raged ever since and the original books have since been republished with the 'offending' characters removed.

1975's *Noddy* was a big hit for ITV and two decades later Cosgrove Hall came back with an even more ambitious remake for the BBC. *Noddy's Toyland Adventures* (1992-1999) was more polished and faster-paced, but was virtually an identical copy of what had gone before. Cosgrove Hall's mastery helped launch Noddy globally, and the little pixie in a tinkling hat now enjoys as much merchandising success as *Teletubbies* and *Bob the Builder* put together. Finally, in 2001 he went all CGI in a $15 million American series, *Make Way For Noddy*. The computer animation has made him more youthful-looking than ever, but who could blame the little lad for a few wrinkles here and there? After all, he's half a century old now.

PADDINGTON

BBC TV / Produced 1975, 1978 and 1983 / A FilmFair Production / Created and Written by Michael Bond / Executive Producer Graham Clutterbuck / Directed and Animated by Ivor Wood / Music by Herbert Chappell / Narrated by Michael Hordern / 56 episodes plus 3 specials / First broadcast 5 January 1976

It's not easy having a wild South American bear about the house, especially when it's a beautiful detached Victorian house in Maida Vale. They create havoc, you see. Buttered toast gets dropped on the carpet, bubble baths overflow and washing machines explode. It takes a calm, stoical family to adopt a bear, so it's just as well Paddington found the Browns of 32 Windsor Gardens, W9.

Paddington is now very famous (he's the only character in this book to be honoured with his own statue in London) but his beginnings were very humble indeed. The brown bear with the inquisitive black eyes first arrived on our shores in 1958, in a novel penned by Michael Bond. *A Bear Called Paddington* told the story of Mr and Mrs Brown, a well-to-do suburban couple who go to collect their daughter, Judy, from the train at Paddington Station. While they're waiting they spot a hairy mammal sitting on a pile of mailbags. The creature has a note hanging round his neck that reads 'Please look after this bear. Thank you.' The animal can speak too and explains that he came to Blighty as a stowaway on a lifeboat. Back in 'darkest Peru' the bear's Aunt Lucy has taken a room at the Home for Retired Bears in Lima and has encouraged him to emigrate. The Browns christen the bear after the station where they find him and take him back to their smart residence to meet their son, Jonathan, and their live-in housekeeper, Mrs Bird. The starting point for Bond's book is silly, but engaging, and the author fills his pages with droll humour, quaint observations and chuckles aplenty.

Over the next decade a further nine Paddington novels arrived, proving so popular that Michael Bond was able to quit his job as a BBC cameraman to write full time. The lovably eccentric bear made

his first appearance on children's television in March 1966, when Thora Hird read out his first adventures on *Jackanory*. However, he didn't materialise in puppet form until the mid-1970s. Bond had previously collaborated with master animator Ivor Wood on BBC's *The Herbs* and together the two men set about bringing Paddington to life. *Paddington*, the series, was made alongside Wood's supreme adaptation of *The Wombles* for the FilmFair studios. But whereas the scavengers of Wimbledon Common are cuddly puppets in a three-dimensional world, Wood diversified for his take on the Peruvian hero. Paddington himself is a furry 3D character, but the world he inhabits, and the people he meets are two-dimensional cut-outs. It is a brilliantly innovative idea. Solely directed and animated by Wood, the 1975 series showcases the animator's absorbing black-and-white line drawings of suburban London, and makes great use of shadows and perspective. It's really like watching a pop-up book with a soft toy poking out from the flat pages.

Self-assured Paddington soon settles into his London life without any problems. 'Good afternoon,' he says to the kindly Mrs Bird, 'I'm from darkest Peru and I've come to stay!' The series remains faithful to Michael Bond's books, portraying the matter-of-fact bear as an innocent abroad, completely unable to understand human absurdities and petty bureaucracy. Paddington speaks as he finds and if he comes across red tape he's more than happy to gnaw through it. You wouldn't want to upset him either because you're liable to be on the receiving end of one of his infamous 'hard stares'. Wood's Paddington puppet is squat and stiff-legged, but his cheerful face and velvety black button eyes make him incredibly expressive. Revered British character actor Michael Hordern (later *Sir* Michael) provides the bear's voice and brings to *Paddington* an air of befuddlement and serene irreproachability. Paddington is the nearest thing children's TV had to a Charlie Chaplin-like character; he's innocent and accident-prone and regularly looks straight to camera in mock bemusement. After all, how is a hairy native from Peru supposed to understand etiquette when eating *hors d'oeuvres* at a fancy restaurant, or remember not to speak at a night out at the theatre? Paddington is a walking disaster area. The poor thing doesn't even realise you have to get undressed *before* you take a bath.

In the original novels Michael Bond relied upon artist Peggy Fortnum to provide the neat pen and ink illustrations, but throughout her tenure in the job she was reluctant to give the bear any clothes at all, (Paddington usually only wore a floppy felt hat). When Bond ceased with the novels in 1972 to concentrate on Paddington picture books, other artists, who put the bear in his trademark duffel coat, replaced Fortnum. It is this unforgettable image that is adopted by Ivor Wood's landmark series. Much is also made of Paddington's love of marmalade sandwiches. He keeps them under his hat, and in his battered briefcase, and likes munching them in bed. He keeps youthful by eating all that vitamin C, although he's also pretty partial to crispy bacon too, and cream buns at elevenses.

Three years after the initial run of *Paddington,* the gentle bear returned in another 30 episodes, this time called *The Adventures of Paddington.* The set-up was exactly the same, as was Ivor Wood's direction, only this time the stories were adapted from Bond's later novels. Paddington continues to visit his German friend Mr Gruber, who owns an antique shop on the Portobello Road, and infuriate the Brown's grumpy next-door neighbour, Mr Curry. ('Bear! What is the meaning of this?') The series was successful exported around the globe, particularly to the United States, where it became an Emmy award winner. As a response, in 1983, a further three 20 minute specials – *Paddington Goes to the Movies, Paddington's Birthday Bonanza* and *Paddington Goes to School* – were made with an eye on the American market. Regrettably, in 1989 the Hanna-Barbera Company got their hands on our furry friend and created a misbegotten cartoon series, simply called *Paddington Bear.* Crudely animated and appallingly Americanised, Paddington became a sort of pseudo-Scooby Doo character. He lodged with a family of awful voice-over actors speaking Dick Van Dyke English and 'solved crimes' in a north London suburb which looked more like downtown Manhattan. When Bond saw what they'd done to his 'essentially English character' he must have choked on his thick cut marmalade. Slightly better was 1997's *The Adventures of Paddington Bear,* a FilmFair production made in Canada and featuring the voice of English actor Jonathan Kydd, but stuck in some 1950s time warp.

The definitive Paddington series will forever be the 1970s original. Possessed of an addictive charm and fresh, breezy innocence, Ivor

Wood's series is what teatime on BBC1 was made for. It's the archetypal 5.35 pm animation – a script full of mirth and naughtiness (dropping sandwiches out of the theatre's royal box sounds great), coupled with quietly effusive animation. As Paddington's adoptive mother Mrs Brown says: 'It's awfully nice having a bear about the house.'

THE PERISHERS

BBC TV / Produced 1978 / A FilmFair and Bill Melendez Co-Production / Created by Maurice Dodd / Executive Producer Graham Clutterbuck / Produced by Graeme Spurway / Directed by Dick Horn / Featuring the voices of Leonard Rossiter, Sheila Steafel, Peter Hawkins and Judy Bennett / 20 episodes / First broadcast 21 March 1979

The *Fred Basset* cartoons were still being repeated in the pre-BBC news slot when a second newspaper strip was being lined up for the small screen. FilmFair (the makers of teatime triumphs like *The Wombles* and *Paddington*) had been working with a London advertising agency on the, now, infamous 'Clunk Click, Every Trip' road safety campaign, fronted by Jimmy Saville. Those adverts were written by Maurice Dodd, who was also responsible for the co-creation of *The Perishers* cartoon strip in the *Daily Mirror*. The cartoon originally only appeared in the northern edition of the aforementioned tabloid, but was not proving to be too popular with readers. In 1959 the newspaper's cartoon editor, Bill Herbert, an old army chum of Dodd, asked him whether he could breathe new life into it. Dodd accepted the assignment and promptly killed off most of the original cast introducing more 'sycophantic creatures on whose aid I knew I could count if ever the need arose.' The new look *Perishers* strip, drawn by Dennis Collins, chronicled the naughty escapades of a bunch of mischievous, and seemingly parentless, cockney kids, based loosely on the experiences of Maurice Dodd's East End childhood. By the early 1970s some 13 million *Daily Mirror* readers were enjoying the strip and their popularity was at an all-time high. Because of the FilmFair connection, Dodd persuaded the company to bring his cheeky creations to life. 'It

was my infectious enthusiasm coupled with some intense grovelling that won them over to my point of view,' he laughs.

A sort of English *Peanuts*, which gave the world Charlie Brown and Snoopy, *The Perishers* were made up of six diverse characters. Wellington is the hero – a bolshy, pseudo-political entrepreneur ('I was born under the flag of freedom,' he boasts) permanently in rubber wellies and wearing a deerstalker on his head. His dog, Boot, is a shaggy Old English sheepdog with ideas above his station, (or should that be kennel?). Unlike Fred Basset, Boot does actually speak, not that anybody hears him though. 'I am an adventurer, raconteur, *bon viveur* and wit,' he says, claiming to be the reincarnation of an eighteenth-century nobleman. Boot's best mate is a dilapidated old Indian blood-hound called 'BH'. Unfortunately the poor old mutt has no sense of smell and is oblivious to the stink emitting from the local fish paste factory. The other kids in the gang are a blonde curly-top called Baby Grumpling and belligerent friends Maisie and Marlon. Maisie is one of the most deliciously self-centred children's characters ever. A conniving little demon who wants to rule the world, she'll resort to any amount of dirty tricks to get her own way and enjoys chastising go-cart obsessed, and brainless, Marlon (catchphrase: 'Vroom, vroom!'). 'You're an idiot Marlon,' she shrieks, earwigs dropping out of the woodwork. 'A proper idiot!' And she's not wrong either.

The gang's halcyon days are spent fooling about in a hot, dreamy British summer: pulling each other around in buggies, playing war games and messing about on the beach, looking for crabs. It's pure undiluted joy and reminds me of happy times at my grandparents' house where I was allowed to read the *Daily Mirror* cartoon page – my father wouldn't have 'that rag' in our house.

Maurice Dodd scripted all the episodes and created some quite intricate plots with political overtones and social comment – certainly not many kids' cartoon series could boast an episode called 'Noblesse Oblige'. In one storyline Maisie attempts to intimidate her classmates into voting her 'Queen of the May' at primary school. Disgusted by her vote-rigging tactics Baby Grumpling says: 'May I express the hope that you'll conduct this year's election in the spirit of honesty and true democracy!' And he's only three. The series remained faithful to the *Daily Mirror* cartoons, although three controversial characters did not make it to the TV screen. The original strip featured two socialist insects (a trade unionist beetle and a bug continually smoking a fag) as well as a dubious Swastika-wearing German tortoise with an uncanny likeness to Adolf Hitler!

The series of 20 episodes was made in conjunction with Bill Melendez Productions, which had made the earlier *Fred Basset* cartoons, and director Dick Horn was brought back on board. 'We were just a gang of silly artists having fun,' he remembers. 'It was not a normal nine-to-five job because we were under so much pressure to get the series finished, but the scripts were so much better than we had on *Fred Basset.* However, we had so much talk there sometimes wasn't enough action.' A cast of accomplished actors including Sheila Staefel, Peter Hawkins and Leornard Rossiter, as Boot, provided that talk. Peter Sallis, who later went on to provide the voice of Wallace in Aardman's *Wallace and Gromit* series, originally auditioned to play Boot, but it was felt that comedy actor Rossiter's acerbic tones were more suitable. 'I sat in during the recordings,' comments Dodd, 'but Leonard had no sense of humour. You just couldn't get a laugh out of him.'

Like Dick Horn, Dodd isn't totally enamoured with the end result of the TV series. 'It was all made in a terrible rush,' the writer comments. 'I sketched out all the storyboards, but there was a total lack of control. I designed a lovely title sequence, but they never used it. Things were galloping ahead all the time and mistakes were made. In one episode ['The Ugly Duckling'] Boot is carrying a basket and then it suddenly completely disappears off screen! I wasn't very impressed.' Even worse was when the BBC first broadcast the series. Dodd noticed that the soundtrack had been tampered with and made more subdued. 'It transpired that the BBC had muted the sound because they thought parents would need a restful period after watching the shenanigans on *Grange Hill,* which immediately preceded my show!' he explains incredulously. Some clunky-looking action figures of *The Perishers* were available in toy shops to coincide with the series, but did they not prove popular and a tie-in soundtrack LP, called *'The Perishers Sing – Well Sort Of',* flopped. 'The vocalist allegedly had a nervous breakdown during the recording,' he explains ruefully. 'I think it was jinxed!'

PIPKINS / INIGO PIPKIN

ITV / Produced 1972-1981 / An ATV Production / Devised, Produced and Directed by Michael Jeans / Written by Michael Jeans, Susan Pleat, Billy Hamon, David Cregan, Denis Bond, Gail Renard, Steve James, Vicky Ireland, Johnny Byrne and Sandy Byrne / Music and Lyrics by Chris Hazel / Original theme tune written by Frank Weston and Ron Roker / Original theme tune performed by Jackie Lee / Puppets originally created by Jane Tyson / Starring Nigel Plaskitt (Narrator / Hartley Hare / Tortoise / Mooney the Badger / Uncle Hare / Angus McHare), George Woodbridge (Inigo Pipkin 1973-1974), Wayne Laryea (Johnny 1973-1978), Jonathan Kydd (Tom 1979-1980), Paddy O'Hagan (Peter 1980-1981) with Jumoke Debayo (Bertha), Sue Nicholls (Mrs Muddle), Billy Hamon (The Genie), Royce Mills (Fred Pipkin) and Heather Tobias (Pig / Topov / Octavia), Lorain Bertorelli (Pig / Topov / Octavia / Pigeon), Elizabeth Lindsay (Topov / Octavia), Anne Rutter (Pig / Sophie the cat), Alex Knight (Pig) and Diana Eden (Penguin) / 313 episodes / First broadcast 1 January 1973

The UK debut of Jim Henson's *Sesame Street* in early 1971 encouraged British programme-makers to try their hand at creating a homegrown alternative. In 1972 the IBA (Independent Broadcasting Authority) commissioned *Rainbow* from Thames Television, swiftly followed the following year by *Mister Trimble* (Yorkshire TV), *Hickory House* (Granada) and, best of all, *Inigo Pipkin* from ATV. *Sesame Street* may well have had Oscar the Grouch, but nothing could have prepared British under-fives for Zippy, or much less a buck-toothed hare with delusions of grandeur. Nigel Plaskitt – later famous for creating Malcolm in the Vick's Synex adverts – is the man responsible for unleashing such a happy horror to millions of viewers. Plaskitt was working in the Bill Kenwright stage production of *Conduct Unbecoming* when a colleague, who was making puppets for a new pre-school TV series, approached him with an unexpected offer. 'She asked me if I did character voices,' he remembers. 'You never say no when you're a young actor, so I said yes, not really knowing what I was getting into.' The performer met series producer Michael Jeans, and was given a brief description of the puppets. 'The funny thing

was he didn't even bother to ask me to do some practice voices!' chuckles Plaskitt. 'But I got the job anyway!' As well as using his own voice in the role of *Inigo Pipkin*'s narrator, Plaskitt breathed life into one of the most neurotic, hysterical, high-pitched herbivores in TV history. His name was Hartley Hare.

'I quickly had to think of a funny voice for Hartley,' recalls Plaskitt. 'One of the reasons I took it so high was because I'd also signed up to play the tortoise as well. I wanted both voices to be very different. The tortoise dictated that he'd be very slow anyway. In the end both seemed to suit their puppets. One was a histrionic hare and the other a pedantic tortoise!' In addition to providing the voices, Plaskitt was persuaded to operate his puppet characters too. 'It was actually more spontaneous doing voices and puppetry in tandem,' he says. 'That's how we were different from *Rainbow*.' Plaskitt was not unaccustomed to fiddling with moth-eaten marionettes. As a youngster, in the 1960s, he had assisted puppeteer Anne Hogarth for Muffin the Mule's farewell tour around the London parks. However, that mute mule's innocent prancing was a world away from Hartley Hare's self-absorbed screeching and sulking. Choosing my words carefully, I ask Plaskitt whether he had intended to create such a loveable control freak? 'Well, yes he *is* selfish and vain and he was definitely *Pipkins*' anti-hero,' he concedes. 'But if he was naughty he'd always get his comeuppance and you'd end up loving him because he was always so contrite. I did make him have the worst human frailties possible, but in the end he was always a sympathetic character.'

Hartley is just one of a collection of puppets made by the jolly craftsman Inigo Pipkin (played by wheezing, ruddy-cheeked Devonshire actor George Wooodbridge). Mr Pipkin's workshop is not dissimilar to Steptoe's Yard, littered, as it is, with piles of junk, fabric and furniture stuffing. From this organised chaos old Inigo creates his puppet friends, who magically come to life in the very first episode. Hartley is made from a dishevelled old woolly jumper, but Topov the monkey originates from a lampshade, complete with floppy fringe around his neck. The Cockney simian – famous for his Swiss Roll-like ears and long limbs – is easily persuaded to do Hartley's bidding, but Tortoise is more cautious and pessimistic, almost to the point of sounding manically-depressed. Tortoise faithfully guards the pennies

in the workshop cash register; the very same pennies Pig wants to spend on Mars bars and Spangles. Pig, an obnoxious hog with a continual look of consternation on his squidgy face, is more than a match for the hare. A Brummie by birth (he refers to himself as 'Peeg'), Pig is a bit of a bruiser ('Oi've lost my kewl,' he squeals) and will eat cocoa right out the tin. If ever a puppet should have been able to dribble it was Pig. Rounding off the puppet team are Mooney, the Irish badger ('I feel a little dizzy, to be sure!'), Octavia, a trashy, coquettish French Ostrich who lives in a sandpit in the back yard and an ex-RAF carrier pigeon, called Pigeon ('Ding dong! Jolly bad luck, what!'). A penguin, a cat and two relatives of Hartley (Uncle Hare and Angus McHare) make occasional appearances too.

Unsurprisingly, it was the thunderously overwrought Hartley who rapidly became the focus for the programme. Hartley's early dialogue, written by series scribe Susan Pleat, allowed him to be as narcissistic and attention seeking as possible. In one episode he persuades the other puppets to vote for him as their official leader, but the power immediately goes to his ears Lounging in the back yard with a cocktail he moans in pseudo-orgasmic pleasure. 'Fan me Topov! Fan Me, fan me!' he groans. 'Octavia, peel me a grape!' He even sings a little ditty to celebrate his newfound role:

'I'm the leader. I'm the leader. I'm a leader, not a hare! I'm so clever and handsome with it. I'm so super everywhere!' Had daytime TV seen anything so obnoxious as this before? Even when a teenage house burglar was in the dock in *Crown Court*?

Aside from his egotistical behaviour ('I've a very good opinion of myself!' he quips), one criticism levelled at Hartley from those (very uneducated) children who disliked the series was that the hare looked, well, slightly, manky. Was it a conscious decision to make him look past his sell-by-date? The answer is a resounding 'Yes!' from Nigel Plaskitt. 'That was the intention. The idea was that he was supposed to look like a well-loved toy; a toy that's gone a bit manky because it's been hugged to bits. But his tatty looks did give him some sympathy.'

The series had a strong student following during the 1970s and the puppet performers had fun injecting some of the episodes with off-the-cuff *double entendres* and topical references. Hartley, who was often prone to hamming it up outrageously, is provocative, to say the least. In one infamous 1975 instalment, when Hartley has become addicted to sucking sherbet fountains, Tortoise accuses the mad march hare of secreting sweets around the workshop. 'Show me, big boy!' Hartley retorts angrily, doing his best Mae West impression. 'Just come over here and show me!'

'Most of those ad-libs were probably unintentional,' laughs Plaskitt. 'I think we tried to stay away from going *too* over the top. Things like 'big boy' were probably not in the script, but I did add little jokes at the end of a take, not expecting it to be kept in. But Michael, the producer, had a wicked sense of humour and occasionally he liked the ad-libs and left them in. We'd mess about with the crew and it was all good fun.'

Halfway through the filming of the second series actor George Woodbridge died suddenly of a heart attack, aged 66. Because *Inigo Pipkin* was filmed out-of-sequence, Woodbridge had only completed shooting series two's latter episodes. Hartley had to comment that Inigo had 'gone fishing for a few weeks' to explain his absence from the early stories. 'By the first episode of series three we decided to say that his character had died,' explains Nigel Plaskitt. 'We did a whole storyline about death and we got a very positive response from parents and children. It was highly unusual for a children's TV show to be potentially controversial like this, but it worked so well that we did another episode about a goldfish dying.'

In August 1974 the series was simply renamed *Pipkins* and Inigo's funky 22-year-old assistant Johnny (played by Wayne Laryea) took over as the show's anchorman. Laryea, who had previously starred in a bizarre American series called *The Boogaloos* (1970) about an insect rock band, is the most fondly recalled of *Pipkins'* human presenters. He was, in many respects, like a black Richard Beckinsale. With his reassuring voice, Afro hair, big flares and knack for making anything out of cardboard and glue, Laryea was the big brother every kid wanted. When Johnny drove the Pipkins' Morris Minor van around the town in the series' opening titles, children everywhere wished it would come chugging down their street. 'Here come the Pipkins. There go the Pipkins... Topov the monkey. Pig's always hungry....'

Laryea sadly left the show in 1978 to star in BBC2's groundbreaking black drama *Empire Road* and was replaced by new presenters Jonathan Kydd (as Tom) and eventually Paddy O'Hagan (as Peter). The puppeteers and voice artistes came and went too, with only Nigel Plaskitt remaining the constant performer for the full 313 episodes. By the late 1970s *The Muppet Show* was being filmed in the studio next door. It influenced the way *Pipkins* was shot and necessitated a radical redesign of the set by Muppet maestro Leigh Malone. The puppets had revamps too – there were three very similar Hartleys over nine years – but several of the other characters had more alarming facelifts. Pig's ears went from pink to black-and-white spotted, and Topov re-emerged in 1977 with a completely new face that *Dallas*'s Miss Ellie would have been envious of.

In 1981 *Pipkins* tragically fell foul of the ITV regional reshuffle and Hartley and company were unceremoniously axed from their lunchtime television slot. Producer Michael Jeans, furious that his extremely successful creation had been dumped, later produced *Let's Pretend* (1982) for Central, one of the blandest (by comparison) kids' TV shows ever. 'In many ways I think *Pipkins* was way ahead of its time,' reckons Nigel Plaskitt. 'People miss it because it had an edge to it which the other shows lacked.' One thing is for sure: they'll never be a puppet as ostentatious as that hare made out of a holey jumper. 'I've really enjoyed creating a cult with Hartley,' laughs Nigel. 'He's certainly the most extreme character I've ever played. He was 'way out there', but that's what made him so enjoyable to play for a decade.'

PLAY SCHOOL

BBC TV / Produced 1964-1988 / A BBC Production / Devised by Joy Whitby / Series Editor Cynthia Felgate / Producers included Anne Gobey, Peter Risdale Scott and Michael Cole / Music by The Paul Reade Ensemble and Peter Gosling / Starring Gordon Rollings, Julie Stevens, Brian Cant, Phyllida Law, Eric Thompson, Rick Jones, Carol Chell, Toni Arthur, Chloe Ashcroft, Fred Harris, Derek Griffiths, Johnny Ball, Don Spencer, Carol Leader, Sarah Long and

Floella Benjamin / Pianist Jonathan Cohen / Over 5,500 episodes / First broadcast 21 April 1964

Hannah's a nice name isn't it? So is Harriet. Even Harmony is pleasant enough. So then, you've got a doll and you want to give it a name beginning with 'H'. How about a pretty name... like Hamble? HAMBLE!!!! What the hell does Hamble mean? It's a river in Hampshire, for God's sake. I suppose, on reflection, she deserved an unattractive name since she was the ugliest doll ever seen on kids' television. I'd even rather have kissed Looby Loo's creepy felt lips than gone anywhere near Hamble's dirty brown vinyl face and screwed-up granny eyes. Nobody liked her, not even the jolly *Play School* presenters. Rumours abound of the doll being intentionally dropped on its head, being scribbled on with indelible marker pen and even having sharp objects stuffed up her backside. 'I did a terrible thing to Hamble,' admitted one-time presenter Chloe Ashcroft. 'She would just not sit up, so one day I got a very big knitting needle, a big wooden one, and stuck it right up her bum, as far as her head!' After two decades as the hate figure for toddlers everywhere, Hamble finally got booted off the show and was replaced by a glamorous black doll called Poppy. Revenge was sweet for Hamble though: the *Play School* revamp flopped and the show was axed, ten days short of its 24th birthday.

Hamble actually looked better in *Play School*'s early days. Filmed in black-and-white, her sickly saffron complexion was unnoticeable. It was only when the show began screening in colour that the hate mail started flooding in. The producers even gave her a feather boa to obscure her ugly mug, but it just didn't work. Her toy box friends were much more cuddly. There was big daddy Humpty, a fat round lump with a cheeky velvet face, Jemima the floppy rag doll with the rosebud lips, and hairy double act 'Big' Ted (who was big) and 'Little' Ted (who was not). These four remained the cornerstones of the series over the duration of some 5,500 broadcasts. However, the very same toys that made their debut in 1964 were not the exact same ones that went down with the ship in 1988. Humpty's sewn on pyjama suit (ouch!) changed more than once, Jemima's woollen 'hair' mysteriously grew longer and the stiff-jointed Teds gave way to a looser, fluffier look in

the 1980s. The toys had to share the screen with some of the most childish and unremittingly cheerful humans ever to have graduated from RADA. Thing is, they were paid to be childish. How cool is that?

Everybody had a good laugh at *Play School* presenters looking stupid, but it would be wise to remember that pretending to be a pork sausage sizzling in a pan is no mean feat. Nor is barking like a dog and nor is singing: 'Let's all bounce together! Bounce, Bounce, Bounce!' The very first show featured lugubrious-faced Gordon Rollings crawling around on the studio floor, snorting like a sow in labour. It was hardly dignified work for trained thespians, but in their own little way, *Play School* made them household names. Rollings was often paired with comedy actress Julie Stevens (she's in *Carry on Cleo*, don't you know), whose impersonation of jelly wobbling on a plate looks like a demented Katharine Hepburn being pushed down a flight of stairs on a trolley. It is quite, quite incredible.

Rollings went back to 'serious acting' and Stevens began to rule the roost with a lanky, silky-voiced actor named Brian Cant. The best loved of all *Play School*'s male presenters, Cant went on to provide the narration for the Trumptonshire chronicles as well as a host of other kids' shows including *Dappledown Farm* and the awe-inspiring *Diggers and Dumpers*. Like all the other *Play School* presenters Cant was a jobbing actor when he went to audition for series producers Joy Whitby and Cynthia Felgate. Whitby gave Cant a cardboard box and told him to 'row out to sea in it.' Cant did so, without hesitation. 'After all,' he later recalled, 'it was a calm day.' Cant has claimed that by acting stupid he got the job, but some weeks into the job he would recoil as the show's scripts fell through his letterbox. 'Oh no,' he would cry. 'I've got to be a pig again!' Cant stayed with the show throughout its run, but other stars came and went. They included motherly, curly-top Carol Chell, talented mimic and musician Derek Griffiths, Eric *The Magic Roundabout* Thompson, Johnny *Think of a Number* Ball, glamorous Floella Benjamin, impish Sarah Long and my personal favourite Toni Arthur. Toni was a girl – with a boy's name, which to a toddler makes no sense whatsoever – and had flowing brunette locks and a nice line in tight sweaters. Toni had a superb singing voice too and listening to her belting out 'One, two, three, four, five. Once I caught a fish alive!' was astounding stuff.

Play School was full of laughter and songs, but quite apart from standards like 'Ten Green Bottles', 'Ride a Cockhorse to Banbury Cross' and 'Wibble Wobble. Wibble Wobble, Jelly on a Plate', the series' producers liked to invent their own rhymes and songs too. Who can forget classics like 'Standing on One Leg Isn't Easy!', 'Scrub your Cheeks Every Day of the Week' and, best of all, 'We are Great Big Splodges'? Each show would reverberate with music and each mime, joke or story enjoyed the accompaniment of a tinkling piano (often provided by Jonathan Cohen). Music was used to accentuate the on-screen emotions and also to signify imminent danger. 'Pretend you're flying like a bird,' encouraged Brian Cant, before swiftly adding, 'but don't climb on anything, because you know you can't *really* fly, don't you?'

Other dangers lurked in pets' corner, where resided temperamental bunnies, razor toothed mice and a vicious crested cockatoo, enlighteningly-named 'Katoo', who bit any fingers which strayed into his cage. The animals didn't appear in every episode because the presenters disliked their unpredictability. Storybooks and stuffed teddy bears were a far safer proposition. The daily story would emerge through one of three studio 'windows', which weren't windows in the traditional sense, but merely big holes, with harp music being played through them. Guessing which window – square, round or arched – the story would emerge from was a perennial favourite of *Play School* viewers. Throughout the country screaming kids let rip at the TV screen, desperate to guess the right aperture. 'Eeny, meeny, miney mo, through which window shall we go?' asks Cant. I always thought the church-like window was rigged to win, although I have no confirmation of this. Having said that, the very first and very last editions of the show both favoured the arch. The *Play School* clock was also a mainstay of the series, evolving from a swirling psychedelic clock of the 1960s to a whirring clockwork contraption in the 1970s and a 1980s monstrosity featuring a stuffed cuckoo (!). Telling the time was one of the presenter's main responsibilities. It had to be done in a particular way. 'Today the clock says... one... o'... clock' ...said verrrrry slowly.

Play School, always broadcast on BBC2 in the morning and then repeated on BBC1 around four o'clock (sorry, that's four...o'...clock),

spawned a more disobedient son in the early 1970s called *Play Away*. Ostensibly helmed by Brian Cant, *Play Away* (first shown 20 November 1971) aimed its inexorable parade of shaggy dog stories and silly nonsense songs at slightly older children. The Saturday afternoon show gave Cant the opportunity to dress up as a schoolboy (in shorts, blazer and swinging a catapult) and do all the naughty things he couldn't do during the week. *Play Away* ran for 13 years, by which time the world's supply of knock-knock jokes had been exhausted. *Play School* disappeared four years later, but for those of you still wanting to remind yourself just how hideous Hamble is, you can see her, and the rest of the toys, on display at the National Museum of Photography, Film and Television in Bradford.

RAINBOW

ITV / Produced 1972-1992 / A Thames Television Production / Devised and Originally Produced by Pamela Lonsdale / Originally Directed by Roger Price / Originally Written by John Kershaw / Presented by David Cook (1972-1973) and Geoffrey Hayes (1973-1992) / Bungle played by John Leeson (1972-1973), Stanley Bates (1973-1989) and Malcolm Lord (1989-1992) / Zippy played by Peter Hawkins (1972) and Roy Skelton (1973-1992) / George played by Roy Skelton (1973-1992) / Music by Telltale (1972-1973), Julian, Karl and Charmain (1973-1974), Rod, Matt and Jane (1974-1976), Rod, Jane and Roger (1976-1979) and Rod, Jane and Freddy (1980-1992) / Puppetry by Violet Philpott, John Thirtle, Ronnie Le Drew, Ian Allen, Tony Holtham and Malcolm Lord / Theme tune: 'Up Above the Streets and Houses' performed by Telltale / Animation by Cosgrove Hall Productions / Over 1,300 episodes / First broadcast 16 October 1972

At the very end of the yellow brick road stands a house with three walls and no roof. Residing there, in fluffy disharmony, are a silver-haired man-child who thinks he's a rock star, a 6ft teddy bear who sulks if he doesn't get to wear a skirt, a gay hippopotamus with extravagant eyelashes and a caustic-voiced alien with a zip for a mouth. In the garden a musical trio are belting out a song about washing machines. Is this just an LSD-induced fantasy? Far from it. This is classic television at its very best. Few kids' TV shows have been heaped with as many accolades or have induced so many warm nostalgic feelings from its grown up viewers as the perennially popular *Rainbow*. ITV's longest running pre-school series is remarkable not just for its longevity but for continuing to capture people's hearts a decade after it was shamefully axed. 'It was the best time of my life,' explains Jane Tucker, one of *Rainbow*'s eternally youthful performers. 'For all those years we had such a laugh and it tied up all my favourite things: comedy, singing and dancing. It was like a big, happy family.'

No children growing up in the 1970s and 1980s can have been immune to the universal appeal of *Rainbow*. It is probably one of the

most influential British kids' TV show of all time; a relentlessly enthusiastic mixture of great songs, classy animation and grown ups acting like five year olds. There were puppets with objectionable habits, double entendres, drunken storytellers and viewers asking for photos of cast members in stockings and suspenders. You mean to say you didn't know any of this? Well, read on because the *Rainbow* story is the stuff dreams are made of.

In 1972 innovative Thames Television producer Pamela Lonsdale was approached to come up with a British response to *Sesame Street.* Pamela, who had previously worked on the first TV adaptation of *The Lion, The Witch and The Wardrobe* in 1967, as well as the brilliant fantasy series *Ace of Wands* (1970), was more used to making programmes for the 8-12 age group and the prospect of making a series for younger children knocked her sideways. 'Lewis Rudd, the head of children's programming at Thames, asked me to do it,' explains Pamela. 'He handed me a blank sheet of paper and told me to go away and think of something. I said "You do know *Sesame Street* costs X million dollars per episode, don't you?" and he replied "Yes, yes, yes. You've got £1,000, so get on with it." I thought he was joking. I knew sod all about pre-school children's shows, but I thought "why not?"'

Pamela went away with her blank sheet of Basildon Bond and her mind went blank. After a drink at the Thames bar with her two researchers, Pamela slowly came up with some ideas. 'We watched episodes of *Play School,* but we were desperately trying not to go down that route,' she says. 'After all, you couldn't have had Zippy on the BBC!'

Ah, Zippy, the key to *Rainbow*'s huge success. 'We called them the Zip-Ups,' says Pamela. 'Zippy had a zip on his mouth, his Daddy had a zip on his tummy, where he kept all his food, and Mummy had a zip on her side where she kept her knitting. It was all quite charming!' I freeze for a moment. So Zippy has parents, then? 'Oh yes,' she replies. 'He has a family, you know.' So what is he? 'Oh, we don't know, but his family never made it onto the screen. We just stuck with Zippy as the naughty character. We were certain we had to have naughtiness on screen!'

At this stage the show was called *Fish and Chips*. 'Don't ask me why,' says Pamela. 'We also had a big bear called Rainbow. He wasn't called Bungle back then. We had ideas all over the place.' After a pretty

disastrous pilot episode, never broadcast, featuring Royal Shakespeare Company actor John Kane ('Sorry I can't be doing this,' he said, 'I'm going back to the theatre'), Pamela and her team went back to the drawing board. When ex-*Play School* writer John Kershaw came on board, plus Peter Hawkins as the voice of Zippy, Brian Cosgrove and Mark Hall doing the animation and studious actor David Cook as the main presenter, *Rainbow* finally started to come together. It made its debut on ITV in October 1972. 'I couldn't have done it without all these marvellous people,' says Pamela. 'It was magic!'

Cook's sidekick was a huge bear, newly christened Bungle, played by actor John Leeson (later the voice of *Doctor Who*'s robot dog K9). Cook had to teach Bungle everything, from how to draw a circle to how to water a flower, but *Rainbow* was the very first ITV series solely concerned with teaching young children. The show aimed to educate, but only with a small 'e'. It was smart and modern, but Pamela also wanted the series to be fun, and it was the furry contingent of the cast that made the biggest comedy impact. Unfortunately, in the early days, Bungle alarmingly looked like a hideous hairy monster from *Tales of the Unexpected* or something along the lines of a giant mutated hamster. He was exceptionally creepy. In 1973 Leeson left the show and was replaced by actor Malcolm Bates. The bear costume was fattened up and redesigned into a more cuddly shape. 'It was a conscious decision to change him,' says Lonsdale. 'We suddenly looked at him and thought how wrong he was. We wanted a warmer, funnier character, not something that looked like an old fox.' Under Bates's tutelage Bungle rapidly evolved into an annoying, mumsy tell-tale who stamped his foot and sulked if he didn't get his own way. Children yearned to smack the big sissy in the mouth, especially after he shouted 'But, it's not fair!' for the umpteenth time.

Around the same time as Bungle was putting on weight, presenter David Cook quit. Then Peter Hawkins also departed, to voice the new colour remake of *Captain Pugwash* for the BBC. With half the cast gone Pamela was left with a problem, but in 1973 *Rainbow* really found its pot of gold. Ex-*Z Cars* actor Geoffrey Hayes auditioned for the part of the new presenter and the producer was immediately smitten with his natural, laid back cheerfulness. 'You don't really want an actor,' says Pamela, 'you are looking for somebody to be themselves and Geoffrey

was exceptionally good at just being Geoffrey.' Hayes stayed with the show for the remainder of its 19-year run and proved to be the perfect foil for the bossy bear and the selfish show-off with the zip up gob. From 1973 Zippy was re-voiced by the incomparable Roy Skelton, the man later responsible for giving *Doctor Who*'s Daleks their buzzing, Nazi-esque screech. With Skelton's help Zippy soon became the Johnny Rotten of the puppet world, shouting and screaming, sulking and mocking in his guttural Mr Punch voice. But it was suddenly two against one: effervescent Geoffrey continually chastising two squabbling 'children'. He was in desperate need of an ally. The production team pondered it for a while: *How about an exceedingly effeminate hippo?* 'We wanted somebody silly to go with the bossy boots,' explains Pamela. 'But he *was* a bit asexual, I suppose!'

George, the sexually ambiguous pink hippo, is a legend in his own lunchtime. He was described in Thames' publicity material as 'shy, but loves making strange noises', but that was only half the tale. George, with his candyfloss voice (again expertly provided by Skelton), is the gayest children's character in broadcasting history. If the BBC might have balked at Zippy, what would they have made of this? 'George was always gay, I think,' comments Jane Tucker. 'I used to love it when he'd wear rollers in his hair at night.' The happy hippo also had a penchant for wearing feather boas, tiaras and fluttering his eyelashes at Geoffrey. What with George cooing over his rag dolls, and Bungle prancing about in a mini-skirt with his hand on his hip, the show took considerable risks, but children just accepted it. Pamela Lonsdale explains: 'A parent accosted me once and said 'Why have you got a bent bear in *Rainbow*?' and I explained that the children didn't know and he wasn't to tell them!' So convincing were the puppet personas that when visitors came on set they would question Zippy and George directly, rather than to actor Roy Skelton, who sat by his microphone in the corner.

Rainbow was twice nominated for a British Academy Award and, finally in 1976, the programme won one for 'Best Children's Programme'. 'It was a complete surprise,' says Pamela, 'but we were all thrilled.' In 1977 Pamela left the show she had nurtured to become the executive producer of children's drama at Thames. Her later successes included *Educating Marmalade* and cult favourite *Chocky*. Pamela left

Rainbow in capable hands, but in subsequent years the show sometimes strayed into *Are You Being Served?* territory. 'It was a great deal more innocent in the early days,' believes Jane Tucker. 'Later on a few double entendres did get slipped in.' The cast played wicked jokes on each other in rehearsals, sometimes utilising, how shall I put it, 'marital aids'. However, it was rare to find anything too risqué actually turning up on screen. In particular, the actors who played the puppets enjoyed practical jokes. In one episode Bungle and Geoffrey are laying out a picnic in the garden. As Geoffrey bends over in his skimpy shorts Bungle exclaims: 'What a lovely spread!' And he's not talking about the egg sandwiches either. It won't be a surprise to learn that one of *Rainbow*'s directors was Dennis Kirkland, later to become producer on *The Benny Hill Show*. After Pamela's departure she sometimes still visited the old *Rainbow* set to see how the gang were getting along. 'They'd say "Oh here comes the headmistress again!"' she chuckles. 'I wouldn't let them get away with things!'

As well as misbehaving puppets, another highlight of the show was the guest star reading from the *Rainbow* storybook. Appearing were such luminaries as Beryl Reid, Mollie Sugden, Judi Dench (who fluffed her lines because she was nervous) and Stephanie Beacham. Not everyone enjoyed the experience though. 'Sometimes the story-tellers would turn up on set drunk,' admits Jane Tucker. 'It happened on two occasions, but I daren't say who because it would be libellous!'

Jane Tucker, sexier than all of Pan's People put together, was the lone female in *Rainbow*'s cast, providing the glamour and the short skirts. 'I used to get lots of flattering letters from viewers' dads,' she says, giggling. 'Some were very naughty. I'd get requests for signed photographs, which was fine, but some were writing "Can I have a photo, preferably on your own, wearing stockings or a bikini." I suppose my legs were quite prevalent in *Rainbow*, but if I was being provocative I hadn't thought about it!' Music was an essential element of Rainbow. The series' first band was called Telltale, five hippies who wrote the programme's iconic theme tune: 'Up above the streets and houses, Rainbow climbing high....'

Telltale only lasted one series and was replaced by a three piece called 'Julian, Karl and Charmain.' In turn they quit after 12 months to concentrate on other projects. One singer, Julian Littman, went

into musical theatre and ended up playing Madonna's brother in the movie version of *Evita* in 1996. However, this is all of secondary importance compared to the real maestros of *Rainbow* – the incomparable Rod, Jane and Freddy. Actress and singer Jane Tucker ('I played a lot of wenches and tarts in Rep!') got the gig after appearing on *Opportunity Knocks*, coincidentally wearing a diaphanous rainbow-coloured dress. Jane and her then-husband Rod Burton auditioned for the series in 1974, singing their own composition 'Great Big Grey Elephants', and were subsequently paired with Matthew Corbett. Corbett bowed out after three series to take over his father's Sooty empire, but it would be another four years before the classic RJF line-up would be established. (In the meantime Roger Walker, later a star of the BBC's ill-fated soap *Eldorado*, joined the cast.) Eventually, in 1980, Freddy Marks completed the trio, but the new mix was not without complications. Jane and Rod's marriage ended in the late 1970s and then Jane began an affair with Freddy. Did this have any effect on their performances? 'I've often thought it could be construed as an emotional entanglement,' Jane says, with a grin across her face. 'It was an odd dynamic in the early days. On occasion they'd get us singing a song while we were all in bed – with me in the middle. It's a bit like Abba isn't it?' In 1981 Jane and her boys got their own spin-off series, predictably called *Rod, Jane and Freddy*. The series won numerous awards but when the musical trio went on tour they hadn't banked on such a rapturous reception from their fans. 'Once we played a gig at the Liverpool Empire,' Jane recalls. 'After the show we were leaving by the stage door, only to be met by hundreds of fans chanting our names, blowing kisses and asking for autographs. We must have been stuck there for a couple of hours. For a moment I felt like Madonna!'

Over the years Jane and Rod have written some 2,500 songs, making them the Lennon and McCartney of kids' telly. 'Yes, it is a pretty amazing portfolio of songs,' she admits, 'but we've never run out of ideas!' Tragically, the music ended when ITV dropped *Rainbow* in 1992, after nearly 1,500 episodes. 'We all knew something was up,' says Jane, 'everybody was in tears, but we were all very emotional people anyway.' There was a national outcry at the decision, and after two ugly, and brief, revamps minus the original cast (combined with the sacrilegious decision to give the puppets two, yes *two*, arms), the series was finally put to bed. It was a sad end to a groundbreaking British institution, but *Rainbow*'s legacy has refused to go away.

In the period following *Rainbow*'s sad demise the show has been endlessly spoofed and several of the more colourful characters have spilled carelessly into real life self-parody. What should never be overlooked is that fact that the architects of *Rainbow* – both on and off screen – had an unflagging desire to celebrate all that is exciting and wonderful about childhood. It extolled the virtues of friendship, creativity and discovery and, for millions of British kids, *Rainbow* really made a difference. 'When I meet young people now,' says Pamela Lonsdale, 'they ask what programmes I used to work on and when I tell them *Rainbow* they get so excited. "*Rainbow*?" they say. "You used to do *Rainbow*?" I love it because all their wonderful memories flood out. Zippy, George and Bungle didn't belong to me. They all belonged to the children. The show was theirs and that's why it has stood the test of time.'

RECORD BREAKERS

BBC TV / Produced 1972-2001 / A BBC Production / Originally produced by Alan Russell / Presented by Roy Castle, Ross and Norris McWhirter, Cheryl Baker, Linford Chrisie, Ron Reagan Jr and Kris Akabussi / 29 series / First broadcast 15 December 1972

'Dedication, dedication, dedication, that's what you need. If you wanna be the best and you wanna beat the rest...'. Indeed dedication *was* what you needed and plenty of staying power too, since no British children's television series endured as much tragedy as *Record Breakers* did – cold-blooded murder, terminal illness *and* Kris Akabussi.

To see all this in context we first have to travel back in time to the 1950s to a damp field with an upper-class shooting party. Old aristo Sir Hugo Beaver (his real name) was out pumping lead shot into game birds one Sunday morning when he got into a bit of an argument with his chums over which bird flew faster – the golden plover or the grouse? The argument rapidly turned heated and Beaver was placed

in the uncomfortable position of being unable to provide a conclusive answer to his quandary. Now Beaver was a very rich man and just so happened to be the managing director of the Guinness Organisation. When he returned to his London office the following day, feathers still ruffled, he immediately called upon the services of statisticians Ross and Norris McWhirter. Could they shed any light on the mysterious case of the grouse and plovers? Unfortunately they couldn't, but Beaver suggested to the 30-year-old twins that they compile a book of the most fantastical statistical information ever collated. The two Oxford University graduates could hardly contain their excitement and over the coming year amassed a vast list of the world's fastest, slowest, tallest, smallest, longest and shortest. Thus the *Guinness Book of Records* was born and the first edition, published in the autumn of 1955, shot to the top of the best-sellers list. Whilst various editions of the tome went on to sell over 80 million copies, translated into 38 different languages, Beaver went back to his gun cabinet in a huff. The world's fastest bird was revealed to be the white-throated spine-tailed swift, but there isn't a lot of meat on them.

Each subsequent edition of the *Guinness Book of Records* created a flurry of worldwide media interest and by the early 1970s it had reached its zenith. Throughout the globe foolhardy bog-snorkellers, mountain climbers and gum-boot throwers were risking life and liberty just so they could gain entry to the world's most famous book. The BBC duly took note of this alarming trend and in 1972 approached the McWhirter boys in the hope that the book could be translated into a children's TV format. They tentatively agreed, but on condition that they could present the show. Unsurprisingly, the two boffins were not the most naturally photogenic. Dressed identically in ties and blazers, and both sporting alarmingly high-foreheads and bouffant hair, they were, ever so slightly, scary-looking. It was decided that a younger, user-friendlier face would have to be brought in as a co-host. That person was the redoubtable Roy Castle.

Castle had been an entertainer since childhood and was beloved by the British public for his tap-dancing and trumpet blowing. His cheery demeanour and smiley face made him a favourite with audiences from an early age. After leaving school aged 15 he entered summer season at Blackpool and never looked back. Although the

Yorkshireman had acted on the silver screen in movies like *Dr Who and the Daleks* (1965) and *Carry On Up The Khyber* (1968), TV and the stage were his natural homes. *Record Breakers* with Roy and the McWhirter twins debuted in 1972 and immediately consolidated the huge success of the book. A seemingly endless parade of majorettes twirling batons, police motorcycle display teams, domino topplers from China and spotty geeks with unfeasibly large balls of elastic (if you follow me) provided the show with some of its finest moments throughout my childhood. Best of all, Roy himself wasn't averse to having a go too.

During the 186 shows he presented, Roy achieved no less than eight entries in the Guinness book. In 1972 he became the world's biggest one-man band, playing 40 instruments at the same time – the obligatory trumpet, plus bongos, xylophone, a kettle (!) etc – performing 'Whistle While You Work'. The next year he was declared the world's fastest tap dancer after registering an incredible 1,440 taps per minute. The following decade he succeeded in completing one million individual taps in 23 hours and 44 minutes. The amazing feat, performed at London's Trocadero complex, nearly finished him off, but not even Kathy Staff egging him on could put him off the job in hand (or foot). Asked by an interviewer from the *Nine O'clock News* whether he was mad to do it, Castle replied, 'Of course I am!'

The horrible records many children really wanted to see, like people force-feeding themselves pork pies, hammering nails into their faces, or jumping off skyscrapers without parachutes etc, were, naturally, never broadcast – much to my dismay – but *Record Breakers* was soon to touch horror like no other kids' show had done before. Ross McWhirter was an outspoken critic of the IRA and in 1975 he famously offered a £50,000 reward for information leading to the arrest of any Irish terrorist. Mainland England had suffered from horrifying bombings for several years and McWhirter was, understandably, incensed. His very public views immediately made him a visible target for the IRA. In November 1975 he had just returned to his Enfield home with his wife when a gunman shot him in the head at close range. His vicious murder created news headlines worldwide. His TV show was thrown into turmoil, but Norris decided to battle on and co-present with Roy. Norris, a private, unassuming man, even put

pen to paper and wrote a moving memoir about his brother entitled *Ross – The Story of a Shared Life* published in 1976. Interestingly, after Ross's assassination, Norris became a bigger star on *Record Breakers*. He was given his own slot called 'Norris on the Spot' in which a studio audience full of spoilt kids fired random questions at him regarding world records. 'Can you tell me who the tallest man was?' Kevin from Oldham asks. 'How deep is the deepest mine?' asks Cheryl from Dudley. Only once was the encyclopaedic-brained Norris stumped when a kid struck lucky. 'What tree has the most leaves Norris?' McWhirter squirmed in his leather seat for several moments before admitting defeat. I tell you that episode was the talk of my classroom the next day. How could he ever have failed us? Norris later revealed on another show that the answer was probably the Cypress, which may have some 40-50 million leaf scales. The following series some smart Alec, who had obviously got off on McWhirter's discomfort, piped up: 'What tree has the most twigs Norris?' You could have heard a pin drop! He was not amused. In 2001, three years before his death, McWhirter revealed that he never thought his memory was that good, but he was no cheat. 'People always said "You knew what was coming", but I never had the slightest idea what was coming,' he said, rather hurt. 'The BBC wouldn't agree to that sort of thing and I wouldn't have wanted it anyway.'

Despite his being one of the most consummate presenters on British television, the producers of *Record Breakers* decided to give Roy Castle another co-host. Viewers were initially suspicious when ex-Bucks Fizz vocalist Cheryl Baker arrived, but her good-natured relationship with the TV star was genuine. She got into the swing of things, in more ways than one, particularly when she and Roy slid down a 1,200ft rope from the top of Blackpool Tower. Baker went a nice shade of green, but Castle, who suffered from vertigo, just sang 'I do like to be beside the seaside' as he hurtled to the ground at 35mph.

By the early 1990s Roy was still breaking personal records, such as wing-walking on top of a bi-plane from Gatwick to Paris airports in three hours and 23 minutes. His stamina and abundant energy touched everyone who ever met him. However his indefatigability was to be tested one last time. In 1992 he was diagnosed with lung cancer. As he had been a life-long non-smoker, Roy's friends were at

a loss to understand how this could have happened to a man who jogged and played squash almost daily. Roy greeted his diagnosis with resolute optimism. 'You mustn't whine. You should laugh!' he joked and attributed his illness to passive smoking whilst working in smoky jazz clubs when he was younger. He continued to work on *Record Breakers* throughout his chemotherapy and impressed his co-stars with his courage. In the summer of 1994 he embarked on a nationwide 'Tour of Hope' walk to raise money for the Liverpool-based cancer charity he had put his name to. Sadly, on 2 September, just two days after his 62nd birthday, he died at home in Middlesex. Roy Castle was a one-in-a-million entertainer, a truly awe-inspiring childhood individual, who lived his life to the full. Alan Yentob, the then-controller of BBC1, called him 'a defining symbol of all that's best in children's programmes.'

Sadly *Record Breakers* was not cared for after Roy's death. Norris McWhirter quickly bailed ship and Linford Christie helmed the programme for a while. Christie was followed, bizarrely, by Ronald Reagan's son, Ron Jr. Worst of all, ex-athlete Kris Akabussi, the man with the most annoying laugh in the Western World, took charge and failed miserably. Like it or not, *Record Breakers* WAS Roy Castle, and his ability to present a top-rated show for 22 series with the same level of enthusiasm and humour throughout is very special. What's more, it takes dedication.

ROOBARB

BBC TV / Produced 1973-1974 / A Bob Godfrey's Movie Emporium Production / Created and Written by Grange Calveley / Directed and Produced by Bob Godfrey / Edited by Tony Fish and Peter Hearn / Music by Johnny Hawksworth / Narrated by Richard Briers / 30 episodes / First broadcast 21 October 1974

London 1973. The wibbliest, wobbliest, wackiest cartoon series is created in a small West End studio. The cartoon is about a green dog, which runs about a lot. This is normal behaviour for green

cartoon dogs. However, this dog continues moving even when it's not doing anything. That's to say it trembles, jerks, wobbles and twitches even when it's supposed to be still. This unusual animation style has become *Roobarb*'s trademark, but was it deliberate or just an odd twist of fate? Opinions are divided. When I met *Roobarb*'s director, Bob Godfrey, some years back he told me it was not intentional. It was just a happy mistake. The series was animated, on a budget, using magic marker pens, which to the uninitiated are like big chunky felt tips. As all budding child artists know, felt tips are difficult buggers to control. They go splodgy, and if you draw over a bit you've already coloured in, the ink goes darker and leaves an unsightly overlap. When this type of drawing is animated you get a noticeable ripple in the movement of the characters. Clever animation experts call this effect 'boiling'.

So there you have it. A green dog called Roobarb 'boils' in a garden and makes your eyes go funny if you look at him for too long. The real Roobarb was a hyperactive Welsh collie that probably couldn't keep still either, but at least he wasn't fluorescent. Grange Calveley, an artist who worked in advertising, adopted the collie and gave him his unusual name after the mutt urinated all over his prize rhubarb plants. They lived together in a gorgeous detached house in St Albans, Hertfordshire, where the garden was big enough for a dog to run about like crazy. There was also a shed, a pond, a conker tree, lots of squawking birds and a cat next door that stared at the dog from atop the fence. Sound familiar?

Roobarb was based on Calveley's life with his manic dog and the leafy environment they lived in. When his mind wandered away from advertising slogans, the artist took to drawing his hairy pet and allowed him to have all the adventures a normal dog could not – like dressing up in armour or turning into an alligator when he was angry. He soon had a notebook full of ideas, in the hope of turning his creation into a book; he hawked the idea round every publisher in London. They all turned him down. He wrote to the BBC to ask if Roobarb would be suitable for *Jackanory*. They said it wouldn't, but Calveley persisted and came up with an idea for turning Roobarb into a cartoon. Calveley hooked up with Australian-born animator Bob Godfrey and together they produced a test sequence of the headstrong hound running through a garden and leaping into the branches of a tree. It was enough to finally persuade the head of Children's BBC to commission 30 five-minute episodes.

That joyous test sequence went on to form the opening titles to *Roobarb*, but what followed in the subsequent episodes was totally, deliriously unpredictable. Roobarb lives in a lovely house in a leafy green garden. There are no unruly humans to boss him about so he's left to his own doggy devices. He's a dreadful show-off and enjoys nothing more than attempting to impress the neighbours. 'What a brilliant idea!' Roobarb says to himself for the millionth time, when he thinks of something totally un-brilliant. Off he bounds into the garden shed and announces his latest stupid scam, using a megaphone. The poor shaggy mongrel is quite obviously deluded. One minute he fancies himself as a movie director, then an aviator, a hypnotist, a scientist (who can create extra-bubbly lemonade) or a famous scoutmaster. Like all his puerile plans, the latter is just a flash in the billy-can.

Mocking Roobarb's arrogant fantasies are the same garden creatures he is so desperate to have on-side. The conker trees team with demented, chattering birds, but these are no ordinary birds; they have teeth and gossip incessantly. 'Oh no! He's at it again. Please go away,' they plead to Roobarb. 'We're not interested today!' The birds laugh and jeer at the stupid green dog ('The birds squeaked with delight because they knew he was mad' we are told), but they invariably take their lead from the smirking pink cat next door, Custard. Fond of giggling like a hyena and blowing raspberries, Custard is much more fun than Roobarb. Such is his popularity that fans mistakenly think he had equal billing in the series' title, but the superior sounding *Roobarb and Custard* never existed. Custard is a thoroughly nasty moggy. He collapses, from his favoured perch on the garden fence, in fits of giggles at every one of Roobarb's mishaps and enjoys seeing the daft dog humiliated week after week. Sadly, though, Roobarb's plans deserve to be discredited, and it's rare to find Roobarb in the pink and Custard green with envy. Roobarb is an idealistic dreamer: a Tony Hancock-type character to Custard's Sid James, and there's no getting away from the fact. *Roobarb*'s rather oblique scripts allow the dog to behave foolishly. In one drought-ridden episode he attempts to find the source of the

pond's water, but instead finds a reservoir of chocolate sauce at the centre of the earth. In another he fancies himself as Thor, the God of Thunder, and sets about firing bolts of lightning around the rose bushes. That is until the real Gods take offence and turns him into a giant jelly. (Puce jellies make regular appearances throughout the series, probably because it doesn't matter that they wobble, even when they are supposed to be still.)

The series' frenzied narration is provided by actor Richard Briers, who was about to take the starring role in *The Good Life* (1975-1978). Briers' voice bounces uncontrollably over the visuals, breathlessly and excitedly breathing a human element into the spasmodic tales. Roobarb can't get his words out quick enough, while Custard's flat rasping is like a saw blade rubbing over corrugated iron. There are other characters who make fleeting appearances too: Betty the carrier pigeon, a fat mole, an educated Rook in a top hat and monocle, and a rascally fox, whose voice sounds uncannily like Briers' real life uncle, actor Terry-Thomas.

Before *Roobarb* even made its debut on BBC1 in October 1974 the pilot episode, 'When Roobarb Made a Spike', had been exhibited in international film festivals in Rome and Paris and had won an award for 'Outstanding Short Film of the Year' at the National Film Theatre in London. Despite being a lot more anarchic than *The Wombles*, the BBC teatime animation that had immediately preceded it, the new series took off virtually overnight, eventually scoring nearly seven million viewers per episode. A lunatic theme tune (by long-time Bob Godfrey collaborator Johnny Hawksworth), which sounded like it had been played on a deranged Hammond organ, topped and tailed each instalment. The bizarre music coupled with gorgeously garish visuals encouraged critics to level the old '*Magic Roundabout* and drugs' argument at the series. This has persisted ever since. In April 2001 TV presenter Richard Madeley suggested that the *Roobarb* animators must have 'been on something' when they drew it. The 80-year-old Bob Godfrey was furious and demanded an apology from Granada Television. 'Drawing a green dog and a pink cat doesn't mean I was on drugs,' he fumed.

SCOOBY DOO, WHERE ARE YOU!

BBC TV / Produced 1969-1970 / A Hanna-Barbera Production / Directed and Produced by William Hanna and Joseph Barbera / Music by Ted Nichols / Featuring the voices of Don Messick (Scooby Doo), Casey Kasem (Shaggy), Frank Welker (Fred), Heather North (Daphne) and Nichole Jaffe (Velma) / 25 episodes / First broadcast (UK) 26 November 1970

Unquestionably, Scooby-Doo is the most enduring and popular of all the unorthodox characters to emerge from the Hanna-Barbera studios. Since he first bounded off his leash in 1969 he has spawned over 25 TV spin-offs, numerous straight-to-video releases, computer games and, most recently, live action theatrical movies. He's the doggy prince of American cartoonery, and although we now take his name totally for granted it's interesting to stand back for a second and think: 'Scooby-Doo, what the hell does *that* mean?' Presumably it means absolutely nothing because America's most famous dog since Lassie allegedly got his name from a bit of mumbling in a Frank Sinatra song. Remember – 'Strangers in the night, Scoo-be doo-be doo....'

Scooby Doo, Where Are You! started life as a relatively laughter-free cartoon pilot called *Mysteries Five*, (later re-named *Who's Scared?*) featuring a bunch of crime-busting teens, dubbed Mystery Inc, and their dippy hound. Hanna-Barbera hoped it would be a move away from the more light-hearted hi-jinx of the likes of *Banana Splits* and *Wacky Races*, and the canine character was only supposed to be a minor element of the series. However, when studio executives saw the proposed episode they feared it was too frightening for the kiddie audience. Going back to the drawing board, literally, the artists re-formatted the characters, injected more corny jokes and gave the dopey dog a starring role.

Premiering on US television on Saturday morning, 13 September 1969, the show immediately scared off all its rivals with its surprising

mix of good-natured hippy philosophy, Abbot and Costello-style slapstick, pseudo-suspense, chills, thrills, monsters and some of the most memorably wacky characters ever to grace children's television. The premise for the show is that four hippy crime fighters, and their huge dog, travel around America in a Ford Transit van decorated in peace 'n' love flowers and emblazoned with the sign: 'The Mystery Machine'. They're hardly an inconspicuous bunch and they're not even hippies, well three aren't anyway. Head of the team is squeaky-clean, square-jawed Fred Jones – the all-American collegiate kid in trademark tight (I mean *really* tight) blue jeans, white sweater and Leslie Philips cravat. His sometime girlfriend is Daphne Blake, the leggy brunette with an hourglass figure more preoccupied with saving her hair than saving her life. The last of the 'squares' is Velma Dunkley (I bet you're thinking 'I didn't know they had surnames until now!'). Poor Velma is the short dumpy one in a polo neck and Deirdre Barlow glasses. She's intelligent, sure, and has a scientific mind, but she's as blind as a vampire bat without her specs. 'Hey, my glasses!' she shrieks when they fall off for the umpteenth time and she scrabbles around on the floor aimlessly looking for them. 'I can't see without my glasses!' Velma is a bookish swot and possibly a latent lesbian.

The only real hippy in the team is Norville Rogers, better known as Shaggy. A round-shouldered dropout with a chin full of bum fluff, Shaggy is the most unlikely crime buster of his generation. As with *The Magic Roundabout, Scooby Doo, Where Are You!* has endured decades of jokes regarding its characters' predilections for smoking dope. Without a shadow of a doubt Shaggy was conceived as a pot-smoking waster, but naturally we never ever see him inhale the wicked weed. All the signs are there though: he's slow, paranoid and has a voracious appetite. Food, and the eating of, is a central element of the series. Shaggy is a glutton and so is his pet dog. The star of the show is the super groovy four-legged Scoobert 'Scooby' Doo, a dog of such gigantic proportions that it would be possible to saddle him up for the 3.15 at Chepstow. He can talk too, well sort of. Given a voice by actor Don Messick (the man also responsible for *Wacky Race*'s Muttley), Scooby spoke in a most peculiar, but surprisingly endearing, manner. 'Sorry Shaggy' would come out as 'Rorry Raggy!' and his oft-shouted catchphrase sounded something like 'Rooby, Dooby Doo!' It didn't really matter how he spoke, as it just provided a new challenge for schoolchildren everywhere, who attempted to mimic his curious vocal abilities.

A Great Dane by breed, but a coward by nature, Scooby is the dog born to be a scaredy cat. He shivers and shakes, whines and cowers at the merest whiff of fear and can only be comforted by a cuddle from his master and a treat from the Scooby Snack carton. Nobody really knows what Scooby Snacks are. They pour out of a cornflake box and look like Oxo cubes, but boy, are they tasty! Whilst the rest of Mystery Inc is busy searching for clues, Shaggy and Scooby are only looking for grub. No refrigerator is safe when the duo, with stomachs emptier than a piggybank on Boxing Day, is around. Their quadruple-decker, liverwurst, Swiss cheese, pepperoni and mayonnaise sandwiches, swallowed whole without chewing, are renowned, but nothing ever seems to sate their obscene appetites.

While the gruesome twosome are hanging around kitchens, Fred, Daphne and Velma are out looking for mysteries to solve. The gang is inexorably drawn to ghosts and all things ghoulish ('Hey guys,' pipes up Velma. 'There's a light on in the window of that haunted mansion!'), and always manage to upset the locals. On entering a haunted house/spooky ship/Transylvanian castle/disused theatre, etc, the gang are never simply told to leave by the caretaker because they are trespassing. No, that would be far too easy. There's always a mystery to be investigated involving cackling freaks, headless spectres, snarling werewolves or marauding apparitions with fluorescent eyes. There's an awful lot of high-speed running up rickety staircases and down corridors where the background artists at Hanna-Barbera just looped the same old doorways, family portraits and huge cobwebs. (That really used to annoy me when I was a boy. Did they not think we'd *notice*?). Fred and his friends always fall for the midnight terrors, never realising that the floating candles and fluttering vampire bats are merely an elaborate scam to frighten off intruders. Behind the scenes, the kooky baddie is slipping into his monster suit once again in order to scare anybody away from his banknote counterfeiting operation/gold smuggling business/discovery of treasure trove etc. The villain is always unmasked at the denouement. The floating candles were, in fact, and here's the ingenious bit, held up on *transparent* cotton. And the vampire bats were *stuffed* and slid down a greased wire!

The series is great, predictable fun and the writers, quickly realising they were onto a winner, camped it up for all its worth. Just before the baddie is cuffed and carted away by the local sheriff he screams abuse at the teenage crime fighters. 'If it wasn't for you meddling snoopers/pesky kids/troublesome troublemakers* (*delete where appropriate), I'd have got away with it!'

The classic show ran for two seasons in the US between 1969 and 1971, becoming the highest rated kids' series on TV, before being replaced by the, frankly bizarre, *The New Scooby-Doo Movies* (1972). By this stage Scooby-Doo had a hyphen in his name and was busy investigating wrong-doings with a gaggle of 'special guest stars' including, and I'm not making this up, peculiar animated versions of The Monkees, Sonny and Cher, The Addams Family and Dick Van Dyke! It is debatable as to whether Cher really did much to harm Scooby's enviable reputation, but far worse was to come. 1977 *Scooby's All Star Laff-A-Lympics* (a-hem!) transformed the greedy dog into an Olympic athlete in order to compete with Hong Kong Phooey, Dick Dastardly and Yogi Bear. During the late 1970s Hanna-Barbera didn't seem to know where to draw the line. Well-established characters were taken out of their natural settings, mixed up with one another and dumped in desperately inappropriate starring vehicles. Fred, Daphne and Velma got unceremoniously dumped from the schedules and Shaggy and Scooby were left to struggle alone but on reflection, not for long enough. A greater terror more frightening than zombies, bloodsuckers and giant rats was about to befall Scooby-Doo. His name was Scrappy-Doo.

Oh hell, here we go. I doubt you remember but Scooby had a sister (they weren't close, so don't worry) called Rooby-Doo. She gave birth to a hyperactive pup called Scrappy, who she understandably couldn't cope with. Placing him in a cardboard box (ventilated, unfortunately) she put her son on a train and delivered him to his kindly uncle. Scooby devotees were horrified because out popped the most distasteful, annoying, exasperating little hound ever seen on television. What's more he got equal billing too in *The Scooby and Scrappy-Doo Show*

(1979). The 160-episode era of 'crappy Scrappy' was upon us. What possessed Hanna-Barbera to give Scooby a canine sidekick is beyond most people's comprehension. To keep him there for so long is just unforgivable. Scrappy, a boisterous, immature little pest, always pitching for a fight ('Lemme at 'em! Lemme at 'em!'), and puffing out his ribcage, became the most unpopular creation ever to emerge from the cartoon super factory. A televisual equivalent of *Star Wars'* Jar Jar Binks, Scrappy will go down in TV history as one of the most vilified characters of all time. Oh, how we endured his pint-sized posturing, his charmless naivety and his constant cries of 'P-p-p-p-puppy power!' I gave up on Scooby-Doo at this stage, but somebody out there must have loved him. *The All-New Scooby and Scrappy-Doo Show* (1983) came next, which even further diluted the formula with the introduction of Scooby's dumb Hicksville cousin Yabba-Doo (a *Flintstones* in-joke methinks). The mystery element which made the original *Scooby Doo, Where Are You!* so unmissable was removed in favour of yucky comedy business involving Scrappy picking fights with alligators, Scooby setting up a hairdressing salon and Shaggy dragging up to enter beauty pageants. Dumbed down to near-catastrophic levels, the various Scooby/Scrappy variations ran for nigh on 20 years until somebody finally realised that Scrappy had to be put back in his kennel.

The 1999 animated TV movie *Scooby-Doo on Zombie Island* triumphantly reunited the original Mystery Inc team after nearly 30 years of obscurity. The 90 minute feature finds Shaggy and Scooby working for Customs and Excise, and snaffling as much illegal tucker as possible, while Velma is running her own backstreet bookshop specialising in murder mystery novels. Only Daphne has really hit the big time. She's now the host of TV chat show *Coast to Coast with Daphne Blake.* Her boyfriend Fred (cravat now binned in favour of a safari jacket) is her cheesy producer. Because Daphne is doing a programme on spooks, the team is brought out of retirement to investigate 'one last mystery'. But, jaded by their experiences of counterfeit monsters and fabricated freaks, the team are cynical about finding 'real' ghoulies. However, this new post-modern take on the original series finds Mystery Inc battling genuine maggot-infested zombies and blood-sucking human-cat hybrids and they can't believe their luck.

Buoyed up by the realisation that rubber masks are now a thing of the past, the revitalised team have since returned in an ongoing series of new made-for-TV specials. The best is *Scooby-Doo and the Legend of the Vampire* (2003), a fans' favourite since it reunites most of the original voice artistes from the 1960s series. It is far superior to the live action theatrical movie *Scooby-Doo*, starring Freddie Prinze Jr, released in 2002. Back on Saturday morning TV the team have come back in *What's New Scooby-Doo?* (2002), a super cliché-ridden return to form with Velma still losing her glasses, Daphne getting kidnapped, Shaggy and Scooby gorging themselves on pizza and Fred talking a load of crap. Best of all though, there's no Scrappy. The pugilistic puppy has been humanely put to sleep by the Hanna-Barbera vet.

SIMON IN THE LAND OF CHALK DRAWINGS

ITV / Produced 1975 / A FilmFair Production / Created by Edward McLachlan / Directed by Ivor Wood / Written by Glyn Frewer / Animation by Alain de Lannoy / Music by Mike Batt / Narrated by Bernard Cribbins / 24 episodes / First broadcast 29 March 1976

Six-year-old Simon is a child prodigy who excels in his artistry, but he's also a bit of a juvenile delinquent. He loves scrawling his chalk drawings on the old wooden park fence as he dawdles to school each morning, but, we are told, he is 'lazy and never finishes his pictures.' This wanton vandalism is made all the worse by the fact that his pictures have been inexplicably coming to life before his very eyes in a parallel universe within the park perimeter. Simon has created the 'Land of Chalk Drawings' and, because of his inability to complete his sketches, paraplegics hobbling around on singular limbs populate this über-land.

Suddenly discovering he has the power to play God, Simon returns to his smart terraced London home and the large blackboard that dominates his bedroom. Whatever he draws on the board manifests itself beyond the park fence and Simon rectifies the sorry situation of

one-legged school children by giving them two of everything. Having made his peace, Simon is invited to visit the chalky world and sets himself the challenge of building them a better society. However, it seems that Simon is not the sharpest crayon in the carton. Via his coloured chalks he single-handedly manages to create, among other things, a rampaging dinosaur, misbehaving robots, traffic jams and an epidemic of measles! Day after day (and episode after episode) his miserable stick-figure best mate, Henry, appears on the fence to chastise Simon for his latest artistic blunder. 'There's trouble again Simon,' explains a gloomy-faced Henry. 'Mysterious things are happening.'

Simon in the Land of Chalk Drawings was the latest in a long line of five-minute wonders created by London's FilmFair studios, helmed by director Ivor Wood. FilmFair had come to the fore on BBC1 with the stop-motion puppet antics of *The Herbs* and *The Wombles*, but here they were attempting something slightly different – a wholly drawn, two-dimensional, series for Thames Television. Based on the classic 1960s book by Edward McLachlan and beautifully animated by Canadian illustrator Alain de Lannoy, the series burst open with an imaginatively original-looking concept. Simon lives in a stark white world where he and his neighbourhood are drawn in thin black lines (similar to *Paddington*'s world). But as soon as he climbs the ladder over the park fence to the enchanting chalk world, fireworks flash excitedly. Thereafter he enters a place where the background is totally black and the doodles of children, birds, trees and clouds are rainbow-coloured. The programme has shades of both *Mr Benn* and *Jamie and the Magic Torch*, presenting as it does a mundane world contrasted with a secret fantasyland. *Simon in the Land of Chalk Drawings* has largely been forgotten in the UK, rarely repeated and consigned to the box marked 'also-rans'.

Despite its impressive pedigree – friendly narration by Bernard Cribbins and a haunting, almost melancholic, score by *Wombles* composer Mike Batt – the series never really took off in Britain. Overseas, the story couldn't be more different. Even today, the bespectacled daydreamer and his box of chalks have near-legendary status in America, Canada and Australia. In the US *Simon* was shown as a segment in the long-running pre-school series *Captain Kangaroo*

(1955-1984), a sort of stateside *Pipkins*, with additional American narration. So well known was the chalk-obsessed character that Mike Myers spoofed him and the theme tune on the satirical late night show *Saturday Night Live*.

Simon in the Land of Chalk Drawings is a beautiful little treasure, long overlooked and ripe for rediscovery. Cinar, the new Canadian owners of FilmFair, obviously think so too since, in 2002, they premiered a brand new 13-part half hour series made in conjunction with a Chinese studio. He's more Americanised now of course and his primary school tie and snappy blazer have long since bitten the dust, but you might just still hear him humming his innocent tune:

'Well you know my name is Simon,
And the things I draw come true....'

THE SOOTY SHOW

BBC TV and ITV / Produced 1955-1992 / A BBC and Thames Production / Created by Harry Corbett / Presented by Harry Corbett (1955-1975) and Matthew Corbett (1976-1992) / Featuring the voices of Marjorie Corbett, Connie Creighton and Brenda Longman (as Soo) / 29 series / First broadcast 16 January 1955

Sooty never said anything at all and Sweep just squeaked. But my overriding memory of *The Sooty Show* is *that* woman's flat reprimanding voice, which seemed to pervade every scene. When I write 'woman's voice' I really mean 'panda's voice', because it was Soo, the black-and-white bear, who drove me mad. Sooty used to enjoy the quiet life – happily shooting his human owner in the face with black ink and dribbling raspberry jam down his suit, but then a panda arrived to ruin all his fun. 'No, Sooty. You mustn't do that!'

This bit of the book should really be subtitled 'How a 37½p hand puppet made £1,400,000' because Sooty's rise to millionaire status is the stuff best-sellers are made of. The little yellow bear started life as a seaside novelty on Blackpool's North Pier in 1948. Harry Corbett, an engineer by trade, but with dreams of becoming a professional

magician, was on holiday in the Lancashire resort with his two young sons. The weather wasn't the best and Corbett purchased the puppet from a stall, hoping that it would amuse his children. 'I'd always had a thing about teddy bears,' he later recalled, 'and this one had a cheeky face!' He splashed out the asking price of seven shillings and six pence (that's old money, 37 1/2p in today's currency) and took the little chap back to his boarding house in a paper bag. Corbett's kids loved the puppet, christening it 'Teddy'. Their dad incorporated Teddy into his magic act and toured the country making kids laugh with his silly antics. Eventually a TV scout from BBC's *Talent Night* (a forerunner to *Opportunity Knocks*) spotted the human-bear partnership and asked the duo to appear. Their television debut, on 3 May 1952, was a roaring success and the controller of BBC children's television, Freda Lingstrom, immediately offered Corbett more work.

Teddy was elevated to special guest star status on a children's variety show called *Saturday Special* (1951-1953), which featured an up-and-coming Tony Hart and a rambunctious parrot called Porterhouse. The audience loved Teddy but not before he'd had a change of name and extensive plastic surgery. The first Teddy was said to look like a rat so Corbett experimented with altering his looks. Eventually he settled on blackening his nose and ears with soot from the chimney and the Sooty we now know and love was born. By 1955 he had his own series – *The Sooty Show* – and the naughty bear was a firm fixture of the BBC's schedules. Sooty's personality can be best described as maniacal. Presumably frustrated that Corbett never gave him an audible voice (although he was prone to whispering in his master's ear), Sooty took out his frustrations with a variety of sharp instruments and toxic liquids. The bear liked nothing better than whacking his puppeteer over the head with a mallet or an umbrella, squirting him in the face with indelible ink and chucking rotten eggs. Their routine was pure slapstick played out in exceedingly brutal, yet miniature, fashion.

Corbett endured three decades of bear abuse, during which time it was suggested that Sooty needed somebody of his own stature to torture. In 1957 Sweep the dim-witted dog with an obsession for plastic bones and pork sausages was introduced, but apart from squeaking very loudly he hardly tamed Sooty's anti-social behaviour.

Because Corbett had to keep at least one of his hands free, his brother Leslie operated Sweep and soon Corbett's wife was muscling in on the action too. The testosterone-fuelled *Sooty Show* needed a feminine touch, so in 1964 Sooty got a girlfriend, Soo the panda. Annoyingly voiced by Corbett's wife Marjorie, Soo set about declaring herself the standard bearer of bear morality. Like a smaller, hairier version of Mary Whitehouse, Soo loved the sound of her own voice and has subsequently spent the last 40 years moaning in the most deflated, prosaic tones yet heard in the puppet world.

The ever-vigilant BBC producers insisted that Sooty and Soo should never touch, since bear sex was disallowed at the time, but I think the little yellow fella had a narrow escape. The smacking, yanking, soaking and throttling (always with Soo telling everybody off) carried on until 1968 when the BBC ordered that this orgy of depravity be removed from the screen. Corbett was furious. He considered Sooty to be a member of his family and saw the axing as a personal insult. However, Thames Television stepped in and recommissioned the series the same year for ITV. The boisterous fun carried on until Christmas Day 1975, when Corbett had a near-fatal heart attack. Greatly incapacitated, Corbett feared this was the end for his favourite right hand bear.

Corbett's son Matthew had been working as a singer and dancer on Thames' *Rainbow* for several years and stepped in as a temporary presenter, but when it became apparent that Corbett Senior would not be returning Matthew bought the rights to Sooty, Sweep and Soo for £35,000. With Matthew in charge *The Sooty Show* looked revitalised and, if anything, became more boisterous and violent. Flour bombs, hammers and water pistols were *de rigueur* as Matthew desperately tried to create some semblance of order in the bestial household. Soo changed her voice twice, but each new actress somehow managed to be as monotonous as the last. However, there was trouble afoot when, in the late 1970s, Harry Corbett recovered enough to ask for the return of his puppet. Harry demanded his bear back: it was his creation. But Matthew stood firm: the bear was now legally his. The ensuing nastiness between son and father was splashed across the tabloids, but after several months of furry unpleasantness the Corbetts came to a compromise. Matthew would continue with the TV series and Harry would take Sooty on the road again.

The Sooty Show ended in 1992, when Thames Television lost their ITV franchise, but was resurrected the following year as *Sooty and Co* (1993-1998). Sooty's naughty cousin Scampy (a schoolboy bear with a liking for catapults) was introduced, so Soo was in her element having somebody else to chastise. Matthew, however, was tiring of sticking his hand up a bear's backside and decided to get shot of him. He retired from a career of animal handling in 1998, but not before selling Sooty and his mates for nearly one and half million quid to a Japanese bank. Sooty now has new human friends and stars in ITV's sitcom *Sooty Heights* about the hotel management industry. A mute, ten-inch glove puppet running a south coast bed and breakfast. Work it out for yourself.

TAKE HART

BBC TV / Produced 1977-1983 / A BBC Bristol Production / Originally produced by Patrick Dowling / Starring Tony Hart with Colin Bennett and Morph / Morph created by Peter Lord and David Sproxton / Music by The Left Bank Two Orchestra / 'Gallery' theme by John Williams / 8 series / First broadcast 15 February 1977

You can have your Dino Chapmans and stuff your Damien Hirsts. There's only one superstar artist still doing the business in Britain and that's Mr Tony Hart. Unmistakably dressed in beige slacks, a stripy open-necked shirt, silk cravat tied around his neck and sporting slightly fluffy golden hair, Hart looks part eccentric theatrical uncle and part creative genius. To several generations of children he was both. His position as the UK's most easily recognisable artist is still unchallenged.

After being demobbed in 1947, Maidstone-born Hart enrolled at the local art college. He graduated with flying crayon colours, naturally, and his first job was as a display artist for a West End store. Disliking the job he went freelance, painting murals on restaurant walls, but after a couple of years eking out a limited existence with his paint brush his luck changed at a friend's party. There he met a BBC TV producer who asked him what he did for a living. Hart responded by doing what he knew best – he drew a cartoon of a fish on a table napkin and gave it to the producer. Within weeks he was working as the resident artist on children's TV series *Saturday Special*. Not quite believing his luck, Hart was promoted through a succession of BBC and ITV series until he really made his felt tip mark on the internationally successful *Vision On*.

I must have been a bit stupid when I was a kid because I never realised that *Vision On* was aimed at deaf kids. I knew that Tony's co-presenter Pat Keysell did funny things with her hands, but I had no realisation that it was something called sign language. And I

certainly never questioned Sylvester McCoy's clever, but at the same time frustrating, attempts at mime and walking around the studio backwards. I thought he was just showing off. In fact *Vision On* was a groundbreaking series for deaf youngsters. Taking over from the unimaginatively titled *For The Deaf*, *Vision On* changed the perception of deaf-themed series having to be stuffy and patronising. Presenter Pat, with her wacky team of Tony, Sylvester and crazy inventor Wilf Lunn, created one of the quirkiest and most original art shows ever broadcast on British television. From the energetic title sequence (designed by Hart), featuring a springing, bug-eyed grasshopper (spelling out the series' name) to the somewhat surreal sketches, interactive art gallery and ear-splitting jazz music (the latter was mercifully lost on the deaf kids of course), *Vision On* went on to win numerous awards before finally being put to bed in 1977, after 13 years.

Aside from Wilf Lunn's extravagant, but totally impractical, designs for mechanical egg timers, the real star of *Vision On* had always been the innovative art of Tony Hart. The same year the series was axed he was given his own starring vehicle, *Take Hart*, and for a while at least he didn't have to share his airtime with anybody, or anything, else. With his wavy hair and trademark cravats, Hart flounced around a vast BBC studio, decorated to look like a New York loft apartment. Beyond its beautiful picture windows and stripped pine floorboards, Hart was able to fill the space with wholly inappropriate *objets d'art*. Piles of messy paint pots, dead tree branches, vases of rushes and crates of tissue paper littered the floor, but there was always a sense of thriftiness among the colourful chaos. Each episode concentrated on a different texture or concept. Thus we enjoyed shows entitled 'Stripes', 'Sand', 'Curves' and 'Links and Chains'. Others were more suspicious or obscure, such as 'Dribbling', 'Rubbing' and 'Various Cats'.

Whatever the subject matter, Hart's artistry was unparalleled in its scope and originality. Children everywhere were inspired to cut, stick, paint and glue any bit of card or scrap they could get their hands on. Hart's mastery with chalks, spray paints and watercolours in the studio was one thing, but when he left his loft apartment he could really get to work on a grand scale. Hart was famed for his massive

open-air artworks executed on sandy beaches, in deserted car parks and grassy hillsides. All filmed from above, the idea was to guess exactly what Hart was creating before the final 'reveal'. Will it be a white horse, a steam engine or a giant starfish?

With viewing figures regularly topping five million the show could do no wrong in the eyes of the BBC, but among viewers it still created a certain amount of consternation. The most popular, and fondly recalled, part of the series was a segment called 'The Gallery'. Here viewers could send in their own artistic creations, which were pinned up on the wall whilst the dreamy theme to the X-rated Robert DeNiro movie *The Deer Hunter* was played over the top. A bored BBC cameraman panned over a dizzying display of papier-mâché pictures and dried spaghetti montages week after week, but while anxious viewers strained to see if their painting had been included they realised there was heartache with *Take Hart*. Tony welcomed children's artwork, but on one condition: 'We're sorry, but we cannot return your pictures.' The *Take Hart* office received some 6,000 paintings each week and to send them back to viewers would have been a costly logistical nightmare. You could spend hours creating a mini masterpiece in the vain hope of fleeting TV fame, but always with the worry that you'd never set eyes on it again. It was a bitter pill to swallow, even more so when you realised that the BBC shipped the finished artworks off to a warehouse in East London where they were 'disposed of'.

Tony weathered the controversy, and *Take Hart* continued its successful run throughout the late 1970s. In 1978 it was awarded a BAFTA for best children's TV series, although the artist had to compete with a new on-screen partner. In an attempt to inject some comedy into the arts programme, BBC producer Patrick Dowling asked animators Peter Lord and David Sproxton, who had previously designed for *Vision On*, to invent a sidekick for Hart. 'In *Vision On* we had created a cartoon character called Aardman – he was half superman and half aardvark,' explains Lord with a groan. 'He was very badly done, but he gave us our company name in the end so he did have his uses. We must have been 16 or something at the time but we weren't very satisfied with it. If we could have afforded to put a letter 'A' on his leotard we would have, but we just didn't have the time to animate that each time!'

After a year working on failed superhero Aardman, Lord and Sproxton went off to university and during their vacations worked on some new ideas using plasticine, every child's favourite malleable art material. 'It was much more fun to do,' explains Lord. 'It was incredibly flexible and also unique because nobody else was doing it on TV. That was its main appeal.' The two young animators went on to create three-inch high plasticine figures (dubbed 'the Gleebies') for *Vision On*, but with the transfer to *Take Hart* came their first iconic character – an anarchic little brown man ('He is terracotta actually,' Lord corrects me) called Morph, who lives in a pencil box on Tony's desk. In the first ever episode of *Take Hart* Morph evolves from a lump of plasticine and interferes with Tony's painting The artist, obviously furious at the interruption, whacks him with his paintbrush and leaves a splattered Morph stencilled all over his paper. 'It is a miraculous shared art experience,' chuckles Lord. Each week much the same thing would happen, until Lord got bored with it and concentrated on mini-stories solely about Tony's little shape-changing nemesis. 'You know, having him morphing into different shapes never really interested me,' says Lord, surprisingly. 'But the people at the BBC thought this was his main selling point. When he was a man he was Morph, but when he was a pencil or a ball or a chair, the person the children cared about was suddenly off the screen. However, the BBC wanted him to change shape, so we kept it in.'

Morph's popularity was instantaneous. During the first season of *Take Hart* in 1977 he appeared in about 13 scenes. By the following year this had risen to 60. Within three years he was opening school fetes! Tony's desktop troublemaker increasingly usurped his master and it could be argued that children began to watch the show solely to see the monkey, rather than the organ grinder. Hart has always strenuously denied any rivalry between him and the little fella, but it must have been galling when Morph was given increasing screen prominence and even his own spin-off series, *The Amazing Adventures of Morph* in 1980.

As if Morph wasn't eating up enough of the series, Hart was given yet another 'comedy' partner, in the form of an obstreperous caretaker. Actor Colin Bennett who played the rather taxing role of 'Mr Bennett' was a BBC jobsworth always going on about health and safety

regulations and asking his tenant to turn down the noise or clean up his paint. Over time he became an integral part of the series, but his participation was often intrusive and frustrating. They should have just hired Terry Scott in idiotic *Terry and June* mode and had done with it. With Bennett's introduction *Take Hart* began to wilt and in 1983, after eight series, the grand penthouse apartment closed its doors. The format was resurrected after a year's layoff in *Hartbeat* (1985-1994), followed by *Tony Hart's Artbox Bunch* (1995-1996) and *Smart Hart* (1999-2000). Today Britain's most famous living artist seldom makes appearances on TV, which is a shame because without him many of us would never have attempted to make a barn owl out of bottle tops, a haunted castle from tree bark or a hot air balloon out of paper plates. Tony Hart – what a class act!

TISWAS

ITV / Produced 1974-1982 / An ATV Production / Executive Producer - Mike Smith / Series Editor - Peter Matthews / Starring Chris Tarrant (1974-1981), John Asher (1974-1976), Sally James (1977-1982), Lenny Henry (1978-1981), John Gorman (1978-1981) and Bob Carolgees (1978-1981). Also featuring Trevor East, Gordon Astley, Clive Webb, Sylvester McCoy, David Rappaport, Dan Hegarty and Fogwell Flax / 9 series / First broadcast 5 January 1974

Weren't Saturdays great when you were a kid? And wasn't Saturday morning TV the best thing ever? Well, it was post 1974 and if you lived in the Midlands (as I just about did). Before then, the two big terrestrial channels just served up a diet of cartoons and black-and-white movies (Bugs Bunny and Laurel and Hardy on BBC1) and repeated puppet series and teenage crime busting (*Captain Scarlet* and *Junior Police Five* on ITV). It wasn't a lot of fun actually, but in desperation you waded through it, especially if it was raining outside and you couldn't go out on your Chopper. By lunchtime television was all set up for five hours of sport with BBC's *Grandstand* and ITV's *World of Sport*. In our household *World of Sport* had the edge because it featured *ITV Wrestling* ('Live from Adwick-Le-Street') and there was nothing more relaxing after lunch than watching flabby middle-aged men tossing each other about, while commentator Kent Walton pumped up the tension 'ringside'.

The phenomenon of 'kids' Saturday morning TV' did not really emerge until January 1974 when a live, three hour long compilation of American cartoons, competitions, phone-ins, pop music and chaotic comedy sketches arrived on ITV. The show was called *Tiswas* and totally revolutionised children's telly, by throwing caution, and a few hundred custard pies, to the wind. The name *Tiswas* is an acronym for 'This is Saturday. Watch and Smile!' although some have suggested it was 'This is Saturday. Wake Up and Smile.' This can't be right since the series would have been named *Tiswuas*, which sounds like a Czech porn actress. Manic Birmingham DJ Chris Tarrant and regional news presenter John Asher presented the first series of ten episodes. Together the two merry men presided over a studio filled with screaming children being drenched by buckets of water. It could have been a recipe for disaster, but the show was recommissioned for a second, extended, series in the autumn of 1974.

For its first five years *Tiswas* was only broadcast in the Midlands by the ATV network. Throughout the rest of the country kids could watch dross like *Saturday Scene*, *Our Show* (both LWT) *Saturday Banana* (Southern TV) and the appalling *Mersey Pirate* (Granada). None of these shows made the same impact as the show creating tsunami waves from ATV's cramped Studio 3 in Birmingham. *Tiswas*'s reputation for unpredictability, unruly kids and unrehearsed bad taste gradually filtered through to other TV regions and bit-by-bit several other local broadcasters began to sit up and take notice. Some companies, like HTV in the West, initially just took selected portions of *Tiswas*, still cautious of the show's more risqué material. As regional shows like *Saturday Banana* deservedly fell by the wayside (taking presenter Bill Oddie with it), schedulers were forced to accept that what was happening in 'ATV-land' had to reach a wider audience. Anglia, Border, Southern, LWT and Yorkshire Television all followed suit and by 1979 *Tiswas* had spread across the UK like an infectious disease.

Two years earlier in 1977 *Tiswas* had begun to change dramatically, morphing into an ever-more riotous and dangerous place to visit. Presenter John Asher had left the series, replaced by a far more

glamorous co-host for Tarrant. Sally James, a petite brunette with a penchant for *really* tight T-shirts, drainpipe jeans and leather boots, caused a sensation among viewers. She doubled the appeal of the show to adults who appreciated the near-the-knuckle banter between the hosts. James, a defector from London's *Saturday Scene*, was the first of a new breed of reckless presenters to infect the safe world of kids' telly. 'One viewer sent me saucy knickers through the post,' James recalled in an interview in 2003. 'He wrote that if I wore my black leather boots on Saturday, then he'd know I was wearing the knickers! I made sure I didn't wear my boots that week.' With an injection of extra sex appeal, the show entered its 'golden age'. The core team consisted of crazy Tarrant, naughty James and laconic baldy John Gorman (aka 'Smello'), moustachioed Bob Carolgees and *New Faces* winner Lenny Henry. At a time when Henry was still genuinely laugh-out-loud funny, the black comedian became a focal point of *Tiswas*'s lawless appeal. Dudley-born Henry was relied upon to play a variety of characters including a spot-on impersonation of botanist David Bellamy (in a bad-fitting ginger beard) and a Rastafarian named Algernon Winston Spencer Castleray Razzmatazz. Algernon's obsession for condensed milk sandwiches and a propensity for saying 'Oooooooooookaaaaaaaaay!' secured the show's place in the history books. Henry's other weekly commitment was the spoof news item when he would dress up as 'Trevor McDoughnut' and wear unfeasibly large glasses. The jokes, unashamedly Midlands-based (break-ins in Bromsgrove, industrial action at the British Leyland factory etc), always finished with Lenny getting a bucket of water thrown over him.

Water, and the chucking of it, was a *Tiswas* trademark. As were custard pies, soot, polystyrene flakes, baked beans, spaghetti, semolina and foam. Billed the 'muckiest show on television', *Tiswas* relished the opportunity to soak, or smear, the studio audience of multi-cultural Brummie kids. The studio was *really* tiny and cameramen, producers and researchers were regularly in full view, dodging pies and hosepipes. The show regularly fell foul of the IBA (Independent Broadcasting Authority) because of its gratuitously messy stunts. However, local children begged to appear on the show just so they could get wet and walk around behind Tarrant and James's studio desk waving placards scrawled with 'Hello Mum' and 'Tarrant is a Looney!' The series upped the gunge and liquid content each successive year and by the time the rest of Britain had begun sampling the anarchic success of the programme, ATV was awash with hundreds of soaking, dripping under-tens. Adults didn't get away with it either. The presenters invariably ended up with more than just egg on their faces and a captive crew of 'especially invited grown-ups' endured several hours locked in the infamous 'cage'. A rickety construction with metal bars, the cage could accommodate around 15 adults who bathed in a torrent of water and sludge deposited from a tilting bathtub suspended above.

In 1980 Tarrant, James, Carolgees and Gorman released a single 'The Bucket of Water Song' ('Whatever the case, we take it in the face,' sang the sexy James) under the moniker of 'The Four Bucketeers'. The accompanying video, shot among the fountains of Birmingham's concrete city centre, was about as cheap as you could get, but the whole point about *Tiswas* was that it was proud to be refreshingly downmarket. Over on the BBC *Swap Shop* stuck to a rigid running order of outside broadcasts, cartoons and competitions. *Tiswas* seemed to make it up as it went along. Noel Edmonds happily interviewed respectable guests like Penelope Keith and David Attenborough. Over on *Tiswas* you were lucky to get Bernard Manning, Big Daddy and Benny from *Crossroads*. On the very first episode of *Swap Shop* there was an item on collecting light bulbs (!) and cooking omelettes with Delia Smith, but on *Tiswas* you were more likely to see a kid from Cannock reading out a recipe for custard pies.

All of *Tiswas*'s guests had to be prepared to get sticky on screen. The series' mascot was a black-clad mystery man named 'The Phantom Flan Flinger' (rumoured to be Jim Davidson), who quite apart from his balaclava-ed SAS looks, was absolutely terrifying. No one knew where he would strike next, pie in hand. Would it be Frank Carson, Noddy Holder from Slade or even an ensemble of lisping stage school poppets? In fact nothing was more satisfying than watching St Winifred's School Choir getting a soaking halfway through their rendition of 'Granddad, We Love You'. Tarrant referred to the ethos of *Tiswas* as 'undisciplined broadcasting' and he wasn't wrong. Watching *Tiswas*'s resident pianist in a sinister pig mask, children being yanked

by their ears and Bob Carolgees's manky punk terrier 'Spit the Dog' gobbing everywhere was not to everyone's taste for sure. Nor were the double entendres, adult jokes and digs at 'the out of work' Noel Edmonds. A hysterical Tarrant ranted, bawled and raged through each episode, barely pausing for breath, but his frustration at having to abide by daytime broadcasting restrictions frustrated him.

Tarrant quit *Tiswas* in 1981, taking Carolgees, Henry and Gorman with him, to concentrate on an adults-only, version of the show, called *OTT* (it stood for 'Over the Top'). Broadcast at 11.00 pm on a Saturday night *OTT* was definitely not for children, yet I remember some of the naughtier kids in my class boasting that they'd stayed up to watch it. From the way they colourfully described it, the show sounded like hardcore pornography to me. It wasn't, of course, but there was plenty of swearing, a character named Captain Custard (a ruder version of the Flan Flinger) and several male cast members doing a stark naked dance with balloons. The series proved to be just too hot (and too stupid) for ITV and it was axed after one season. Back on Saturday mornings *Tiswas* wasn't doing much better. Without Tarrant at the helm it was dying a dirty death. Sally James didn't gel with her new team of Gordon Astley, Fogwell Flax and some bloke with a quiff from the pop group Darts. American cartoons began to replace most of the perilous parts of the show and by 1982 James announced she was quitting too. I remember watching the last season with utter disbelief as one joke fell flatter than the last and bearded Astley desperately attempted to hold the crumbling show together. Despite his best efforts to be manic it was obvious to all that he was drowning not waving. Not even maniacal special guest Spike Milligan could lift the mood of the very last episode. *Tiswas*'s rival *Swap Shop* had the decency to throw in the towel at the same time, but thereafter it was the BBC, who ruled Saturday mornings. ITV's best efforts, like the lame *Saturday Show* (1982-1984) (presented, uncontroversially, by Tommy Boyd and Isla St Clair. Yawn!) failed hopelessly against BBC's safe, but entertaining *Saturday Superstore* (1982-1987) and *Going Live* (1987-1992). It wasn't until *SM:tv* (1998-2003) that ITV finally regained old ground and offered kids something risky and rude again: custard pies and double entendres reign freely once more on Saturday mornings. However, some three decades after it was first broadcast,

Tiswas still sets the standards of nuttiness – nothing quite matches the sheer pleasure of 'The Dying Fly' on the lounge carpet. *Tiswas* was always the perfect antidote for a tough week of maths and history at school. It was Saturday escapism at its very best, where there was only one rule: there are no rules.

TOP CAT

BBC TV / Produced 1961 / A Hanna-Barbera Production / Produced and Directed by William Hanna and Joseph Barbera / Music by Hoyt S Curtin / Featuring the voices of Arnold Strang (Top Cat), Allen Jenkins (Officer Dibble), Maurice Gosfield (Benny the Ball), John Stephenson (Fancy-Fancy), Leon DeLyon (Brain and Spook) and Marvin Kaplan (Choo-Choo) / 30 episodes / First broadcast (UK) 15 May 1962

In Britain *Top Cat* wasn't called *Top Cat*. It was known as *Boss Cat*. This really bothered me as a kid because the lead character was endearingly referred to as 'TC' by his feline chums, not 'BC'. And the singer of the theme tune warbled: *'... close friends get to call him TC.'* Why was this, I pondered? Finally, 30 years later I know. The BBC clamoured to buy this classic Hanna-Barbera cartoon, keen, as they were, to screen a rival to *The Flintstones*, already a ratings success on ITV. There was one small problem though. The BBC is a non-commercial channel and on supermarket shelves across the land were tins of pet food called, you guessed it, 'Top Cat'. Unable to screen a cartoon which appeared to endorse succulent lumps of lamb in thick gravy, the BBC persuaded the American studio to substitute part of the series' title sequence with 'Boss Cat'. It's rather annoying and not very inspired. Considering how annoyingly self-assured the character is, Cocksure Cat or Conceited Cat would have been much better.

The American *Top Cat* debuted on US TV in September 1961 in a prime-time evening slot on the ABC channel. As with many Hanna-Barbera cartoons of the period it was based on a popular live action sitcom, in this case, *The Phil Silvers Show* (originally entitled *You'll Never Get Rich*; 1955-1959). Like *Top Cat*, this series was re-christened for sensitive BBC audiences as *Sergeant Bilko*, but I don't think that

had anything to do with pet food. *Bilko* starred American comedian Phil Silvers as a shirking sergeant in the transport pool of the US Army base at Fort Baxter, Kansas. His money-grabbing schemes rarely bore real fruit, but he enjoyed the support of a band of gullible eccentrics who believed every word he uttered. The Top Cat character was a direct lift from Bilko, even going so far as having voice-over artiste Arnold Strang mimic Silver's unmistakably explosive tones.

Vaudevillian wisecracks and physical comedy business are the order of the day as the egotistical, yellow-furred TC operates various scams in the back streets of New York. The cool cat's gang are the rather fey Choo-Choo ('Hey there, TC!'), brainless Brain, beatnik, hep-talking Spook, the super smooth pussy-killer Fancy-Fancy and trusting Benny the Ball. Benny, a blue cat, as wide as he is tall, is TC's innocent charge who naively tries to make a buck or two from unsuspecting tourists. (Another link to the *Bilko* series is that Maurice Gosfield, the actor who played Silver's dopey sidekick Private Duane Doberman, provides Benny's voice.) TC resides in Hoagy's Alley, a less-than-luxurious address, littered with fish carcasses and filthy trash. The cats seem to like it, though. TC's comfortable bed is a trash-can, which doubles up as a table for playing poker on, and he has easy access to an NYPD phone on a nearby telegraph pole. The man responsible for cleaning up this disreputable fish-stinking neighbourhood is long-suffering Officer Charles Dibble. Patrolman Dibble's dilemma is that he's stuck between a rock salmon and a hard plaice (ouch!) since he grudgingly respects the cats, but has a duty to evict them at the same time.

Over the duration of 30 episodes the cat and cop game was played out for all its worth, with TC and his gang invariably getting the upper paw. Despite the series being a relative flop in the States (it was yanked from its evening slot and relegated to Saturday mornings) *Top Cat* was a staple of the BBC's schedules throughout the sixties, seventies and eighties. Hanna-Barbera left the wily cat in his foul-smelling trashcan for the best part of 25 years, only allowing him a brief cameo role in the abysmal *Yogi's Treasure Hunt* (1985) and his own lousy spin-off movie, *Top Cat and the Beverley Hills Cats* (1987) where he swapped cod roe for caviar.

WACKY RACES

BBC TV / Produced 1968 / A Hanna-Barbera Production / Directed and Produced by William Hanna and Joseph Barbera / Music by Hoyt S Curtin / Featuring the voices of Paul Winchell (Dick Dastardly), Janet Waldo (Penelope Pitstop), Don Messick (Muttley), Daws Butler (Peter Perfect) and Dave Willock (Narrator) / 34 episodes / First broadcast (UK) 7 October 1969

Get your motors running! Hanna-Barbera is proud to present the 'Way-Out Wacky Races'. Watch in wonderment as the most bizarre menagerie of men, women, talking animals, prehistoric creatures and the scrapings off the floor of Dr Frankenstein's laboratory compete for the prestigious title of the 'World's Wackiest Racer' and, well, that's it. There is no financial reward, no clunky gold-plated medal and certainly no Moët & Chandon sprayed over a podium. You may think that drivers risking their lives travelling thousands of miles for the sake of a cartoon certificate must be completely off their rockers and you'd be totally correct in that belief. Basically 11 crazy bone-shakers race against each other from one side of America to the other in all its dizzying, nauseous, flower-power glory. Of course it's easily the most repetitive and wearily relentless cartoon ever to infect children's TV throughout the world, but hey, was it terrific fun!

Wacky Races was inspired by a couple of live-action movies which were doing the business at cinemas across the US and Europe during the mid-1960s. *The Great Race* (1965), starring Tony Curtis, was a slap-stick car-caper, which promised a '20,000 mile or one million laughs guarantee!' The other movie, released the same year, was *Those Magnificent Men in their Flying Machines*. The latter movie also enjoyed a rubber-wheeled sequel, *Monte Carlo or Bust!* (1969). These films offered crazy contraptions, pie-throwing escapades, moustache-twirling baddies and vehicular sabotage on a grand scale. *Wacky Races* attempted to re-create these movie successes for the small screen – and, with the greater artistic license that animation afforded, pro-

duced some of the most dangerous stunts and hair-brained plots yet seen on Saturday morning telly.

For the completists out there reading this let me, for a brief moment, go misty-eyed and remember those daring young participants in their jaunty jalopies. First off the starting line were the unfortunately named 'Slag Brothers' – hairy, club-wielding cave dwellers driving the Boulder-Mobile, an automobile expertly crafted from a lump of granite. The Creepy Coupe looked like the house from The Addams Family, complete with fluttering bats, but obviously on wheels. It was driven by two extras from a Hammer Horror picture, Big Gruesome, an enormous Frankenstein's monster with a floppy fringe, and his 'twin' brother, Lil' Gruesome, a mauve midget vampire. In the number three place we had Professor Pat Pending (very droll) and his part boat, part car, part plane, part helicopter contraption named 'The Ring-a-Ding Convert-a-Car'. Nice one. Next up was the easily-forgettable Crimson Haybailer (yes it was crimson, no it was not a haybailer), manned by the Nazi-esque Red Max. The fifth automobile was the stunning Compact Pussycat, driven by the even more stunning Penelope Pitstop. Her curvaceous pink car, complete with pouting lips for a radiator and come-hither eyelashes around the headlamps could break even the hardest of hearts. Following close behind was the Army Surplus Special, a converted tank-cum-steamroller piloted by Private Meekly and his knuckleheaded Sergeant. Don't worry, we're nearly done now with this list.

Driving car number seven were the Ant Hill Mob, self-styled mini-Mafiosi in sharp suits and stubble. Their vehicle of choice was a hearse-like creation named The Bullet-Proof Bomb. A creaky old cart with a wood-burning stove was stamped with entry number eight. Called the Arkansas Chugabug, this flimsy rust bucket was driven, somewhat half-heartedly, by bare-footed, tobacco-chewing hillbilly Lazy Luke and his cowardly bear, Blubber. Amazingly, they managed to steer their contraption whilst both balanced on a rocking chair. In position number nine was big-jawed, oily-voiced Peter Perfect in his zoop-de-zoop Turbo Terrific, a flashy racing car with smooth lines, ideal for impressing the ladeez. Hot on his heels came the log-chopping Buzzwagon with frighteningly lethal-looking buzz saws for wheels and driven by a buck-toothed beaver and a goonish lumberjack. The final car did not sport the number 11 emblem but instead stuck with a double zero, just to be different. This vehicle, the Mean Machine, was driven to distraction by *Wacky Races'* most enduring creations – Dick Dastardly and his mongrel sidekick Muttley.

Despicable Dastardly has proven to be one of the best cartoon villains of all time, up there with Cruella de Ville and the Hooded Claw. Wearing a wonderful purple coat, extravagant elbow-length leather gloves and a magnificent striped motoring cap, Dastardly looks every inch the perfect camp über-villain. His nasty cackle and waxed moustache owes much to the sort of rascally rogues English actor Terry-Thomas had been playing for decades and Dick's Anglo-American tones were provided by voice artiste, and ex-ventriloquist, Paul Winchell. His second-in-command, Muttley, is a smirking, snickering disloyal reject from Battersea Dogs' Home who speaks like this: 'Snukn'-fstkn'-rawwa-grr', although I cannot be entirely sure of his exact regional dialect. Dastardly, the self-styled 'Dracula of the drag strip', fails at every hairpin bend to get ahead of the other wacky racers. He creates endless detours and booby-traps involving amazing artilleries of gadgets and evil schemes. These include swapping chilli sauce for fuel, creating artificial landslides and directing his competitors down an endless series of holes and dead-end tunnels. A sperm whale even gets involved at one stage. 'Drat and double drat' Dastardly splutters each time his evil plans come to nothing, while the ever-grinning Muttley reluctantly takes the blame.

The series ran to 34 episodes, by which time the over-excitable (and unseen) commentator had narrated each leg of the race over rickety bridges, up mountains and under water, into alligator-infested swamps and through snow flurries and sand storms. Despite driving without road tax or, presumably, up-to-date insurance cover and with little due regard to passing pedestrians, the Wacky Racers did not trouble the authorities. The police let them get on with some of the most careless and murderous driving ever known and all for the sake of winning a certificate. And who actually won the final race anyway? The final leg of the competition proved that beauty beats brains any time when vacuous blonde Miss Pitstop finally passed the finishing line first. The self-styled 'meanie of the motor

world' Dick Dastardly went home with nothing, but he lived to drive another day.

Wacky Races' most memorable characters were rewarded with their own spin-off series. The villains of the piece returned in *Dastardly and Muttley in Their Flying Machines* (1969), (aka *Stop the Pigeon!*) hopelessly trying to capture a sweet little carrier pigeon in a flying helmet. Meanwhile, Penelope Pitstop, not, if you recall, the most positive role model for young ladies, took her Southern Belle manicurist skills to *The Perils of Penelope Pitstop* (also 1969). In her new home Penny was allowed to shout 'Hey-elp, hey-elp' as often as she liked as her evil uncle, The Hooded Claw, attempted to murder her and claim her life insurance. Rather than just shooting her with a Kalashnikov, he preferred to devise elaborate fetishistic ways of bumping her off, such as tying her to a train track or poisoning her flower bouquet. Attempted homicide and children's TV had never been so delightfully mixed.

WAIT TILL YOUR FATHER GETS HOME

ITV / Produced 1972-1974 / A Hanna-Barbera Production / Executive Producers William Hanna and Joseph Barbera / Featuring the voices of Tom Bosley (Harry Boyle), Joan Gerber (Irma Boyle), Kristina Holland (Alice Boyle), David Hayward (Chet Boyle), Jackie Earle Haley (Jamie Boyle) and Jack Burns (Ralph the Neighbour) / 48 episodes / First broadcast (UK) 2 September 1973

I must confess that I hated this show as a child. Really hated it. My older sister on the other hand thought it was hysterical. Perhaps she saw something in the series that echoed our own family life. Looking back, I hope not. I was always a big fan of Hanna-Barbera cartoons but much preferred ones with wise-cracking cats who lived in trash cans and taunted the police, desperate oddballs careering around a wacky racetrack or cowardly ghost-hunting dogs stuffing their mouths with double-decker cheese and pastrami sandwiches. However, *Wait Till Your Father Gets Home* had none of these exciting elements. It was, by contrast, an animated situation comedy about, shock horror, a middle-class suburban nuclear family.

The schedulers totally cheated me with this one. I equated Hanna-Barbera with Technicolor fun and high-speed hi-jinks, not satire. If I'd wanted satire I'd have begged my mother to let me stay up late to watch Clive James (and she probably would have let me, too). In their stupidity, ITV imagined that six year olds would mistake it for another episode of *Hong Kong Phooey.* Alright, so *Wait Till Your Father Gets Home* did have a moth-eaten old-school comedy dog called Julius. BUT HE DIDN'T TALK OR WALK ON HIS HIND LEGS! The 5.20 pm slot after *Magpie* just wasn't a happy home for this travesty of cartoon entertainment, and Saturday mornings, where it was eventually shifted, was even more sacrilegious. Unsurprisingly, nose-picking school kids were never intended as the series' core audience. In America the show was one of the very first animated productions to be aimed at adults and is now considered a groundbreaking forerunner to *The Simpsons*.

The cartoon's chequered history stretches way back to 1969, when a short animated filler about a suburban family, headed by downtrodden white collar worker Harry Boyle, featured in the popular anthology series *Love, American Style* – a comedy show documenting the ups and downs of l'amour in middle-class America. The series spawned several spin-offs, including *Happy Days* (1974-1984), much loved by the British public who idolised The Fonz, the series' leather-clad king of cool. That show featured American character actor Tom Bosley as a put-upon middle-aged dad struggling to keep his rock 'n' rolling offspring under control. Coincidentally, Bosley also provided the voice of put-upon middle-aged dad struggling to keep his hippy offspring under control in *Wait Till Your Father Gets Home* The actor obviously enjoyed being typecast.

Such was the popularity of the one-off animated segment, then called *Love and the Old Fashioned Father,* that the Hanna-Barbera studios were encouraged to produce extended half hour episodes which eventually debuted on US TV in September 1972. Re-titled *Wait Till Your Father Gets Home,* the new series chronicled the generational gap comedy of the Boyle family who lived in downtown Los Angeles. Dad Harry was a paunchy 40-something who struggled to make ends meet as the president of Boyle Restaurant Supply Company. His mumsy wife Irma was a shocking Su Pollard-lookalike,

who occasionally shook off the shackles of her housewife duties and became a feminist, but it never lasted long. Harry and Irma's children were 22-year-old hippy Chet, a longhaired college dropout (in Shaggy from *Scooby-Doo* mode), Alice, a 16-year-old clinically obese, diet-obsessed tragic romantic and up-and-coming eight-year-old whiz kid capitalist Jamie. The scene was set for dozens of generation clashes between old-fashioned parents and freethinking kids, along with some incisive observations about the all-American way of life.

The storylines bubbled over with adult themes involving unemployment, politics, feminism, gender roles, pollution, mortgages and even public nudity. Not the sort of themes that really had me creased up with laughter on the sofa. Well maybe nudity did. Next door to the Boyles lived their fascist neighbour Ralph. Looking suspiciously like President Nixon, Ralph was a stars-and-stripes-loving bigot who waxed lyrical about the 'Red Chinese', the 'Yellow Peril' and 'them pinkos'. Now let us remember again I wanted cartoons to be about talking bears stealing picnic hampers; instead I got a male chauvinist who staged war re-enactments in his back garden and led a band of liberal-hating OAP vigilantes on neighbourhood demos. The series wasn't for kids, but over here it seems that the ITV programme buyers hadn't even bothered to view it before it was unleashed on a generation of confused kids.

With hindsight, *Wait Till Your Father Gets Home* was pretty revolutionary stuff for its time and certainly innovative. But even its creator Joe Barbera admitted that it was made on the cheap and never really lived up to his high expectations. In stark contrast to his other more famous cartoons the colours are a muted muddle of browns, greys and washed-out blues and the animation overall is pretty shoddy. The American laughter track is more intrusive than ever, appearing throughout the shows like a swarm of angry locusts, although on some episodes it is carelessly omitted altogether. The show was successful enough in the US to run for 48 episodes over two series until 1974. On this side of the pond it only stuck in the mind because of its jaunty theme tune, sung by daughter Alice: *'...every time the slightest little thing goes wrong, mom starts to sing this familiar song... wait 'till your father gets home.'* But apart from that, I hated the series when I was a kid and I still hate it now.

WILLO THE WISP

BBC TV / Produced 1981 / A Nicholas Cartoon Film Production / Created, Written and Directed by Nicholas Spargo / Animated by Ron Murdoch, Ted Percival and Mike Pocock / Edited by Michael Crane / Music by Tony Kinsey / Narrated by Kenneth Williams / 26 episodes / First broadcast 14 September 1981

If you go down into Doyley Woods today, you're in for a big surprise. Fat fairies, gnomes and talking caterpillars you can probably deal with, but a malicious walking television set is quite another matter. This is the enchanted world of *Willo the Wisp*, a spooky dingly dell where wicked sorcery lurks among the moist ferns and careless merriment erupts from mossy crevices. The series owes its creation to a short in-house publicity film made for British Gas in the late 1970s, extolling the benefits of natural gas. The film, entitled *Supernatural Gas*, won numerous awards for its director Nicholas Spargo and begat one of the most witty teatime comedies of the 1980s.

Spargo, an architect by profession, applied to work at Rank's animation studios in 1947 and rapidly moved up the ranks to the position of Head of Story Development. A naturally funny man with a flair for script-work, he gradually moved sideways into the art department, using his architect's drawing skills to best effect. Spargo honed his artistry on the famed 1950 animated movie *Animal Farm*, but as his family recall 'he was so far down the pecking order he didn't warrant a credit on the finished movie.' Hugely enjoying the experience, Spargo set up his own production company – Nicholas Cartoon Films – with his wife Mary in 1954 and produced a string of celebrated TV commercials for everyone from BP and Shell Oil to Schweppes drinks and the Race Relations Board. In between times he was producing a cartoon strip for the now-defunct *Daily Sketch* and drawing for the fabled British comic *The Eagle*. Spargo's long-lost cartoon series *The Arnold Doodle Show*, featuring the voice of Valerie Singleton, whet the animator's appetite for TV. Throughout the 1960s and 1970s he worked in various capacities on more commercials and television shows, including *Fred Basset* (1976), for which he wrote the droll scripts.

It wasn't until the *Supernatural Gas* film came along that Spargo realised he had hit on the perfect concept for a children's series. *Supernatural Gas* featured a flame-like apparition who lived in a boggy marsh and who spoke with the unmistakable fruity tones of Kenneth Williams, the ostentatious star of stage and screen since the 1950s. Alongside his work in the *Carry On* films and in TV series like *International Cabaret*, Williams had long been a favourite voice-over man for advertising companies (he was also the voice of the fey toilet in the *Bloo Loo* adverts) and considered the British Gas engagement to be just another job. Spargo, however, had bigger ideas.

'I think he saw something in the character of Willo which he knew he could take somewhere else,' recalls the animator's daughter Bobbie. 'He was always beavering away at his desk and had so many ideas in the pipeline. In many ways he was an obsessive with *Willo the Wisp* because he just went off and started creating all these extra crazy characters.' Working at his storyboard, Spargo sketched out an entire cast whom the central character of Willo could gossip about. With his vision set out on paper he contacted Williams and asked him whether he would be interested in doing a five-minute pilot called *Willo the Wisp*. Williams agreed to the idea and in December 1978 went into the studio to record his narration. The recording went well and the BBC readily accepted the resulting cartoon, although some BBC bigwig foolishly thought Williams' nasal effeminacy would be 'wrong... just before the news.' The old buffer obviously hadn't experienced the enthralled reaction to Williams' regular virtuoso appearances on *Jackanory*.

Williams' amazing ability to do funny voices was stretched to the limit by *Willo the Wisp*'s hugely inventive scripts. Willo himself is a gossipy, ethereal wood spirit who absolutely adores spreading tittle-tattle about the residents of Doyley Woods. For this role Williams basically plays himself and his animated character has an uncanny likeness to the comedian's famous features. Floating in the damp air, one hand resting on transparent hip, the other defiantly limp-wristed, Willo's huge flared nostrils and pursed lips are unmistakably Williams'. Willo is, simply put, a diaphanous vision of supernatural pre-eminence, presiding, rather loftily, over 'the small people'.

These 'small people' as Willo refers to them, aren't people at all; they're things. Despite being the titular star of the show, Willo rather

takes a narrator's backseat, rarely interfering with the series' main double-act: Mavis and Arthur. Mavis Cruet is the fat fairy. A pretty useless fat fairy, in fact, who can't do proper magic to save her life. Her wonky wand invariably gets the spells wrong and her romantic, idealistic way of thinking gives her nothing but grief. She also worries constantly about her weight, too. Mavis is so heavy that her pretty gossamer wings can't even lift her off the grassy woodland floor. Thankfully, she's got her philosophical working class mate Arthur the caterpillar to boost her confidence. 'You are not fat and ugly, Mavis,' he reassures her. 'You are plump and plain!' With friends like that who needs enemies? Well there's actually a pretty good enemy here already. The baddie of Doyley Woods is an old television set named Evil Edna. A malevolent, vindictive old crone stuck in a veneered cabinet, Edna glares her icy stare from within a cathode ray tube. She has a whim for turning people into frogs, too, with the crackle of her TV antennae. Original? Yes, but certainly very weird; children's BBC of 1981 hadn't seen anything like her before. But I, like millions of other kids, just accepted that a cranky old TV set could quite easily be a four-legged villain. 'I don't know where my father got the idea from for Evil Edna,' explains Bobbie, 'but she is a magnificent baddie. In a way I think he was being quite prophetic. He was trying to say that we'd all be dominated by television one day and in a way, he's been proved right!'

Bad-tempered Edna spends her days stomping round the forest casting demonic spells and she's lucky enough to have many creatures to persecute. Aside from drippy Mavis and clever-dick Arthur, there's Twit the idiotic yellow bird, who only says 'twit!', Carwash, a supercilious blue cat, voiced by Williams in a clever take-off of Noel Coward ('I am unique!') and The Beast, a big whiskery ignoramus who used to be Prince, sorry Pwince Humbert the Handsome, a minor member of the Royal Family who can't sound his 'r's.

Willo has rather become a cult in recent years, but none of the above characters have induced such feelings of adoration as The Moog. Described as a 'sort of dog-type animal' The Moog is quite possibly the single most brainless individual ever to grace British TV. He is, to put it bluntly, so vacuous, he's almost semiconscious. Chubby, stunted and moronic, The Moog reaches the height of sophistication when he says: 'Eh?' or 'Huh?' He is so stupid he can't even think.

('Moogs can't think,' Willo helpfully explains.) He loves digging for bones, but ask him what they are and he'll look at you blankly. The poor wee pup is beyond redemption, but Spargo's talent is that he actually makes you love the imbecile. The whole script sparkles with clever witticisms and hysterical one-liners, made all the more delightful by Kenneth Williams' stunning delivery. That's not to say that Williams found the project easy. He confided in his diary that he was unhappy with several of the voices he helped create. 'I sounded like a strangulated soprano for Evil Edna,' he wrote, but 'laughed immoderately' on hearing the playback. From 1979 to 1981, a further 25 episodes of *Willo the Wisp* were made with Williams recording his narration in batches. 'He was a consummate professional,' says Bobbie Spargo of Williams. 'He would record all those voices in just one take, seamlessly slipping from one character to another. My father didn't have to give him any direction at all. Kenneth did it exactly as my father had envisaged it. He was wonderful.'

Apart from the main core of characters, Williams also had to twist his vowels around the voices of several guest 'stars' including a West Country gnome, a Chinese woodworm, the teeny-weeny dragon from Wales, a West Indian mole, who works for the London Underground, and a giant Australian rabbit from 'Watership Down-Under', no less. The series took several years to finally come to television, partly because Spargo had to go away and find the required finance to bring it to life. In 1979 he directed Bill Melendez's cartoon production of *The Lion, The Witch and the Wardrobe*, which won an Emmy in America, but which Spargo disliked immensely. 'His mind was always focused on *Willo*,' explains his daughter. 'He only did that film to finance the *Willo* project.' His much-cherished series finally debuted on BBC television in September 1981, by which time Spargo was exhausted. The series was a hit with viewers, who loved its cheeky bonhomie and it was soon notching up eight million viewers ('More than *The Jewel in the Crown*,' chuckles Bobbie). Unfortunately, there's no pleasing some people and when Kenneth Williams saw the finished product he was not happy. In his posthumously published diaries he wrote that the series lacked 'drive and energy' and that the jokes weren't 'good enough'. Perhaps manic depression clouded the actor's judgement and Williams' bile, aimed not just exclusively at Spargo, was a sad characteristic of his journals. He was clearly wrong in this case. *Willo* was, and still is, a resounding triumph.

Nicholas Spargo refused to sell *Willo*'s copyright and throughout the 1980s he continued to produce all the series' merchandising, licensed to the BBC. Everything from the *Willo* annuals to the jigsaws and the T-shirts were drawn and overseen by Spargo and his wife, Mary. In 1991 he started work on a new pilot cartoon called *Jones* about a Welsh sheepdog, narrated by Nerys Hughes, but suffered a major stroke soon afterwards. Unable to return to full-time work, he died six years later.

Thankfully, the spirit of *Willo* has not been extinguished. Spargo's daughter Bobbie has taken over the reigns of the Doyley Wood empire and in 2003 launched her new version of the classic series. Bobbie, a trained illustrator herself, was working on the 1990s revival of *Captain Pugwash* when she realised that so many of her fellow animators adored her father's show. 'People who had been brought up with *Willo the Wisp* – people now aged 30 or more – kept coming up to me and asking me to bring the characters back,' she explains. 'So that's what we've done.' The millennium edition of *Willo* has seen some changes though. Actor James Dreyfus, star of outrageous BBC2 sitcom *Gimme Gimme Gimme*, is the new storyteller, Mavis has lost some weight and Arthur has more arms, but it is Evil Edna who has enjoyed the most drastic makeover. 'Children nowadays wouldn't recognise the old Edna as a TV set. She was too dated,' says Bobbie. 'She's now got a sliver casing and skates around on castors. She's got a digibox too and she can even pick up satellite TV.' Edna's a truly amazing sorceress. She can cast spells even without being plugged in!

THE WOMBLES

BBC TV / Produced 1973-1975 & 1991 / A FilmFair Production / Created and Written by Elisabeth Beresford / Directed by Ivor Wood / Animated by Ivor Wood and Barry Leith / Edited by Martin Bohan / Music by Mike Batt / Narrated by Bernard Cribbins / 60 episodes plus 2 specials / First broadcast 5 February 1973

The Wombles: never has a children's TV series owed so much of its success to its theme tune: '*... Wombles of Wimbledon Common are*

we.' It's the sort of song that methodically plods around your head at the most inopportune moments and has you humming it till bedtime. It's a work of complete genius, of course, straight from the fertile mind of British composer Mike Batt. Less than a year after the animated series debuted on British TV, Batt and his fellow musicians were dressing up in hairy costumes and singing 'The Wombling Song' on *Top of the Pops*. He must have been totally mad, although sweating his arse off whilst dressed in fake fur paid off in spectacular style. 'The Wombling Song' was a number four hit and stayed in the charts for nearly five months. Seven other hit singles followed, as did the accompanying albums and live concerts. It was the sort of success Jackie Lee and the *Rupert* song could only dream of. During the mid-1970s the Wombles were nothing short of bona fide superstars. The Bay City Rollers' teenage fans screamed for 'Rollermania', but the under tens dribbled for 'Womblemania', and it was so, so much more exciting. For a while Orinocco and his hairy belly even gave the tartan-trimmed Les McKeowen a run for his money in the heartthrob stakes.

Before becoming unlikely pop idols The Wombles started off as characters in a novel, written by Paris-born author Elisabeth Beresford. Beresford moved to London to raise her children, and although she lived and worked near Wandsworth Common, it was another green area of the capital that was to be the inspiration behind the furry creatures. She recalled in 1974: 'Wimbledon Common means a lot to me, because it was right in the middle of it that I discovered the Wombles. Or perhaps it would be more accurate to say that they discovered me.' Wimbledon Common is a vast open space in southwest London, home to dense woodland, the famous Queen's Mere Lake and a haven for British wildlife. But among the squirrels and chaffinches lurks a far less common species: the Wimbledon Womble. It was Beresford's son Marcus, on whom she based the most loveable of the creatures, who invented the word 'Womble'. 'The character Orinocco was based on me,' he explained in an interview in 2003. 'He was the laziest and tubbiest of all the Wombles and ate the most. Even though it wasn't terribly cool at the time and I was slightly embarrassed, I was secretly proud.'

Being immortalised as a fat furry lump hasn't traumatised Marcus Beresford, which is just as well since Wombles are now established as cultural icons in Britain. The Wombles' *Greatest Hits* albums still get reissued regularly, new adaptations of the stories have appeared on TV and the books are still read by millions of children in over 40 different languages. The Wombles even run the London marathon every year, cheer on the British players at the Wimbledon tennis championships and, in 2002, paraded in front of the Queen for her golden jubilee. Are they annoying self-publicists, or is it that we just love them too much? The answer is probably a bit of both.

The British love affair with the Wombles started in earnest in 1973 when they first starred in their own television series, in the fabled pre-BBC News slot. *The Wombles* introduced Wimbledon's finest to a television audience of millions and jump-started one of the biggest kids' merchandising successes in British TV history. The London-based animation studio, FilmFair, and their chief model-maker Ivor Wood, veteran of *The Magic Roundabout* and *The Herbs*, masterminded the original series of 30 episodes. The BBC loved *The Wombles* and Wood couldn't churn out episodes quick enough to satisfy a public baying for grey fur. These five minute classics were such a hit for the corporation that a further 30 instalments were filmed and eventually screened in September 1975. By this time everybody knew what a Womble was. But here's a reminder, just in case you've forgotten.

Wombles are hairy, dwarf-like creatures, no taller than a park bench, with long snouts that wrinkle when they eat cream buns. Their job is to roam Wimbledon Common all day picking up litter left behind by negligent humans. It doesn't matter what quality of litter it is either: bicycle wheels, sweet wrappers, tin cans, cola bottles, umbrellas, crisp packets, even old TV sets and gas ovens are all deemed useful. (Tins of Special Brew, used condoms and fag packets are conspicuous by their absence.) The junk is then taken back to the Womble's secret underground burrow and efficiently recycled. The burrow is no common badger sett either, but a state-of-the-art subterranean chamber wallpapered with *The Times* and boasting its own internal telephone exchange. Great Uncle Bulgaria even has central heating in his study provided by a disused Rolls Royce radiator. Did somebody *really* leave that on the Common? Bulgaria is the head of the household, a stately gentleman in a tartan shawl who likes to check his stocks and shares in the daily papers. He's a bit of an old

tartar too, bossing the youngsters about and shouting: 'Get on with your cleaning up!'

It's the teenage Wombles who spend their days clearing up after delinquent litterbugs. There's the aforementioned Orinocco – torpid, tubby and terminally tired and who likes nothing better than wrapping his red scarf round his head and having '35 winks'. Slightly more motivated is cap-wearing Bungo ('See a worm. Pick it up. All the day you'll have a worm!'). He's pretty stupid, as you've probably guessed, but not as thick as Tomsk. Keep-fit addict Tomsk is cretinous and clumsy and gets more gormless as the second series progresses. Far better is Wellington, the bespectacled brain box who can climb trees, but not get down again. Back at the burrow, Great Uncle Bulgaria's right hand Womble is Tobermory, the moustachioed inventor with a knack for mending leaky pipes. He's also got a crush on the only lady Womble of that era, Madame Cholet. My sister had a poster of Madame Cholet on her bedroom wall. Back in the 1970s, when nobody knew any better, little girls aspired to being Cholet. She did all the things that girls apparently enjoyed doing back then, like cooking muffins, sweating over the kitchen sink and making beds. She was also a Gallic sex bomb with a feisty temperament and a sexy voice. Little boys thought her tightly permed hair and frilly lace pinny was a major turn-on. Cholet became one of the best-loved characters, but it's interesting to note that she was largely absent from the first series of *The Wombles* and only really made her mark as a domestic goddess in 1975. Can Nigella Lawson cook buttercup crumpets or dandelion pie with raspberry cream as well as Cholet does? Hardly. (There weren't any more female Wombles, but when the series briefly returned on ITV in 1997 two girls – Alderney and Shansi – who had appeared in the original 1970s tie-in annuals, joined the gang and redressed the testosterone imbalance.)

Even though the Wombles tried to set a good example for recycling and conservation, the actual residents of Wimbledon SW19 once complained to the BBC that the television series was spoiling the look of their neighbourhood. *The Wombles* had been adopted by the 'Keep Britain Tidy' campaign in 1974, but local children enjoyed dropping Spangles wrappers and Monster Munch packets on the Common, in the vain hope that they might spot a 'real' Womble, poised and ready to recycle it. I'm sorry to report this but Wombles *do not exist.* Except the six feet tall ones who appear on Christmas Day editions of *Top of the Pops*.

WORZEL GUMMIDGE

ITV / Produced 1979-1981 / A Southern Television Production / Created by Barbara Euphan Todd / Produced and Directed by James Hill / Written by Keith Waterhouse and Willis Hall / Music by Neil Cameron and George Evans / Starring Jon Pertwee (Worzel Gummidge), Una Stubbs (Aunt Sally), Geoffrey Bayldon (The Crowman), Charlotte Coleman (Sue Peters), Jeremy Austin (John Peters), Mike Berry (Mr Peters), Megs Jenkins (Mrs Braithwaite), Norman Bird (Mr Braithwaite), Joan Sims (Mrs Bloomsbury-Barton), Norman Mitchell (PC Parsons) and Michael Ripper (Mr Shepherd) / 30 episodes plus Christmas special / First broadcast 25 February 1979

Nowadays, if you ask a child what a scarecrow is, they'll stare back at you in bemusement. Back in 1979 every self-respecting eight-year-old would be able to give you a detailed description of the smelly, carrot-nosed, straw-stuffed ragamuffins which supposedly littered the English countryside scaring off thieving birds. Actually, scarecrows weren't very common in the 1970s either, but thanks to TV we all could identify one at 100 furrows. I yearned for a filthy scarecrow of my own when I was a boy and, if on the rare occasion we spotted one standing lonely in a field, I bristled with excitement. The nearest I got to owning one of my own was when a neighbour donated an old shop mannequin to us. It had an ear missing and only one leg, but I was thrilled nonetheless. That is until my dad chucked it on the bonfire on 5 November. I don't think I ever got over that experience. Worzel Gummidge was altogether a much more viable proposition than a dirty old shop dummy though. For a start he could speak and had a robin redbreast in his stomach. Oh, and he could take his head off. That was the best bit.

Britain's best-loved walking talking scarecrow was born in 1936 in a story – *Worzel Gummidge or the Scarecrow of Scatterbrook* – written by

Barbara Euphan Todd (1890-1976). The book has the distinction of being the very first children's novel to be published by Puffin and spawned a further ten sequels, each introducing more mangy bird-scaring stinkers. Worzel is the crusty chief scarecrow at Scatterbrook Farm, standing in the middle of the newly ploughed Ten-Acre Field. He's not much good at stopping the feathered vermin from eating Farmer Braithwaite's corn seed since he's always leaving his station to wander round the village looking for cake. He absolutely loves cake. Worzel has a mouldy turnip for a face and his body is an old suit stuffed with straw, but in case you think he takes no pride in his appearance you'd be wrong. His grassy hair is combed each day... with a dead hedgehog. Euphan Todd's stories were extremely funny and imaginative, but at the age of 73 she penned her last and settled into Worzel-free retirement. Her favourite character made his TV debut in a forgotten BBC series *Worzel Gummidge Turns Detective*, but it was only after Euphan Todd's death that her estate allowed Worzel to return to the small screen.

The man hired to breathe human life into a pungent concoction of rotting root vegetable and dead grass was burbling comedy actor Jon Pertwee. A star of radio and film since the 1940s, Pertwee helped to create two of the most idiosyncratic characters in children's television. His portrayal of Doctor Who, a part he played between 1970 and 1974, typified by debonair flair and extravagant velvet smoking jackets, was in stark contrast to Worzel Gummidge's muddy wellies and moth-eaten rags. Established TV writers Keith Waterhouse and Willis Hall had optioned the Worzel stories for a possible feature film and approached Pertwee with the notion of casting him in the lead role. It was the starring role he had been looking for and he signed immediately. Unfortunately, the required finance for a movie did not materialise, but by tweaking the script the writers were able to sell the idea for a seven-part Worzel series to Southern Television.

The series slotted perfectly into the popular Sunday teatime *Muppet Show* slot in February 1979 and within weeks was a ratings winner. *Worzel Gummidge* is a ribald, hilariously funny romp topped off with a master class performance by Pertwee. Playing the character as a greedy, self-pitying man child, fond of sulking ('It t'aint fair!' he wails. 'Humans gets cups o' tea and slices o' cake and I don't!'), but also showing a heart-breaking yearning for affection and companionship, Pertwee's characterisation is perfectly complemented by Una Stubbs' selfish, rosy-cheeked bitch Aunt Sally. In the original books Sally was actually Worzel's aunt. His 'real' girlfriend was a scarecrow called Earthy Mangold, but Waterhouse and Willis jettisoned her in favour of the more glamorous former sideshow toy Aunt Sally. Fashioned out of wood so that fairground children could chuck balls at her, Sally has evolved into a petulant social climber intent on taking advantage of anybody and everybody who comes into view. A compulsive liar who oozes faux-breeding, Sally regularly promises to marry the lovelorn Scatterbrook scarecrow, but is inwardly disgusted by his country bumpkin ways and beggarly appearance. 'What a vulgar scarecrow you are, Worzel Gummidge,' she insults him. 'You look disgusting. A peasant! Certainly not for the likes of me!' Like her scruffy suitor, Sally is also motivated by her love of fondant fancies. Believe me, there's nothing quite as funny as watching Una Stubbs trying to be refined whilst she stuffs a cream horn in her cakehole.

The Pertwee-Stubbs double act became one of the most talked-about partnerships of the era. Much imitated and celebrated, the two actors were rarely out of the tabloid newspapers of the early 1980s. Their on-off screen relationship was nearly as compulsive as that of Den and Angie Watts from *EastEnders* but, at times, Sally's extreme cruelty and Worzel's muddy tear-soaked cheeks became almost too sorrowful to watch. It is testament to the two stars' acting skills that the relationship between a turnip head and an ex-coconut shy became irresistibly believable. A cast of experienced actors offset their rocky romance in a selection of comical supporting roles. Megs Jenkins excels as the kindly farmer's wife, Mrs Braithwaite, Michael Ripper is terrific as crotchety Mr Shepherd and former *Carry On* star Joan Sims is perfectly cast as snobby Mrs Bloomsbury-Barton, the overweight cornerstone of the local Women's Institute. ('I do carry a lot of weight in the county!' she boasts.)

In the very first episode Worzel appears as a somewhat sinister figure, looming large over his bleak field with an umbrella hanging off his tatty arm. Two young kids from town, John (Jeremy Austin) and Sue Peters (the late lamented Charlotte Coleman), come to live in a caravan in the country with their lazy loafer father. Not used to

rural ways, little John only discovers that Worzel is alive when he goes for a pee in the field and sees a man shifting behind him. Looking back at the scene now it is charged with unpleasant undertones, but undeterred John and his sister let their curiosity get the better of them and pursue the scarecrow's secret. In another change from Euphan Todd's original books, Worzel has been given life by the altogether terrifying scarecrow-maker, The Crowman (beautifully underplayed by actor Geoffrey Bayldon). Referred to throughout the furrowed land as 'His Magnificence', the black-clad Crowman is both feared and revered, and he has no time for Worzel's irresponsible gallivanting around with 'titchy humans' and Aunt Sally. Bayldon, more than used to playing mad eccentrics in *Catweazle* (1970-1971), delivers just the right amount of menace and malevolence to the series and relishes the power of life or death over his straw creations.

Is has to be said that Worzel is not one of The Crowman's best efforts. Cross-eyed and simple-minded, the bumpkin scarecrow's only real talent is for pulling his head off. Remembered with fascination and horror by children, the act of twisting off Worzel's head was a plot device attributed to Jon Pertwee. He suggested to the series' writers that Worzel should have a stockpile of different brains to suit every occasion. They liked the idea and duly filled the Braithwaite's barn with an ever-expanding array of alternative turnip topknots. With just three violent twists Worzel's bonce flies off ready to be replaced with the 'adding-up head', the 'singing head', the 'riddle-me-re head' or the 'party-going head'. Considering Aunt Sally's continual lying I always wondered why Worzel didn't just keep his 'Sherlock Holmes head' on all the time so he could sniff out her deceit.

Pertwee's extensive make-up is both inventive and repulsive, whatever head he's 'wearing'. When the series started in 1979 the veteran actor had to endure a full 90 minutes sitting in the make-up chair to get the effect spot-on. Three years later he'd whittled it down to 50, but the make-up artiste's tricks remained the same: Pertwee's whiskers were made from roots of real turnips, his eyebrows were strips of wheat and his warts made of Sugar Puffs. A thick smearing of brown yuck across the face and a blackening of the teeth later and the effect was complete. Looking like that, it's quite a surprise Pertwee managed to forge a short-lived pop career from the dishevelled scarecrow.

Pertwee had helped create a particular vernacular for Worzel's speech. In the original series, the character demonstrates how to spell his name in 'Worzeleze', set to music written by composer George Evans: '*... A wor after L, a zel after wor, And you're left... with me!*'

It was gibberish, of course, and quite impossible to understand when delivered at high speed by Pertwee. The actor took to the new nonsensical language like a worm to a rotting cabbage and proceeded to go into the recording studio to complete an entire album of silly songs for Decca in 1980. 'Worzel's Song', the almost incomprehensible spin-off single, even managed to get to 33 in the charts. Southern Television, a relatively small ITV company, saw £ signs wherever *Worzel Gummidge* went and quickly cashed in with a selection of merchandise. Alongside the albums were spoken-word cassettes featuring Worzel's words of wisdom, tie-in books and annuals, scarecrow costumes and Worzel and Aunt Sally dolls. The Worzel doll, now extremely collectable, even had a detachable head.

For three years the series continued to be a winner for ITV with Waterhouse and Willis writing an abundance of priceless parts for the cream of British comedy talent. Among those who guest-starred were Bill Maynard as red-faced Sergeant Beetroot, Lorraine Chase as shop dummy Dolly Clothes-Peg and *Fawlty Towers'* Connie Booth as a 'nice' Aunt Sally. Also appearing: John Le Mesurier; Beryl Reid; Bernard Cribbins; and even Billy Connolly as Scots scarecrow Bogle McNeep in the 1980 Christmas special. Most memorable was Barbara Windsor as the bodice-busting ship's figurehead Saucy Nancy. Whilst Worzel is attracted to Nancy's barnacle-encrusted portholes, his unrequited love for Stubbs' Aunt Sally remains undimmed. But rather than saying 'I do' to Worzel Hedgerow Gummidge, sadistic Sally callously jilts him at the altar.

Even though the public had yet to tire of the show's marital mishaps, *Worzel Gummidge* was one of the first casualties when Southern Television lost its ITV franchise in 1981. Pertwee was furious at the show's cancellation. He immediately put his name to a 'Bring Back Worzel' campaign in a national tabloid, complete with accompanying car stickers, but ITV would not budge. The cast took to the stage in a touring musical version of the show, but in 1983 a proposed new series, to be set in Ireland, fell through when the new financial

backers suddenly pulled out. It wasn't until 1986 that Worzel finally reappeared, but sadly not back on home turf. *Worzel Gummidge Down Under* (first broadcast on Channel Four on 4 October 1987) transported Pertwee and Stubbs' on-off love affair to luscious New Zealand. Despite it being a lavish production, the new series never really recaptured the magic of the original. A Maori actor replaced Bayldon's creepy Crowman and the scripts re-trod all too familiar ground. After 22 episodes the series was dropped. Pertwee hoped that his favourite role would be resurrected again in Britain, either as a continuation of the original series or as a 3D animation using his voice, but sadly neither happened. He died in 1996, aged 76, taking Worzel's gurning face, bow-legs and turnip nose with him forever.

THE YOGI BEAR SHOW

ITV / Produced 1960–1962 / A Hanna-Barbera Production / Directed and Produced by William Hanna and Joseph Barbera / Music by Hoyt S Curtin / Featuring the voices of Daws Butler (Yogi Bear), Don Messick (Boo-Boo and Ranger John Smith) and Julie Bennett (Cindy Bear) / 32 episodes / First broadcast (US) 30 January 1961

Whatever you might say to the contrary, children love to laugh at gluttons. Kids' entertainment is littered with gormandising heroes like the infamous Billy Bunter, cruelly billed as 'the fattest schoolboy on Earth', Greedy Pigg, the pudgy schoolmaster from *The Dandy*, Roger Hargreaves' Mr Greedy, Muskie from *Deputy Dawg* and Rowland Browning 'the fat one, who got teased' from *Grange Hill*. Perhaps the biggest American snack-snafflers emerged from the Hanna-Barbera cartoon studios. Scooby-Doo and his hippy sidekick Shaggy were exclusively motivated by their love of all things edible, but the guy who really started the Swiss cheese rolling was Yogi Bear, a native American grizzly who crammed as much grub into his mouth as he could, without ever putting on a pound.

Yogi Bear first appeared on American television in a regular segment of *The Huckleberry Hound Show* (1958). Huckleberry – a lackadaisical blue dog with a hiccupy voice – was soon overshadowed by his guest star and eventually Yogi was given his own starring vehicle, sort of. As was the case with all these early Hanna-Barbera series the show was divided into three parts. Yogi and his rumbling stomach was the main attraction, but he also shared screen time with two less-remembered stable mates. Snagglepuss was an effete mountain lion, who quoted Shakespeare and regularly uttered 'Heavens to Murgatroyd'. Yakky Doodle was a cloying cute duckling, forever getting his feathers ruffled. Despite the dim duck and laconic lion, Yogi blossomed into a cartoon god.

America's favourite bear wasn't totally original. He acquired his name from Yogi Berra, a famed New York Yankees baseball player, and

his vocal characterisation (courtesy of Hanna-Barbera favourite Daws Butler) was based, in part, on actor Art Carney's role as Ed the sewer cleaner from cult sitcom *The Honeymooners* (1955-1956). Yogi's laid-back approach to life, where all he cares about is eating, sleeping, and occasionally romancing lady bears, made him a cartoon first. His unfettered hedonistic philosophy and casual arrogance made him one of the studios biggest money-spinners of the 1960s. Yogi became the instantly recognisable face on millions of boxes of Kellogg's Corn Flakes and boasted his own weekly comic, syndicated newspaper comic strip and reams of children's toys. In 1964 Hanna-Barbera even made their first foray onto the big screen with a spin-off movie called *Hey There, Yogi Bear!*

Cool, self-confident Yogi was born to be a star, yet he doesn't live in the most salubrious of surroundings. Home for him is a damp cave at the heart of Jellystone National Park. He hibernates for half the year, but on the first day of spring wakes from his slumber, with only one thought on his mind: picnic baskets. Jellystone is open to the general public and where humans go, food soon follows. Yogi's not fussy; he likes pastrami sandwiches, pumpkin pie, stilton cheese, fresh olives in brine, honey pots, Coca-Cola. You name it, he'll eat it. In fact, Yogi's never met a picnic basket he didn't like. Grizzly bears are a protected species so Yogi can't be shot at, but in this artificial, sterile environment he can't hunt as nature intended. The paying hordes don't want to see a grizzly ripping a racoon's head off, so what's a bear to do, but steal?

Yogi's obsession with 'pic-a-nic baskets' lies at the very heart of this classic series, but his passion for filching food puts him seriously at odds with Park Ranger Smith, a smug stickler for the rules and a man who likes to run a tight ship. 'There are strict rules here Yogi,' he tells his most meddlesome bear. 'You must not stop on highways and beg for food. You must not enter the log cabins and you must *not* steal picnic baskets!' Despite Ranger Smith's constant battles with Yogi, the two characters endure a grudging respect for each other and the regular intervention of Boo Boo smoothes over the cracks. Boo Boo! You've not forgotten Boo Boo have you?

For all Yogi's machismo and puffed-up posturing, his true sexuality is in some doubt. For six months of the year he shares his bed with a diminutive grizzly with a girly name. Boo Boo, good-natured, gentle and, unfortunately, very drippy, is Yogi's ever-present conscience. His cautious criticism of Yogi's best-laid plans prevents his big buddy from being carted off to a bear's idea of hell – Toledo Zoo. The two chums obviously love each other, but perhaps their relationship is more innocent than we think. Yogi promises to tell his tiny charge about the birds and the bees, but when pressed, is unable to give him the hard facts. If there was any suspicion in conservative America's minds that their friendship was, indeed, 'unhealthy' (as was suggested by some religious organisations) it was quashed in 1962. That year Yogi was given a female bear, called Cindy, to sniff around; although, tellingly they never shared a duvet.

For 32 episodes Yogi tried every trick in the hamper to get his greasy paws on some pilfered provisions. But with his waistline still intact, he disappeared for a decade. He returned in 1973, but the magic was sorely missing. In perhaps one of the worst Hanna-Barbera spin-offs ever, *Yogi's Gang* saw the 'smarter than the average bear' forced out of Jellystone Park by pollution and board an ark with Snagglepuss and Huckleberry Hound as they searched for a new paradise. It was, in a word, diabolical. Yet worse was to come. *Yogi's Space Race* (1978) and *Yogi's Treasure Hunt* (1985) merit no comment and *Yogi and the Invasion of the Space Bears* (1988) was probably just somebody's idea of a sick joke. The studio's desecration of a once-great cartoon institution is unforgivable, but for those purists out there who still yearn for a bit of grizzly action, there is hope. Throughout America are now several Jellystone Park Resorts where happy holidaymakers can stay in real log cabins, eat as much picnic food as they desire and get hassled by out-of-work actors in Yogi and Boo Boo suits. Pure bliss!

Time for bed...

BIBLIOGRAPHY

Elisabeth Beresford, *The Wombles*
(Ernest Benn Ltd, 1968)

Michael Bond, *A Bear Called Paddington*
(William Collins Sons & Co, 1958)

Jeff Evans, *The Penguin TV Companion*
(Penguin Books, 2001)

Tove Jansson, *The Summer Book*
(UK Edition by Random House, 1974)

Oliver Postgate, *Seeing Things, An Autobiography*
(Sidgwick & Jackson, 2000)

Geoff Tibballs, *The Golden Age of Children's Television*
(Titan Books, 1991)

Tise Vahimagi, *British Television, An Illustrated Guide*
(Oxford University Press, 1996)

Kenneth Williams, *The Kenneth Williams Diaries,*
Edited by Russell Davies
(HarperCollins, 1993)

PICTURE CREDITS

Front cover

Central image: Sally James © Rex Features
Clockwise:
Evil Edna from *Willo the Wisp* © Spargo Sisters
Zippy from *Rainbow* © Rex Features (*Rainbow* © Thames Television/FremantleMedia)
Danger Mouse © Thames Television/FremantleMedia
Sooty © Rex Features
Worzel Gummidge © Rex Features
Bod © The Estate of Michael Cole

Back cover

Alberto Frog © The Estate of Michael Cole
Keith Chegwin © Rex Features
The Swedish Chef from *The Muppet Show* © Rex Features (*The Muppet Show* © The Jim Henson Company)

Picture pages

Picture pages 1 (top), 2 (top), 3 (bottom), 5 (bottom), 7 (top), 8 (top) © Rex Features
Picture page 4 (top) © Aardman Animations Ltd, 1980
Picture page 5 (top) courtesy Brian Cosgrove
Picture page 6 courtesy Jane Tucker; George © Rex Features
Picture page 8: Ludwig © Mirek and Peter Lang; Aunt Flo © The Estate of Michael Cole